Infe

MW01195806

This unique textbook provides an introduction to statistical inference with network data. The authors present a self-contained derivation and mathematical formulation of methods, review examples, and real-world applications, as well as providing data and code in the R environment that can be customized. Inferential network analysis transcends fields, and examples from across the social sciences (from management to electoral politics) are discussed, which can be adapted and applied to a panorama of research. From scholars to undergraduates, spanning the social, mathematical, computational, and physical sciences, readers will be introduced to inferential network models and their extensions. The exponential random graph model and latent space network model are given particular attention, and, fundamentally, the reader is given the tools to independently conduct their own analyses.

Skyler J. Cranmer is the Carter Phillips and Sue Henry Professor of Political Science at the Ohio State University.

Bruce A. Desmarais is the DeGrandis-McCourtney Early Career Professor in Political Science at Penn State University.

Jason William Morgan is Vice President for Behavioral Intelligence: Aware and a visiting scholar in political science at the Ohio State University.

Analytical Methods for Social Research presents texts on empirical and formal methods for the social sciences. Volumes in the series address both the theoretical underpinnings of analytical techniques as well as their application in social research. Some series volumes are broad in scope, cutting across a number of disciplines. Others focus mainly on methodological applications within specific fields such as political science, sociology, demography, and public health. The series serves a mix of students and researchers in the social sciences and statistics.

Series Editors
R. Michael Alvarez, California Institute of Technology
Nathaniel L. Beck, New York University
Stephen L. Morgan, Johns Hopkins University Lawrence L. Wu, New York University

Other Titles in the Series:

Inferential Network Analysis

SKYLER J. CRANMER
The Ohio State University

BRUCE A. DESMARAIS
The Pennsylvania State University

JASON W. MORGAN
The Ohio State University

CAMBRIDGE
UNIVERSITY PRESS

CAMBRIDGE
UNIVERSITY PRESS

University Printing House, Cambridge CB2 8BS, United Kingdom

One Liberty Plaza, 20th Floor, New York, NY 10006, USA

477 Williamstown Road, Port Melbourne, VIC 3207, Australia

314–321, 3rd Floor, Plot 3, Splendor Forum, Jasola District Centre,
New Delhi – 110025, India

79 Anson Road, #06–04/06, Singapore 079906

Cambridge University Press is part of the University of Cambridge.

It furthers the University's mission by disseminating knowledge in the pursuit of
education, learning, and research at the highest international levels of excellence.

www.cambridge.org
Information on this title: www.cambridge.org/9781107158122
DOI: 10.1017/9781316662915

First published 2021

Printed in the United Kingdom by TJ Books Ltd. Padstow, Cornwall

A catalogue record for this publication is available from the British Library.

ISBN 978-1-107-15812-2 Hardback
ISBN 978-1-316-61085-5 Paperback

Contents

PART III LATENT SPACE NETWORK MODELS

Figures

Tables

Notation and Acronyms

Some symbols in this book reflect multiple mathematical constructs. We do this to keep the book's notation consistent with the notation of the literature on the various models we discuss and to make clear the context of the symbols; interpretation where necessary.

Model Acronyms

ERGM	exponential random graph model
TERGM	temporal exponential random model
GERGM	generalized exponential random graph model
LSM	latent space model
LPMC	latent position cluster model
QAP	quadratic assignment procedure
CUG	conditional uniform graph
SAOM	stochastic actor-oriented model

Notation and Terms

edge	The link between two vertices
vertex	Nodes or actors in a network; the elements connected by edges
subgraph	Some subset of the network N, also known as a subnetwork
N	A network
$\mathcal{N}$	The set of all possible permutations of network N with the same number of vertices

E	The set of all edges in network N
V	The set of all vertices in network N
n	A node (i.e., a vertex)
i	Primary/ego vertex index
j	Secondary/alter vertex index
k	Third vertex index
l	Fourth vertex index
X	A covariate matrix of the same dimensions as N
X_i	A vertex-level covariate value for vertex i
x	Weighted network edges bounded on $[0, 1]^m$
Y	A dependent network with the same dimensions as N
Y	The weights of network edges modeled by the GERGM
$y_{i,j}$	A weighted tie between i and j
Z	A potential confounder of Y in an ERGM; the latent social space in the LSM or set of positions in that space
Z	A vertex-level covariate
z_i^s	Location of vertex i in the sth dimension of the latent social space
$\mathbf{z}_i$	Location of vertex i in an s-dimensional latent social space
K	The order of temporal dependence (i.e., the number of previously observed networks to condition upon) in a longitudinal setting
M	Sample size for Monte Carlo maximum likelihood; number of iterations in the basic LSM MCMC algorithm
m	Number of adjacency matrix elements that reflect the ties between nodes
m	Blocks in the blocked Gibbs approach to interpretation
t	A temporal observation (e.g., a network snapshot at a given point in time)
T	Number of time steps in longitudinally observed networks
T	A one-to-one function for transforming x to y
$t_{i,j}$	An edge-specific one-to-one transformation function
θ	A vector of parameters
h	A statistic computed on network N
$\mathbf{h}$	A vector of statistics h
N^*	An element of the set $\mathcal{N}$ that is not necessarily N
θ'	Transpose of the vector of parameters
n	A dimension that corresponds to the number of vertices under consideration (e.g., a $1 \times n$ vector or $n \times n$ adjacency matrix)
r	An index to indicate a particular element (so as not to confuse the meaning of i and j)

S	Number of saved samples in the basic LSM MCMC algorithm
$S(m)$	Updating sequence for the blocks
S_k	Degree of the star in an alternating k-star
s	MCMC sample size in the MC-MLE algorithm; dimension of the latent social space in the LSM
N_b	A block in the block Gibbs approach to interpretation (Chapter 3)
d	A distance metric used in the LSM
d_{ij}	The distance between vertices i and j in the LSM
G	Group/cluster in the latent cluster model; indexed by g
P_{ij}	Number of trials in a binomial process weighting the edge between vertices i and j
u	Iteration number in the MC-MLE algorithm
w	A random sample from a truncated normal distribution
U	A uniform random variable
δ	Coefficient to be estimated on Z
$\delta_d^{(ij)}(N)$	Captures the change in the value of h_d that would occur if the edge N_{ij} were changed from off (o) to on (1)
δ_i	Sociality/sender random effect for vertex i in the random effects LSM
γ_j	Receiver random effect for vertex i in the random effects LSM
ε	Theoretical error term in QAP
ϵ	Empirical error term in QAP
π	A matrix permutation operator on ϵ
π	Denotes a probability model [in Section 4.4]
β	Regression coefficient in QAP; coefficient for exogenous covariate in the LSM
θ	A parameter to be estimated
η	A nonlinear function of θ for use in curved ERGMs
α	Geometric penalty for use in geometrically weighted statistics
λ	A weight for use in geometrically weighted statistics
ψ	A weighting parameter based on λ for use in geometrically weighted statistics
ν	A positive scalar that controls the rate at which the weights attributed to edges change with the number of shared partners in GWESP
λ	Rate-of-change function in the SAOM
ρ	"A statistical parameter" according to Snijders (2016)

γ		A parameter vector for the marginal distribution of edge values in the GERGM
$q(\cdot \mid x^{(t)})$		A truncated multivariate normal proposal distribution
$q_\sigma(w \mid x)$		Truncated normal PDF on the unit interval
$\psi(\cdot \mid \mu, \sigma^2)$		Normal PDF
$\Phi(\cdot)$		Standard normal CDF
$\tau(\cdot)$		Acceptance probability in the Metropolis–Hastings algorithm
η		Linear component of the LSM
μ_g		Mean of cluster g in the latent cluster model
$\sigma_g^2 I_s$		Variance of cluster g in the latent cluster model
λ_g		Probability of membership in group g in the latent cluster model

Preface

AIM OF THIS BOOK

This book grew out of graduate courses that Skyler Cranmer and Bruce Desmarais have been teaching at the Ohio State University and Pennsylvania State University, respectively, over the last five years. It began as our lecture notes and slide decks, evolved into a series of handout notes, and eventually became a book concept. Our courses were attended by a wide range of social and behavioral scientists (political science, sociology, communication, psychology, sports science, social work, public policy, and many others), statisticians, and computer scientists. We benefited greatly from the discussions in these classes and now seek to pass this content on to researchers outside our classes.

The goal of this book is to provide an introduction to statistical inference with network data. There are many excellent books on network analysis, but they tend to be focused on descriptive analysis rather than on the comparatively new and quickly evolving world of inferential analysis with networks. For many, particularly in the social and behavioral sciences, a focus on description is dissatisfying since deductive hypothesis testing is the bedrock of our disciplines. In this book, we aim to introduce the reader to inferential network models theoretically and to provide code and empirical examples through which the reader may learn to conduct their own analyses.

This book assumes some limited knowledge, consistent with having taken an introductory course, in basic statistics, regression analysis (with nonnetwork data), and basic techniques for descriptive network analysis.

We have worked hard to make the text stand on its own to the extent possible, but readers unfamiliar with these concepts may wish to consult reference material or introductory texts on these subjects.

LEARNING OBJECTIVES

As this book grew out of graduate courses, it is structured by topic and with specific learning outcomes intended for every part and chapter within.

Part I of this book is designed to familiarize the reader with the concept of inferential (as opposed to descriptive) network analysis, its problems, the opportunities it presents, how it can be used to both test and help develop substantive theories, what goes wrong when networks are modeled inappropriately, and how we can detect the presence of network dependencies. Part II focuses on a powerful and popular technique for inferential network analysis: the exponential random graph model (ERGM). After reading this part of the book and working through the examples and problems, the reader should be able to specify, run, troubleshoot, and interpret an ERGM with a single binary network, a set of temporally observed networks, or a weighted (valued-edge) network. Part III focuses on another powerful and popular approach to modeling networks: the latent space network model (LSM). After reading this part and working the examples and problems, the reader should be able to specify, run, troubleshoot, and interpret an LSM with binary, weighted, or longitudinal network data.

The specific learning objectives of the book are as follows:

- Part I: Understand the concept of statistical inference with network data, how that differs from inference with nonnetwork data, the problem and opportunity of network dependence, and how to identify network dependence when it exists.
    - Chapter 1: Understand what inferential network analysis is, how it can be used to test substantive hypotheses, opportunities it presents for theoretical development, and what goes wrong if network data are mistreated.
    - Chapter 2: Be able to detect and (sometimes) adjust for network dependencies via tools like the conditional uniform graph test (CUG) and the quadratic assignment procedure (QAP).

- Part II: Gain an understanding of and proficiency in applying the exponential random graph model (ERGM) and its extensions to temporal and weighted networks.
    - Chapter 3: Be able to estimate, interpret, and assess the fit of a basic ERGM.
    - Chapter 4: Be able to specify an ERGM with endogenous and exogenous effects that correspond to theory.
    - Chapter 5: Understand ERGM estimation, the problem of degeneracy, and how to troubleshoot degenerate specifications.
    - Chapter 6: Be able to specify, estimate, assess, and interpret temporal ERGMs and SAOMs for longitudinally observed networks.
    - Chapter 7: Be able to specify, estimate, assess, and interpret a generalized ERGM for use on weighted networks.
- Part III: Gain an understanding of and proficiency with the latent space network model (LSM), being able to apply it to binary, weighted, and temporal networks.
    - Chapter 8: Understand the basics of the LSM's mechanics, fitting, specification, and interpretation.
    - Chapter 9: Gain a deeper understanding of how the model is estimated and how to interpret the latent space itself.
    - Chapter 10: Gain facility with extensions to the basic LSM such that the reader could use the model on weighted networks, run cluster models, run random effects models, and run latent factor models.

DATA AND CODE

All data and code for this book are bundled in the R package `ina`, which we developed for this book. The package can be downloaded from `https://github.com/jason-morgan/ina`. The first chapter of this book provides code and a walk-through of how to access and download the package.

SUGGESTIONS FOR TEACHING A COURSE WITH THIS BOOK

As this book grew out of the graduate courses we teach, we believe it follows a logical topic progression (and indeed the progression we use when we teach). An alternative progression would be to teach Part III (the LSM) before Part II (the ERGM). As our discussion of the LSM does not require knowledge of the ERGM, the order of these topics could be switched without causing confusion among the students.

To aid in teaching courses with this book, we have structured most of the problem sets at the end of each chapter to support students in writing research papers using the tools covered in the chapter. When we teach, we prefer problem sets to contribute to a final product rather than being "busy work" that does not necessarily help a student achieve a research aim.

Acknowledgments

We are grateful to all those who helped us craft this book. This book highlights methodological developments that were supported by a number of grants from the National Science Foundation, including SES-1558661, SES-1637089, SES-1514750, SES-1461493, SES-1357622, and SES-1357606, and from the National Institute on Drug Abuse (NIH R-34, DA043079-01A1). We are deeply grateful to our families for their support throughout the writing process, especially to Mirjam, Rebecca, Hadleigh, Emerson, Evelyn, Marin, and Danielle. Thanks are due to Caleb Pomeroy and Caleb Costa for their valuable research assistance. The book also benefited greatly from the comments of Ohio State and Penn State graduate students who read early drafts of this book's chapters as part of their network analysis courses. Thanks too to Mark Lubell and Matt Robbins for providing the replication code and data we used as an example in the discussion of bipartite ERGMs. Not least, we are grateful to Robert Dreesen at Cambridge University Press for his early and consistent support of this project. We are in debt to you all.

PART I

DEPENDENCE AND INTERDEPENDENCE

Promises and Pitfalls of Inferential Network Analysis

With the explosive digital technologies of the information age (e.g., the Internet, digital messaging, online social networks), we may be tempted to think of a networked society as a rather modern phenomenon. However, as a conceptual structure, networks lie at the heart of foundational works in the study of society. The founders of social contract theory (Locke, Hobbes, Rousseau) characterized society as arising from a set of dyadic and groupwise contracts that permitted people to transition from an independent, individualistic, and zero-sum "state of nature" to a more peaceful and interactive form of coexistence. Hobbes famously characterized this hypothetical state of nature:

Whatsoever therefore is consequent to a time of war, where every man is enemy to every man, the same consequent to the time wherein men live without other security than what their own strength and their own invention shall furnish them withal. In such condition there is no place for industry ... no knowledge of the face of the earth; no account of time; no arts; no letters; no society; and which is worst of all, continual fear, and danger of violent death; and the life of man, solitary, poor, nasty, brutish, and short. (as quoted in Ryan 2015, 140)

Hobbes also explains the route to escaping this "solitary, poor, nasty" state as dependent on mutual interaction and compromise – a state of coexistence that can best be conceptualized as a sociopolitical network in which ties between individuals represent mutual adherence to the social contract:

From this fundamental law of Nature, by which men are commanded to endeavour peace, is derived this second law, that a man be willing, when others are so too, as far-forth as for peace and defence of himself he shall think it necessary, to lay down this right to all things, and be contented with so much liberty against other men as he would allow other men against himself. (as quoted in Ryan 2015, 145)

The interdependence between individuals that is so fundamental to society makes network science a substantively fruitful approach to social research. In the 1933 *New York Times* article that accompanied his famous sociograms, psychologist Jacob Moreno aptly defined the promise and importance of studying society through the perspective of networks. About networks, he wrote,

Such an invisible structure underlies society and has its influence in determining the conduct of society as a whole. Deep psychological evolutions have been evident throughout the world in the last few years in clashes between groups within nations, and between nations themselves. Until we have at least determined the nature of these fundamental structures which form the networks, we are working blindly in a hit-or-miss effort to solve problems which are caused by group attraction, repulsion and indifference.

However, while interdependence in social processes makes the network perspective so illuminating, it also raises major challenges for conventional approaches to statistical inference. In most frameworks for statistical analysis, it is assumed that the units under study are drawn independently at random from some underlying distribution or data-generating process (i.e., the probabilistic sequence and/or structure of events that gives rise to the observed data). But when we study networks, it is typically inappropriate to assume that the units under study are independent of each other. In fact, we are often interested in studying how the units depend upon each other. Consequently, applying conventional tools of statistical inference could amount to assuming away the very phenomenon that we are interested in studying.

Over the last few decades, a robust literature and set of tools have been developed to address the challenges inherent to statistical inference with network data. In this text we present a broad cross section of these methods and summarize a tool kit that can be used for explanation, exploration, and prediction with network data, all through the framework of statistical inference.

1.1 A BASIS FOR CONSIDERING NETWORKS

We begin this section by discussing a hypothetical research problem that illustrates the challenges of statistical inference with networks. The context is a hypothetical political party leader (e.g., a majority leader) in a legislature who is trying to increase the support – in the form of bill cosponsorships – for legislation offered by the leader of a legislative caucus. Suppose ties (bill cosponsorships) in the network are generated according to a simple formula whereby the number of cosponsorships offered to legislator j by legislator i is governed by a formula that includes a constant, a count of the number of cosponsorships offered to legislator i by legislator j, and some random noise. As such, we say that cosponsorship ties are reciprocal, since the number of cosponsorships sent from i to j increases, in expectation, with the number of cosponsorships sent from j to i. Suppose that, in past legislative sessions, party leaders have awarded committee chair positions to legislators according to a formula that includes a constant, the count of the number of cosponsorships they have received from other legislators (i.e., legislators are rewarded for writing popular legislation), and random noise.

In data from past legislative sessions, based on these two formulas for generating cosponsorships and committee chair positions, committee chairs will, on average, have sent more cosponsorships than nonchairs. However, this correlation is spurious, as being a committee chair does not factor into the formula for generating cosponsorships. Rather, committee chairs will have sent more cosponsorships because they are legislators who received more cosponsorships. If the party leader does not consider the network dependency – reciprocity – an exercise in conventional approaches to statistical inference (i.e., regressing cosponsorships sent on an indicator of committee chair status) would lead to the conclusion that, to increase support for legislation offered by the caucus leader, the caucus leader should be offered a committee chair position. This committee chair assignment would result from an error in statistical inference, attributable to the inaccurate assumption that cosponsorship ties are independent of each other.

Statistical inference is the methodology by which a sample of data can be used to learn about the population parameters that generated those data (Casella and Berger 2001). The concept of independence is fundamental to nearly all methods in statistical inference (Dawid 1980). When two data points are independent, the value or state of one provides no information about the likely values of the other. The assumption of independence, when applied to an entire data sample, implies that each data point provides unique and unconditional information regarding the population or process from which the data were drawn. The independence assumption has proven essential to deriving and establishing normality in the sampling distributions of statistics under the classical framework of inference and deriving likelihood functions for use in the Bayesian framework. Despite its usefulness, the assumption of independence, like all assumptions adopted in the application of statistical methods, must be scrutinized. The independence assumption adopted without justification could result in inefficient estimates at best or completely erroneous inferences at worst (Ernst & Albers 2017).

Consider, for example, World War II, a conflict that involved at least a dozen countries. The conventional approach to studying dyadic conflicts as independent outcomes among pairs of countries would treat the disputes between pairs of countries on separate sides of the war as independent wars (Poast 2010). Aside from being theoretically unrealistic, the treatment of dependent multivariate observations as independent single observations creates two types of errors in statistical inference. First, since the processes according to which observations depend upon each other are omitted from conventional regression models for dyadic data, the independence assumption reflects a form of omitted variable bias (Desmarais & Cranmer 2017). Second, when independence is inappropriately assumed, p-values are subject to the problem of data multiplication (Stevens & Verhoest 2016), whereby observations contribute less independent information than is reflected in the standard errors, p-values are too small, and statistical inference is subject to a heightened rate of Type 1 errors.

The fundamental challenge posed in statistical inference with networks is that data points that are either embedded in networks or consitute the relationships in the networks cannot be assumed to arise independently (Cranmer & Desmarais 2016). To illustrate the first type of data, consider individuals embedded in a friendship network. The attitudes and behaviors of the individuals, voting behavior, for example, often depend upon the attitudes and behaviors of those to which they are connected. These are data that involve a network. Now consider data that *are* a network: the fundamental unit of analysis is the relationship between two observations. A simple friendship network might be measured by coding a relationship 1 if a pair of individuals are friends, and 0 otherwise. In such data, the status of a relationship (e.g., friends/not friends) will rarely be independent of the statuses of other relationships in the network (e.g., if you and I are friends, we are likely to have some other friends in common).

Several frameworks for statistical inference have been developed in the context of dependent data. These include hierarchical modeling (Lee &

Nelder 1996), time series (Box-Steffensmeier et al. 2014), spatial analysis (Wang et al. 2013), and copula modeling (Genest & MacKay 1986). However, none of these methodological frameworks are sufficient to capture the complex structure and long reach of dependencies that we observe in networks.

In this book we will present the most common approaches to statistical inference with network data. We will present methods for adjusting variance estimates and p-values for the presence of network dependence when estimating conventional regression models. We will present a modeling approach for fully specifying the forms of dependence in the network. And we will present a parametric latent variable modeling approach to fitting leftover structure in network data without making precise assumptions regarding the form of the dependence structure.

The models and methods we describe in this book can be used for several related research objectives. First, each method we introduce can be used to characterize a network generation process using interpretable parameters and to test hypotheses regarding those parameter values. For example, an exponential random graph model (ERGM) can be formulated to simultaneously represent the degree of partisan homophily (homophily meaning "love-of-like," in this case, the tendency for ties to form between actors affiliated with the same political parties) and preferential attachment – the tendency for new ties to be sent to actors who already have many ties, among other properties, in a political communication network. Hypothesis tests regarding the presence and nature of these properties can be performed using the results from an ERGM. Other objectives include the realistic simulation of a network and, relatedly, forecasting or prediction of tie values. All of these objectives (explanation, simulation, and prediction) can be addressed with the methods we present in this book because most of these methods involve the formulation and estimation of probabilistic models for networks.

Consider the problem of maximizing the degree of interracial friendship formation in a classroom of schoolchildren by manipulating an assigned seating chart. If we learn a realistic model of the friendship network, as it relates to the seating chart, simulations from that model can be used to identify the seating chart that maximizes interracial mixing. The models presented in this book have also been used in applications of forecasting or prediction of unseen link data (e.g., Li et al. 2005; Ward et al. 2007; Lu et al. 2010; Desmarais & Cranmer 2013).

We assume that the reader of this book has two categories of background knowledge. First, we assume that the reader has taken some graduate-level coursework in which they were exposed to classical statistical inference, from either an applied or theoretical perspective. The reader should be familiar with concepts such as confidence intervals, correlation, standard errors, and logistic regression. Readings that would serve as sufficient background material on statistical inference include Casella and Berger (2001) and Hogg (2018). Second, as we do not fully cover several foundational concepts from network theory on which we draw, we assume that the reader has a basic understanding of descriptive network analysis. Readings that would serve as sufficient background material on descriptive network analysis include Wasserman and Faust (1994) and Newman (2010).

1.2 NETWORKS AND COMPLEX STATISTICAL DEPENDENCE

A network is a data structure defined by connections (often referred to as edges or ties) between vertices (i.e., nodes). The objective of inferential network analysis is to make empirically sound statements about the distribution or process that generated a network or sample of networks that exhibits complex interwoven structures. This, of course, is analogous to the objective of statistical inference, generally speaking. The feature of networks that is at once scientifically interesting and methodologically challenging is that the probability of an edge forming between any two vertices depends upon the structures formed by classes of other edges throughout the network (Cranmer and Desmarais 2011). Consider an example – the structural tendencies of inter-organizational edge formation within a policy network. Berardo and Scholz (2010) theorize that well-connected organizations will accumulate more ties because of their potential to help their partners coordinate across the network. They also posit that organizations prefer to have relationships with trustworthy partners. These hypotheses represent dependence and covariate hypotheses, respectively. Valid approaches to statistical inference with network data must simultaneously account for two separate classes of generative processes. The first class represents the structural consequences of the dependence of ties upon each other. For example, if a network exhibits reciprocity, we will be more likely to observe a tie from i to j when we also observe a tie from j to i. If we do not observe a tie from j to i, a tie between i and j would be less likely. The second class represents dependence of ties on exogenous covariates (e.g., i is more likely to send a text message to j if i and j reside in close geographic proximity). Appropriate methods for modeling network data can simultaneously incorporate dependence processes and covariate effects. Several broad classes of methods have been developed to address the fundamental challenge of inferential network analysis. These methods offer network researchers a powerful methodological tool kit for building models, testing theories, and exploring the generative nature of networks.

In discussing dependence throughout this book, we will repeatedly return to several important concepts from network theory. These include, but are not limited to, *reciprocity* – the tendency for a tie from vertex i to vertex j to be predictive of the presence of a tie from j to i (Garlaschelli & Loffredo 2004); *transitivity* – the tendency of vertices that are tied to one or more of the same third vertices (i.e., shared partners) to be tied to each other (Karlberg 1997; Vera & Schupp 2006); and *popularity* (i.e., preferential attachment) – the tendency for ties sent to a vertex to predict additional ties being sent to that same vertex (Barabási & Albert 1999). Reciprocity has been found to characterize, for example, follower networks of members of the US Congress on Twitter (Peng et al. 2016), networks of economic sanctions issued between countries (Cranmer et al. 2014), acquaintance networks of German university students (Kuhnt & Brust 2014), and dominance interactions among birds (Dey & Quinn 2014). Transitivity has been found to characterize, for example, discussion of childhood obesity on Twitter (Harris et al. 2014), trade between countries (Chu-Shore 2010), and job moves between stores in a grocery store chain (McDonald & Benton 2017). Popularity has been found to characterize, for example, collaboration between scientists (Kronegger et al. 2012), connections between cities via firm locations (Liu et al. 2015), and the formation of liking networks in an online health care community (Song et al. 2015). These properties do not, by any means, constitute an exhaustive list of dependence processes, but they serve as common network properties that pose considerable challenges to the use of conventional approaches to statistical analysis with network data. The methods that we present in this book permit the researcher to model and test for properties such as reciprocity, transitivity, and popularity, while also using covariates to predict tie formation in networks.

1.2.1   Inferential Network Analysis

Perhaps the strongest empirical regularity discovered and replicated in the quantitative study of international conflict, starting in the late

1980s and 1990s, is termed the "Democratic Peace." The Democratic Peace refers to the finding that two countries with democratic forms of government are very unlikely to go to war with each other – especially when compared to pairs of countries with other combinations of government types (e.g., autocratic and democratic, both autocratic) (Elman 2001). The evidence for the Democratic Peace was derived via the analysis of conflict data with regression models (see references in Ward et al. 2007). Ward et al. approached the analysis of conflict from a different perspective – as a network of conflicts in which countries are vertices, conflicts are undirected edges, and the network changes over time. For the first time, Ward et al. used methods for the analysis of conflict that could simultaneously account for dependence processes (e.g., was the decision of the United States to declare war on Germany in 1941 related to its decision to declare war on Japan in 1941?) and the effects of covariates (e.g., two countries' governing systems). In an analysis of the international conflict network spanning 1950–2000, Ward et al. find that once latent network structure and dependencies are accounted for, the evidence for the Democratic Peace and the broad theoretical framework from which it is derived lack robustness. They also find that the latent network structure is much more valuable when it comes to predicting conflict out-of-sample than are the measures of the Democratic Peace. This study provides an example of how estimates of covariate effects (e.g., the Democratic Peace) can be biased, and often overconfident, if network dependence processes are ignored in the statistical analysis of relational data.

In most applications of inferential network analysis, and indeed most quantitative analyses in the social sciences generally, researchers are interested in interpreting results in an explanatory or causal fashion (Cranmer & Desmarais 2016) – providing theoretical evidence regarding which specific factors lead to structure formation in the network. This is very much analogous to the sort of regression modeling often employed to analyze nonnetwork data. The model used for analysis is formulated such that (1) all of the hypothesized dynamics of network generation are represented and (2) several dynamics of interest are represented by distinct parameters in the model. Once the parameter values have been estimated, the researcher can interpret an individual parameter as evidence for the strength and direction of a specific generative dynamic, adjusting for the other dynamics represented in the model. If inferences of this explanatory/causal form are to be valid, the model used for inference must provide a fairly accurate representation of the true process that generated the data; otherwise, the inferences are subject to misspecification bias (Cranmer & Desmarais 2016).

When it comes to statistical analysis of network data, one of the common forms of misspecification risked in substantive applications is the risk that arises from not modeling dependence at all (see, for example, regression-based approaches to modeling international trade networks; Konstantinos Kepaptsoglou & Tsamboulas 2010). These studies often use dyadic regression methods – regression models that predict ties based on covariate values but do not account for any of the complex dependencies among the dyadic observations. When ignoring or insufficiently modeling network dependencies, structural tendencies in the network (e.g., popularity) can be attributed to covariate effects (Cranmer & Desmarais 2016). This misspecification bias presents a double-edge risk – by insufficiently modeling network dependencies, researchers lack understanding regarding important components of the generative process and incorrectly attribute network structure to patterns in vertices' covariate values.

Though misspecification bias is reason enough to use appropriate methods for inferential network analysis, not all applications of statistical analysis with network data are intended for explanatory interpretation. Some researchers are interested, instead, in developing models that can be used for predicting edges. An established and growing literature on edge prediction indicates that the consequences of ignoring network dependence in predictive studies are equally as negative as in explanatory studies.[1] The link prediction literature – a literature dedicated to predicting the future or unobserved states of edgesa (e.g., friendships in online social networks, militarized conflicts between states, hyperlinks connecting websites) (Adamic & Adar 2003) – has drawn upon concepts such as shared partners, structural equivalence, preferential attachment, and reciprocity in specifying and training time series models for link prediction. These approaches to prediction and forecasting exploit the long-range dependence inherent in networks (i.e., the tendency for the value of an edge from i to j to depend on the configuration of ties far away from i or j in the network). Long-range dependence, while posing a challenge to the formulation of explanatory models that account for all

---

[1] See Shmueli (2010) for a discussion of the difference between explanatory and predictive objectives in statistical modeling.

of the generative processes that give rise to networks, serves as a valuable resource in predictive research, since one part of the network can be informative about the structure of the network many hops or time steps away. For a rather extreme example of the effectiveness of using network structure for predictive purposes, see Cranmer and Desmarais (2017), who show that models based solely on network structure perform better at predicting international conflict than sets of covariates drawn from decades of international relations research. It follows, then, that ignoring network dependence in formulating predictive models may result in considerably suboptimal predictive performance relative to what is possible given available data and methods.

1.2.2 Network Theory: A Worthy Scientific Frontier

Our connections affect every aspect of our daily lives ... Beyond our own social horizons, friends of friends of friends can start chain reactions that eventually reach us.

Christakis and Fowler (2011, p.7)

The pattern of connections in a given system can be represented as a network...the structure of such networks, the particular pattern of interactions, can have a big effect on the behavior of the system

Newman (2010, p. 2)

Networks are a transparent yet flexible data structure through which researchers can reason about complex systems. The theoretical benefit of conducting principled statistical inference with networks is that rigorous empirical testing can be applied to these complex systems. Multiple complex structures that have motivated theoretical and statistical developments can be represented as networks. Common systems that can be represented as networks include, but are not limited to, spatial lattices (e.g., a grid of city streets), hierarchies (e.g., an organizational chart), and joint distributions themselves (e.g., a correlation or covariance matrix that describes how different variables in a multivariate normal distribution are associated; Pearce et al. 2015). Network theories about these systems can apply at different levels of the system. For instance, when analyzing an organizational chart, we might ask whether individuals with advanced degrees are located at the top or bottom of the chart. This would be a vertex-level theoretical question. If we were using a covariance matrix to describe a network among stock prices, we could ask whether the stocks of two companies that have a lot of the same corporate board members tended to have high covariance between their stock prices. This would be a dyad-level theoretical question. In terms of a city represented as a spatial lattice, we could ask whether it would be possible to partition the lattice according to the types of buildings (e.g., residences, businesses, government offices) that were located in the blocks along the lattice. This would be a network-level theoretical question.

Inferential network analysis has led to innovations in countless domains of scholarship. These include, but are by no means limited to, the study of friendship networks in sociology (e.g., Mouw & Entwisle 2006; Wimmer & Lewis 2010; Johnson et al. 2012; Heidler et al. 2014), interactions between countries in political science (e.g., Cranmer, Desmarais, and Menninga 2012a; Kinne 2013; Ward & Hoff 2007; Ward et al. 2007), social relations among animals in ecology (e.g., Nomano et al. 2015; Fletcher et al. 2011; Fletcher Jr et al. 2013), business and organizational interaction in economics (e.g., Lomi & Fonti 2012; Gallemore et al. 2015; Dass & Fox 2011), and brain connectivity in neuroscience (e.g., Simpson et al. 2011, 2012; Sinke et al. 2016).

Consider an example from neuroscience. Recently, neuroscientists have begun analyzing brain network architecture from the perspective of inferential network analysis. Simpson et al. (2011) model the associations between the activity levels of different regions of the brain (as measured using fMRI) as a network. They use inferential network analysis to model the brains of several subjects – some younger and some older. Based on the modeling approach they use, they are able to formulate a model that represents the "global efficiency" of brain coactivation as a network statistic. The statistic they use is designed to evaluate whether, if two vertices i and j are connected indirectly through one or more third vertices k via coactivation ties, they are less likely to be directly tied. It is inefficient for i and j to be directly tied if they have shared partners since they can communicate neural signals through their shared partner(s). Simpson et al. (2011) find that brains of older subjects are more efficient in terms of demonstrating a lower tendency toward forming redundant coactivation ties. This study serves as an example of how a global system property can be precisely characterized and tested using an inferential network analytic approach.

1.3 METHODS COVERED IN THIS BOOK

In this book we present three broad categories of approaches to inferential network analysis. The first approach is only presented briefly in Chapter 2 because it is a more limited method relative to the other approaches we present. Broadly cast, the first approach constitutes the comparison of observed patterns in the network with what we would expect those patterns to look like if the process for which we were testing did not play a role in network generation. For example, we could count the number of times we observe a pair of vertices in which i sends a tie to j and j sends a tie to i (i.e., a mutual dyad) and compare that count in our observed network to the count we would observe in networks that we simulate from a process that we know does not involve tie reciprocation (e.g., there's a tie from i to j if a biased coin lands on tails). Within this approach, we cover the quadratic assignment procedure (QAP), a method for permutation testing with networks, and conditional uniform graph (CUG) testing, a method for evaluating network statistics against simple null distributions. Both of these methods, the QAP and CUG, constitute methods of hypothesis testing that account, to a degree, for network dependence. However, these methods do not lead to the formulation of generative models for networks.

A major portion of this text is devoted to presenting the exponential random graph model and its extensions. The ERGM is defined as a probability distribution for graphs (i.e., a mathematical model that can be used to generate entire networks). The ERGM can be customized to incorporate virtually any combination of conceivable network properties. We will cover the canonical ERGM and present its extensions on weighted and longitudinal networks. The costs of the flexibility of ERGM come in two different categories: questions about specification and computational complexity in estimation. We will address both of these topics in detail.

The latent space approach represents another powerful framework for statistical inference with networks. Where the ERGM offers explanatory flexibility – allowing the researcher to specify and test any form of network dependence of interest – the latent space framework allows the researcher to test for covariate effects, while incorporating unmodeled network structure through flexible formulations of latent variable effects, akin to mixed effects models for networks. The latent space model and its extensions consist of a regression equation that can be used to predict tie formation with covariates and a latent variable interaction model that predicts the structure in tie formation that cannot be explained using the covariates.

We have designed the chapters of this book to each incorporate four features. The first comprises the essential methodological, mathematical, and statistical definitions required to understand the concepts introduced in the chapter. The second comprises running data examples with which we present original applications of the methodology introduced in the chapter. The third is reference to the scholarly literature in which the methodology has been applied. The fourth component is supplementary data and code for the R statistical software, which can be accessed via the R package associated with this book, ina, which is available at https://github.com/jason-morgan/ina.

Getting Started

Throughout the book we include running example applications to illustrate the use of the methods introduced, and we demonstrate how to apply them using real-world data and available software. The running examples are presented in specially structured sections, such as this. All of the datasets we use in these sections are available in the R package ina, which we developed for use with the applications in this book. The R package can be installed from https://github.com/jason-morgan/ina. The code snippet below illustrates how the package can be installed and then uses the help() function sequentially to bring up the documentation for each dataset included in the package.

```
 1  library(devtools)
 2  install_github("jason-morgan/ina")
 3
 4  ## Look at the help files for the data included in the package
 5
 6  help(ACCBasketball)
 7
 8  ## This directed network of 15 nodes represents scoring between teams
 9  ## in the Atlantic Coast Conference in the 2016 men's basketball
        regular
10  ## season.
11
12  help(Books)
13
14  ## This network consists of 105 vertices, each representing a book
15  ## about politics sold in the early 2000s in Amazon.
16
```

```
17  help(cosponsorship)
18
19  ## This undirected weighted network consists of 101 vertices, each a
20  ## U.S. Senator in the 106th Senate.
21
22  help(estuaries)
23
24  ## This is a directed network with 194 total nodes, spread over
25  ## separate networks that cover ten U.S. estuaries.
26
27  help(gaoh)
28
29  ## This is a directed network of film actors with 55 nodes, over seven
30  ## time periods covering the 'Golden Age of Hollywood'
31
32  help(Hookups)
33
34  ## This undirected network consists of 44 vertices representing
        hookups
35  ## among characters in the Grey's Anatomy television series.
36
37  help(Krackhardt)
38
39  ## This directed network contains the advice communication network
40  ## between 21 managers in a high-tech manufacturing company
        (Krackhardt
41  ## 1987).
42
43  help(Senate)
44
45  ## Cosponsorship network among the 5 most liberal and 5 most
46  ## conservative. In this directed network an edge from i to j
        indicates
47  ## that senator i cosponsored at least two bills sponsored by j in the
48  ## 106th Congress.
49
50  help(Strike)
51
52  ## This undirected network contains the informal communication network
53  ## between 24 striking sawmill workers (Michael 1997). See Details
54  ## below.
```

2

Detecting and Adjusting for Network Dependencies

Throughout most of this book we will focus on building complete statistical models that represent how vertex features predict ties, as well as how ties relate to each other. In this chapter we take an intermediate step toward that end. We present methods that permit researchers to test either for ways in which edges relate to each other or for the effects of vertex features, but not both simultaneously. The methods presented in this chapter help to build bridges between descriptive network statistics and conventional regression models to the full featured models we cover throughout the remainder of the book.

Running Example: Cosponsorship in the US Senate

Throughout this chapter we will use a single application to illustrate methodological concepts and application in software. For this chapter, that application is a network of US senators. The senators are the vertices. The edges in the network are directed and are based on the process of bill cosponsorship. After a bill is introduced in the Senate, and before either the bill is passed or the session ends (whichever comes first), any senator can sign on as a cosponsor of the bill – indicating their endorsement of the legislation. In the network that we study, we draw an edge from each cosponsor of a bill to the sponsor of the bill – the senator who introduced the bill. The network data included in the ina package named cosponsorship includes a list called 'senlist' – a list object that contains a 101 × 101 adjacency matrix in which the i, j cell gives the number of times senator i cosponsored a bill introduced by senator j during the 108th Congress (2003–2005), as well as a character vector of senator names. Also included in `cosponsorship` is a 101 × 2 data frame object that gives two-dimensional ideological scores for each senator. These data were originally collected by Fowler (2006). Bill cosponsorship is a relational process that has been regularly studied using network analysis (Tam Cho & Fowler 2010; Clark & Caro 2013; Bratton & Rouse 2011).

In the code below we load in the data from the cosponsorship network. In line 12 we threshold the matrix to produce a network in which there is an edge from senator i to senator j if senator i cosponsored at least ten bills that were sponsored by senator j. Note that this is not necessarily a great idea for scientific analyses, but we do it here for the purposes of simplicity in illustration. The problem is that the network produced through such thresholding may be sensitive the the arbitrarily chosen threshold. At the very least, we lose much quantitative information in the process of binarization. It would be more principled to analyze the network as one with weighted (i.e., valued) edges, but we do not discuss methods for this type of analysis until later in the book.

In this application, we make use of one other variable associated with senators. The data frame `dwnom` is a two-column dataset that contains ideology scores for the senators. The ideology scores are two-dimensional, with the first column containing the senator's score on economic conservatism and the second column containing the senator's score on cultural conservatism. The higher the value, the more conservative the senator. These scores are derived by scaling senators' roll call votes. Interested readers can read more about how these scores are derived from Poole and Rosenthal (2000). At the end of this code snippet we produce a simple network plot that visualizes the network. We color vertices such that the lighter the color the more conservative the senator. We see from this visualization that senators who are close to each other in the cosponsorship network are typically similar in terms of their ideological scores. We will analyze the structure of this network throughout the remainder of this chapter.

```
1  library(sna)
2  library(ina)
3
4  ## Read in the cosponsorship data (108th Senate)
5  data(cosponsorship)
6
7  ## grab the adjacency matrix
8  SenNet <- senlist$net
```

```
 9
10 ## create a thresholded network
11 ## i must cosponsor j at least ten times
12 SenNetBinary <- 1*(SenNet > 9)
13
14 ## plot this network
15 ## use liberal/conservative score to color nodes
16 conservatism <- dwnom[,1]
17
18 ## convert to grayscale color
19 node.color <- gray((conservatism-min(conservatism)) /
20                    max(conservatism-min(conservatism)))
21 set.seed(1234)
22 plot(network(SenNetBinary), vertex.col=node.color,
23     edge.col=rgb(150, 150, 150, 150, maxColorValue=255))
```

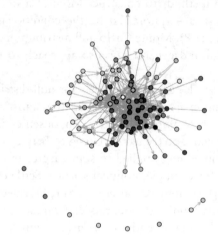

2.1 DETECTING DEPENDENCIES: CONDITIONAL UNIFORM GRAPH TESTS

Studying the complexity of network structure often involves the application of network descriptive statistics such as centralization, graph transitivity, and graph reciprocity. Network descriptive statistics can shed light on vertex positions, subgraph features, and whole network properties. However, due to the complexity of network structure, we often have little sense of how statistics should look under various network generation processes (e.g., does a graph-level clustering coefficient of 0.9 mean that a network exhibits a high degree of clustering?). Moreover, there are often structural features underlying the networks that affect the values of descriptive statistics. For instance, descriptive statistics on legislative networks in the United States are affected by the two political parties that make up the legislature, and transportation networks are affected by major infrastructure such as freeways. The fundamental problem is that one should have a well-defined benchmark or null distribution against which to compare the values computed on the observed network. What we mean here by a null distribution is a probability distribution for generating networks that does not involve a significant tendency regarding the process under study. For example, if the researcher is interested in testing for reciprocity in a network, the null distribution would not involve a tendency for ties to reciprocate each other. The construction of such null distributions has generally been approached through the use of simulation methods to construct Monte Carlo null distributions for network statistics – epitomized by the conditional uniform graph (CUG) test (Butts 2008). Monte Carlo null distribution construction represents a powerful and general purpose approach to network statistic benchmarking.

The use of network generative models for null distribution construction is very common in the literature on the statistical mechanics of networks (Rybarsch & Bornholdt 2012, Simonsen et al. 2004, Maslov, Sneppen & Zaliznyak 2004, Łuksza, Lässig & Berg 2010, Dianati 2016) and has been adopted and applied to some degree in other subfields of network science, for example, political science (Settle et al. 2010), sociology (Neal 2014), ecology (Croft et al. 2011; Freckleton & Watkinson 2001), and security studies (Desmarais & Cranmer 2013). Null model benchmarking holds the potential to be used in any field that has made fruitful use of descriptive network measures. Comparison with a null distribution enhances the use of descriptive network measures by creating a relevant metric for normalization of the network statistic(s) of interest that is customized to the respective application.

2.1.1 Methodological Overview

The CUG test (Butts 2008) is a powerful and general-purpose framework for evaluating whether a specific feature of a network, as represented by a network descriptive statistic, is present at a statistically significant level in the network.

Before presenting the specifics of the CUG test, we briefly review the components of classical hypothesis testing. Consider the classical test that a population mean is equal to zero, as applied to an independent

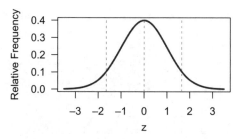

FIGURE 2.1 Standard normal distribution, which is the distribution of the
z-statistic.

and identically distributed random sample from that population (i.e., the
z-test). Under these testing conditions, if the sample size is large, if the
null hypothesis of zero-mean is true, we know that the sample mean
divided by the standard error of the mean would have a standard normal
distribution – the classic bell curve (Warner 2013), which is depicted in
Figure 2.1. The observed value of the sample mean divided by the SE of
the mean can be compared to this distribution to evaluate the probability of observing a sample mean as extreme as that observed if the null
hypothesis holds.

There are three important ways in which the z-test, and other classical
statistical hypothesis tests, fall short when it comes to testing network
hypotheses. First, we are typically interested in complex configurational
statistics that cannot be easily characterized as a mean or other common
statistic, such as the number of triangles in the network, the number of
mutual dyads, or the centralization of a network. Second, the sample
size is not large. In fact, there is often just one network and one corresponding statistic value. Third, even if the statistic of interest results in
multiple values when applied to the network (e.g., eigenvector centrality),
the observations are not independent. As such, we need an alternative
framework for constructing null distributions for network statistics.

In the CUG test, the null hypothesis is constructed by drawing networks from a uniform distribution of networks defined on the space of
networks that exhibit one or more fixed conditions (e.g., have a fixed
number of ties, a fixed degree distribution). Figure 2.2 depicts the in-
degree distributions that would arise from a six-vertex directed network
in which each vertex sends ties to other vertices that are selected uniformly at random. In other words, 2.2 gives the in-degree distributions
that arise from a distribution of directed six-vertex networks in which
each network where each vertex has out-degree 2 is equally likely. To
construct a null distribution for a statistic (e.g., the number of triangles),

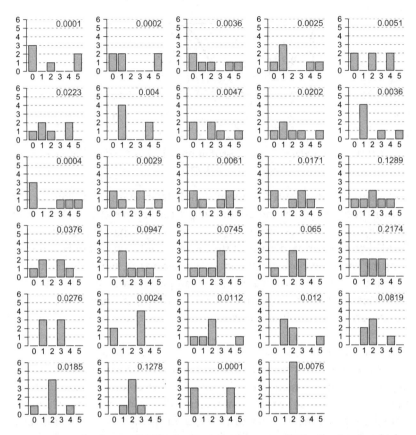

FIGURE 2.2 In-degree distributions arising from a null distribution in which each vertex sends ties to two vertices selected uniformly at random. The *x*-axis gives the in-degree. The *y*-axis gives the number of vertices with the respective in-degree. All twenty-nine possible in-degree distributions from a network of six vertices are depicted. The text gives the probability, rounded to the ten-thousandth, of the respective in-degree distribution.

one randomly draws networks from the null distribution of networks, and calculates the statistic of interest on the networks from the null distribution, as well as on the observed network. A left (right) tailed *p*-value is then calculated as the proportion of simulated statistic values that are less (greater) than the observed values. The null distribution represented in Figure 2.2 controls for the out-degree distribution of the network, forcing each vertex to have out-degree 2. Other controls used in the literature include controlling for the network size, density, in-degree distribution, and dyad distribution. The features for which researchers control should be selected to account for lower-order generative properties that could affect the network configuration being tested (e.g., the number of edges in a network affects the number of reciprocated edges in a network).

Suppose one observed a network of six students in a classroom, in which each student was asked to select the two best informed students among them, excluding themselves. Suppose one student is selected by the five other students, and you wonder whether that is a strong sign of the popular student's expertise, or if it is likely that at least one of the students would have been selected by the other five if students were selecting others uniformly at random. We can use the probabilities listed in Figure 2.2 to calculate the probability that at least one student has an in-degree of 5. By adding up the probabilities associated with all of the distributions in which there is at least one in-degree of 5, we find that the probability of at least one student being selected by five others is 0.0612 under the null distribution. If we use the 0.10 threshold for evaluating statistical significance, we would reject the null hypothesis that the in-degree of 5 was generated by students selecting other vertices uniformly at random. In other words, 5 would be a statistically significantly high maximum in-degree under the null distribution depicted in Figure 2.2.

2.1.2   Applications in the Literature

The CUG test has been used in a variety of applications in the network science literature (Holme 2005, Jasny 2012, Desmarais & Cranmer 2013; Neal 2017, Dokuka, Valeeva & Yudkevich 2015). We will discuss one in detail. Desmarais and Cranmer (2013) studied the degree to which network dependencies in the transnational terrorism network could be used to forecast transnational terrorism ties between countries. They focused specifically on triadic structures in the network, and how they unfold over time. Desmarais & Cranmer (2013) used the CUG test to evaluate the level of transitivity in the graph. Transitivity is a network concept that is related to both hierarchy and clustering in networks. To measure transitivity, they used the graph transitivity statistic implemented in the R package sna. Graph transitivity is the proportion of configurations $i \rightarrow j \rightarrow k$ in which there is an edge from i to k (i.e., the proportion of two-paths in which the first vertex in the two-path sends a tie to the last vertex). They looked at transnational terrorism ties between countries in every year from 1980 through 2002. In all but two years – two years in which there were no triangles in the network – they found that the network exhibited a statistically significantly high level of transitivity. This finding served as an important precursor to the development of their forecasting models, which were based largely in transitivity and other triadic patterns.

Running Example: Cosponsorship in the US Senate

Returning to the cosponsorship example, the simple code snippet below shows how to run the CUG test for graph transitivity. The cug.test function in the R package sna implements the CUG test. The first argument is the network. The second argument, gtrans, is the statistic to which the CUG testing will be subjected – a function that takes a network object or adjacency matrix as an argument. The third argument indicates the feature of the network to hold constant in the distribution of random graphs. Since the cosponsorship network is directed, and we are testing a triadic feature, we hold the dyad distribution constant. The dyad distribution is simply the number of dyads in which there are no edges, one edge, and two edges (i.e., no edges between i and j, an edge from i to j *or* an edge from j to i, and edges from i to j *and* from j to i). The final argument is the number of networks to simulate to construct the null distribution. The number of networks to simulate is typically set to at least 1,000. The more networks simulated, the more accurate the calculation of the p-value. To assess whether the number of simulations is high enough, the researcher should at least rerun the test with a different seed value, to assure that conclusions regarding statistical significance are consistent across the two runs.

```
1  ## Set seed for replicability
2  set.seed(1234)
3  ## Example of a conditional uniform graph test
4  ## test for transitivity in the network (gtrans in the SNA package)
5  ## control for dyad distribution via dyad.census option
6  ## Null distribution constructed using 500 draws
7  cugResults = cug.test(dat=SenNetBinary,
8          FUN=gtrans,
9          cmode="dyad.census",
10         reps=500)
11
12 ## Look at results with just p-values
13 cugResults
```

When printing the object, cugResults, we see the results print out below. The last three lines of this output give the testing results. The first line indicates that the value of graph transitivity, when applied to the observed graph, is approximately 0.37. The next row indicates that none of the graph transitivity values generated using the null distribution of networks exceeds the value of transitivity in the observed network. The next row indicates that all of the transitivity values derived from the null distribution of networks are less than the value in the observed network. These numbers provide strong evidence that there is a high degree of transitivity in this cosponsorship network. One characteristic that may be contributing to this high transitivity is ideological clustering. In the next section, in which we present the quadratic assignment procedure, we illustrate how to test for such clustering.

```
 1  Univariate Conditional Uniform Graph Test
 2
 3  Conditioning Method: dyad.census
 4  Graph Type: digraph
 5  Diagonal Used: FALSE
 6  Replications: 500
 7
 8  Observed Value: 0.3658105
 9  Pr(X>=Obs): 0
10  Pr(X<=Obs): 1
```

In the histogram below we take another look at the results of the CUG test. This is a common way to visualize CUG results, and is generated by running `plot(cugResults)` in R. The histogram depicts the distribution of transitivities resulting from the null distribution of networks. The red line is drawn at the observed transitivity value. This plot demonstrates, perhaps more clearly than the simulated *p*-values, that the observed transitivity value is much higher than those generated under the null distribution.

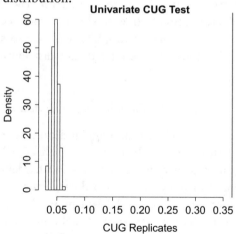

Univariate CUG Test

CUG Replicates
Conditioning: dyad.census Reps: 500

2.2 THE QUADRATIC ASSIGNMENT PROCEDURE (QAP)

The CUG test offered a method for testing the significance of a network dependence pattern, but it is limited in terms of the number of patterns for which it can either test or control. This is problematic when we consider the goal of estimating a regression-like equation in which covariates are used to predict the existence and/or value of ties between nodes (i.e., dyadic regression). Dyadic regression represents a historically common approach to modeling and testing hypotheses regarding the correlates of relational outcomes. For example, Barr, Dekker and Fafchamps (2012) use dyadic regression to model the likelihood of insurance pooling between individuals; Hafner-Burton and Montgomery (2008) use dyadic regression to model economic sanctions between countries; and York and Cornwell (2006) use dyadic regression to model influence relationships between a sample of jurors. The statistical pitfall of using regression with dyadic data is that network dependence violates the independence assumptions commonly used in formulating both estimators and confidence intervals (or p-values) for conventional regression methods. The quadratic assignment procedure (QAP), first developed for network regression by Krackhardt (1987b), is a method of hypothesis testing that is robust to the presence of network dependence. QAP builds upon Mantel (1967) permutation procedure developed for spatial regression, and computes the statistical significance of parameter estimates when the dependent variable is itself a relational matrix (e.g., distance, correlation, network adjacency matrix). The QAP is a form of nonparametric permutation testing in which row and column shuffles of the dependent and independent variables are used to simulate the null condition, which results in a simulated null distribution of regression coefficients.

2.2.1 Methodological Overview

Before presenting the QAP methodology in detail, we need to define the basic data structures on which it operates. The QAP is a method of hypothesis testing that is applied to regression modeling, and has seen most development in the context of ordinary least squares regression. The dependent variable in the QAP is a network adjacency matrix in which the value in the ith row and j^{th} column is an indicator of the existence or measure of the strength/value of the tie sent from vertex i to vertex j. The independent variable (of which there can be many), call it X, is a matrix representation of vertex or dyadic features. It can be somewhat complicated to define how the covariate should be specified as a matrix. The following list covers how major covariate effects can be represented for use with the QAP:

- *Homophily* with respect to a vertex attribute: X_{ij} is the absolute difference between the attribute values of i and j.
- *Sender* effect of a vertex attribute: X_{ij} is the attribute of i.
- *Receiver* effect of a vertex attribute: X_{ij} is the ideology of j.

To illustrate the basic methodology of the QAP, we offer an example of bivariate permutation in Figure 2.3. The QAP boils down to randomly shuffling rows and columns of the adjacency matrix (N). An adjacency matrix is a matrix in which the i, j element represents the value of the edge from i to j. If the network is undirected, the adjacency matrix is symmetric. This maintains the structure of the network right down to the edges, but by shuffling the vertices, the relationship between N and a hypothetical dyadic covariate X, is broken. In the QAP, some measure of relationship (e.g., correlation coefficient, regression) between N and X is calculated on the un-permuted data, then the same measure is calculated on many permutation based replications of the data. A two-tailed p-value to assess the null hypothesis that there is no relationship between N and X can be calculated as the proportion of relationships calculated under permutations that are at least as large, in magnitude, as the value calculated on the observed data. The intuition for QAP is that, the observed association between N and X is significant if it is greater than the association between X and a large proportion (e.g., 0.95) of the networks that can be randomly drawn among the nodes that have the same structure (e.g., number of edges, number of triangles, degree distribution) as N.

N			
	A	B	C
A	0	1	1
B	1	0	0
C	0	1	0

X			
	A	B	C
A	0	3	-2
B	1.2	0	-4
C	0	6	0

	B	C	A
B	0	0	1
C	1	0	0
A	1	1	0

	A	B	C
A	0	3	-2
B	1.2	0	-4
C	0	6	0

FIGURE 2.3 Illustration of a bivariate QAP. Example of dependent network (i.e., N) permutation.

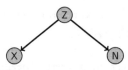

FIGURE 2.4 Causal diagram illustrating the role of a confounder (Z) in creating a spurious correlation between X and N.

Using the QAP with three or more values is more complicated than using either the N or X permutation, which are equivalent in the bivariate case. Suppose there are three relational variables – the dependent network N, the independent variable of interest X, and a potential confounder Z, for which we would like to control in a regression calculating the effect of X on N. Figure 2.4 depicts the causal diagram of Z inducing a spurious correlation between X and N. Consider N permutation, in which the rows of N are permuted to reflect the null hypothesis of no relationship between N and X. Doing this also breaks the relationship between Z and N, which amounts to assuming away one leg in the confounder diagram. Now consider X permutation, in which only X is shuffled. This would break the relationship between Z and X, also assuming away a leg in the confounding diagram.

Dekker, Krackhardt, and Snijders (2007) propose an algorithm, termed double semipartialing, that is intended to balance between X and N permutation, and they show performs better than X or N permutation. Let $\hat{\delta}Z$ be the estimate from $N = \delta Z + \varepsilon$. Define $\hat{\epsilon}_{XZ} = X - \hat{\delta}Z$. Define $\pi(\hat{\epsilon}_{XZ})$ to be a matrix permutation of $\hat{\epsilon}_{XZ}$. Denote the regression coefficient under QAP testing as β. The nonparametric null distribution of β is derived by estimating $N = \pi(\hat{\epsilon}_{XZ})\beta + \delta Z + \varepsilon$. QAP testing is done for each variable in the regression equation by iteratively rerunning the double semipartialing procedure for each variable. The QAP is a useful methodology when the researcher is solely interested in testing hypotheses regarding the relationship between covariates and the network, without interest in testing hypotheses about network dependence or in building a model that can accurately reproduce network structure.

2.2.2 Applications in the Literature

For applications of the QAP in political networks research see Mizruchi (1990), Weible and Sabatier (2005), Bochsler (2009), Shrestha and Feiock (2009), Henry (2011), Lee, Feiock, and Lee (2012), Heaney et al. (2012), Desmarais et al. (2015), Andrew et al. (2015), and Chen, Suo, and Ma (2015). Considering the work of Heaney et al. (2012) as an example, the authors were interested in understanding the conditions under which political party activists become members of the same associations, and particularly in assessing the extent to which co-partisanship affected this likelihood. Drawing upon surveys they conducted at the 2008 Democratic and Republican National Conventions, Heaney et al. (2012) estimated models predicting organizational co-membership as a function of co-partisanship. They also controlled for ideology, sex/gender, race/ethnicity, age, educational attainment, income, and religious participation. The empirical analysis is particularly interesting given our discussion above, because the authors specified three types of models: logistic regression, the QAP, and an ERGM. Results from all three models showed that being in the same party is a strong positive predictor of being in the same organization, even after controlling for alternative explanations for co-membership. In fact, only 1.78 percent of co-memberships crossed party lines: the association network is strongly polarized by party. The results illustrate one of the many barriers affecting partisan polarization: party activists rarely come into contact with activists from the other party in their civic and political associations.

Running Example: Cosponsorship in the US Senate

Like the CUG, the QAP can be applied using the R package sna. Continuing with our analysis of the cosponsorship network, we compare hypothesis tests using standard parametric OLS results with those calculated using 500 QAP permutations. The code for running this example is provided below. Note that to use the QAP, the covariates must be represented as matrices that are equal in dimension to the adjacency matrix. We can see this with the `ideoDist`, `ideoSend`, and `ideoRec` objects in the R code below. `ideoDist` is a distance matrix in which cell i, j, gives the absolute difference between the ideology scores of vertices i and j. `ideoSend` is a matrix in which cell i, j, gives the ideology score of vertex i (i.e., the potential sender of edge ij). `ideoRec` is a matrix in which cell i, j, gives the ideology score of vertex j (i.e., the potential receiver of edge ij).

```
1  library(sna)
2  library(ina)
3
4  ## Read in the cosponsorship data (108th Senate)
5  data(cosponsorship)
6
7  ## Extract the adjacency matrix
```

```
 8 ## i/j element is the number of times senator i cosponsored senator j
 9 ## in the 108th Congress
10 SenNet <- senlist$net
11
12 ## The covariate-creation operations that follow will be applied
13 ## to each column in dwnom--each of two network covariates
14
15 ## Create Distance Matrix for homophily
16 ideoDist <- as.matrix(dist(dwnom[,1]))
17
18 ## Create Sender covariate
19 ## element ij is i's value
20 ideoSend <- matrix(dwnom[,1], nrow(dwnom), nrow(dwnom), byrow=FALSE)
21
22 ## Create Receiver covariate
23 ## element ij is j's value
24 ideoRec <- matrix(dwnom[,1], nrow(dwnom), nrow(dwnom), byrow=TRUE)
25
26 ## Create Distance Matrix for homophily using the second dimension of
27 ## DW-Nominate
28 ideoDist2 <- as.matrix(dist(dwnom[,2]))
29
30 ## Create Sender covariate
31 ideoSend2 <- matrix(dwnom[,2], nrow(dwnom), nrow(dwnom), byrow=FALSE)
32
33 ## Create Receiver covariate
34 ideoRec2 <- matrix(dwnom[,2], nrow(dwnom), nrow(dwnom), byrow=TRUE)
35
36 ## Create the 'graph stack' of covariates
37 #
38 covariates <- list(ideoDist=ideoDist, ideoSend=ideoSend,
       ideoRec=ideoRec,
39                    ideoDist2=ideoDist2, ideoSend2=ideoSend2,
40                    ideoRec2=ideoRec2)
41
42 ## Run QAP for continuous outcomes (netlogit is for dichotomous ties)
43 ## First OLS (nullhyp="classical")
44 ## Second QAP
45 ols <- netlm(SenNet, covariates, nullhyp="classical")
46
47 set.seed(5)
48 qap <- netlm(SenNet, covariates, nullhyp="qap", reps=100)
```

The results from this example, as can be seen by printing the objects ols and qap, are presented in Table 2.1. The results indicate that cosponsorship is strongly related to the first dimension of ideology scores – economic conservatism. Coefficients are interpreted in the conventional way for a linear model. For example, the expected number of times legislator i cosponsors legislator j decreases by approximately 2.8 with every unit of ideological distance between them. The coefficients associated with D1 are statistically significant based on both the QAP and conventional OLS p-values. However, when it comes to D2, the sender and receiver effects are only statistically significant based on the OLS p-values. This indicates that drawing inferences based on the conventional p-values would lead to a Type 1 error that would arise from inappropriately assuming that the elements of the dependent variable matrix arose independently.

TABLE 2.1 Regression coefficients and p-values from QAP analysis.

	OLS β	OLS p	QAP p
Intercept	4.082	0.000	0.000
Homophily (D1)	−2.825	0.000	0.000
Sender (D1)	−1.710	0.000	0.000
Receiver (D1)	−1.403	0.000	0.014
Homophily (D2)	−1.297	0.000	0.026
Sender (D2)	−0.418	0.001	0.234
Receiver (D2)	−0.459	0.000	0.538

Note. Dependent variable: count – number of times sender senator cosponsors legislation sponsored by receiver senator over the two-year period 2005–2006.

2.3 WRAPPING UP

Structural network features represent both interesting theoretical objects of inquiry, and characteristics that need to be controlled for when analyzing data that are embedded in networks. CUG and QAP testing represent methods that adapt conventional approaches to hypothesis testing to the setting of network structure. These methods are intuitive and powerful, but exhibit a couple of important limitations. First, when it comes to the CUG test, there is a limit on the number of structural characteristics for which the researcher can control in the null distribution. Once the researcher controls for several structural features, the conditional uniform distribution may be defined over just a handful of graphs. Second, when it comes to QAP, it is possible to conduct hypothesis tests for covariate effects that do not assume away network dependencies, but it is not possible to estimate and/or test hypotheses about network dependence using QAP. In the next section of the book we move on to a modeling framework that overcomes both of these limitations – exponential random graph models (ERGMs).

2.4 SELF-STUDY PROBLEMS

Select a network dataset to study using CUG testing and/or QAP, but avoid using the datasets from ina that were used for the current chapter. If you do not have a dataset that you would like to use for this exercise, we recommend using the Krackhardt dataset in ina, which is introduced in Section 3.1. Be sure that the dataset provides information about the ties in the network, as well as some form of exogenous covariate. Using this dataset, write up a brief report that includes the following information and analysis:

1. **Description of the dataset:** What does the dataset cover? Where did it come from? Has it been used in any prior studies (especially those that use inferential network analysis)?
2. **Description of the network:** Visualize the network. Calculate and comment on the values and distributions of descriptive quantities, noting especially anything that you think should be considered in conducting statistical modeling and testing with the network. You could calculate measures of, for example, transitivity, reciprocity, and centrality.
3. **Structural hypothesis:** Describe at least one hypothesis regarding the prominence of a network structure (e.g., reciprocal dyads, clustering).
4. **Covariate hypothesis:** Describe at least one hypothesis regarding a relationship between the network structure and an exogenous covariate in the data.
5. **Hypothesis test:** Use CUG and/or QAP to test your hypotheses.
6. **Present results:** Present your results in a tabular or graphical form, and discuss the interpretation of your hypothesis test results.

PART II

THE FAMILY OF EXPONENTIAL RANDOM GRAPH MODELS (ERGMS)

3

The Basic ERGM

3.1 INTRODUCTION

The first part of this book examined the challenges and opportunities faced by analysts working with network data. In this first chapter of the second part, we introduce a powerful and popular technique for conducting statistical inference on network data: the exponential random graph model (ERGM). We discuss the logic and formulation of the technique, as well as its basic specification and interpretation, concepts that will be discussed in more detail and extended throughout this part of the book.

What does it mean to model a network? The basic objective is to construct a probability distribution that can be used to generate networks with structural features of interest – either matching an empirically observed network or fitting some theoretical structure. Examples of these structural features include, but are not limited to, the number of ties, number of triangles, and the number of reciprocated ties. No statistical model will ever recover the network exactly, as that would reflect over-fitting, but models of networks may be useful to the extent that they can capture the *essential generative features* of the processes that produced the observed network(s).

The construction of network models has three major practical purposes: the testing of hypotheses, the simulation of complete networks, and the prediction of edge formation/dissolution.

First, hypothesis testing is the primary reason most social and behavioral scientists are interested in network analysis. The ERGM is a good choice as a network modeling framework for cases where the outcome of interest is the presence or absence of edges. When theory presents a hypothesis about how something causes the formation of edges between vertices, that hypothesis can be tested deductively through the construction of a network model. For example, do friendship ties tend to be reciprocated (e.g., Skyler considers Bruce a friend and also Bruce considers Skyler one as well) (Dokuka et al. 2017)? Do countries with similar regime types tend to go to war with one another (Dorff & Ward 2013)? Do migratory flows tend to form triadic structures (Vögtle & Windzio 2016)? In each of these examples, we see an actor (i.e., node, vertex) embedded in a larger outcome network. This is the environment in which ERGM-style network models are useful for deductive hypothesis testing.

Second, modeling networks allows the analyst to simulate those networks for the purposes of counterfactual exploration. For example, how should seats be assigned in a classroom to encourage cross-racial friendships? A well-fitting model of friendship formation (the edge-level outcome) based on, among other things, race and classroom seating assignments will allow the analyst to simulate the friendship networks expected to emerge from many (or even all, depending on the size of the class) configurations, and select the seating assignment that encourages the desired outcome. This sort of simulation is highly useful for understanding the real-world implications that changes to vertices or the relationships among them are expected to have on the network outcome of interest.

Third, and somewhat related to the above point about simulation, network models may be used to predict tie formation or dissolution (Betancourt et al. 2017). For example, Desmarais and Cranmer (2011) used a temporal extension of the ERGM (temporal ERGMs are discussed extensively in Chapter 6) on a network in which the vertices are countries, and are connected by transnational terrorist attacks, to forecast those terrorist attacks based on the topological structure of the network. The results were powerful. Predictive accuracy was over 95 percent, and probabilities assigned to edges that formed were several orders of magnitude higher than the probabilities assigned to edges that did not form. While prediction is viewed by many as a tool of "applied researchers" rather than the sort of basic research with which science is usually concerned, we believe that prediction offers much to the analyst, both in terms of advancing basic science and producing policy-relevant results.

The major advantage of the ERGM as an approach to modeling networks is that it can model how edges depend upon each other. To be more precise, let us distinguish between two classes of generative questions about which the analyst may form hypotheses: exogenous and

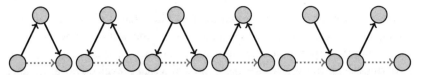

FIGURE 3.1 An illustration of how the connections among three vertices can be thought to impact the probability of the focal (indicated in dashed grey) edge forming. We see three forms of transitivity, one form of cyclicality, one form of popularity, and one form of sociality.

endogenous effects. Exogenous effects are those occurring outside the outcome network and typically correspond to the types of covariates with which analysts are used to working in a regression context. For example, do legislators in the same political party collaborate more frequently than those in opposite parties (Bratton & Rouse 2011)? Because political party is a vertex attribute, and can be observed separately from legislative collaboration, we can study the effect of party as an exogenous predictor of collaboration.

Endogenous effects are those occurring within the outcome network of interest. That is, dependencies among the ties whose presence or absence is the object of inquiry. For example, are there popularity effects in the choice of co-authors, whereby co-authorship begets more co-authorship (Biancani & McFarland 2013)? Are two authors who have both co-authored with a third more likely to coauthor with each other? Figure 3.1 illustrates the six ways in which the structure of connections among three vertices can impact the probability of the focal edge, indicated in dashed grey, forming. Endogenous effects of this sort represent a type of process that has received very little theoretical attention in the social sciences, at least by comparison to the attention dedicated to exogenous effects. This is likely because the technology to model endogenous processes is relatively new. Indeed, the ERGM is the major statistical innovation that allows for the modeling of endogenous effects, and the ERGM is a particularly attractive choice for modeling network data because it integrates both endogenous and exogenous effects into a unified statistical model.

Running Example: Krackhardt's Advice Network

The data originally collected for Krackhardt (1987a) seminal study of the advice network among twenty-one managers in a high-tech firm provide a nice running example with which we can explore the basic ERGM. In this network a directed edge is formed when one manager goes to another for professional advice. The edge is directed from the recipient of the advice to the provider of the advice. The network contains twenty-one vertices and has a density of 0.452. In addition to the advice network, we have several vertex-level covariates: age, department, level/rank in the organizational chart, and tenure. We also have an edge-level covariate: `reportsto` indicates when one vertex reports to another in the corporate hierarchy, with the supervised sending the tie to the supervisor. Further details of the data may be found in Krackhardt (1987a).

It is always good practice to approach a new dataset with an exploratory descriptive analysis. Such analyses can reveal important properties of the network or challenges that might have to be addressed in the modeling process (e.g., very high or low density of connections, which can pose estimation problems for the ERGM).

We begin by loading the `network` package (Butts et al. 2008), a useful and well-featured package for handling network data and conducting basic descriptive analyses. We then load the `ina` package – the package developed as a companion to this book. The `ina` package contains the dataset `Krackhardt`, which includes a network object named `Krackhard`. The network object includes the advice adjacency matrix, vertex attributes, and the matrix of supervisory relationships among the nodes. Thus, we have everything we will need to work with in a single object, called `Net`.

```
## Load the network package
library(network)

## Load the ina package
library(ina)

## load the Krackhardt data
data(Krackhardt)
Net <- Krackhardt
```

We may then produce descriptive plots and statistics of the network. For example, looking at plots of the network with the vertices colored and labeled by tenure, age, and department, respectively (Figure 3.2), we see that those with the longest tenure in the company tend not to be the most central figures in the advice network. At the same time, the most central figures tend not to be the oldest, with the exception of the sixty-two-year-old vertex with only five years' tenure in the company.

Finally, we notice that Department 2 is interesting because it houses some of the most central and some of the most peripheral actors in the network.

```
## Set up a 1x3 plot
par(mfrow=c(1, 3))

## Set the random seed
set.seed(1)

## define the color palette
Pal <- colorRampPalette(c("#e5f5e0", "#31a354"))

## create a temporary object housing the vertex attribute
tenure <- get.vertex.attribute(Net, "Tenure")

## assign different colors based on the vertex attribute
col.tenure <- Pal(length(unique(tenure)))[
    as.numeric(cut(tenure, breaks = length(unique(tenure))))]

## plot the network, including vertex color options
plot(Net, edge.col="gray", label.col="black", vertex.cex=1.5,
    vertex.col=col.tenure, label=tenure,
    main="Tenure")

## repeat the above steps for age and department
set.seed(1)
Pal <- colorRampPalette(c("#e5f5e0", "#31a354"))
age <- get.vertex.attribute(Net, "Age")
col.age<- Pal(length(unique(age)))[
    as.numeric(cut(age, breaks = length(unique(age))))]
plot(Net, edge.col="gray", label.col="black", vertex.cex=1.5,
    vertex.col=col.age, label=age,
    main="Age")

set.seed(1)
dept <- get.vertex.attribute(Net, "Department")
cols <- c("#a6cee3", "#1f78b4", "#b2df8a","#33a02c","#fb9a99")
col.dept <- cols[match(dept, unique(dept))]
plot(Net, edge.col="gray", label.col="black", vertex.cex=1.5,
    vertex.col=col.dept, label=dept,
    main="Department")
```

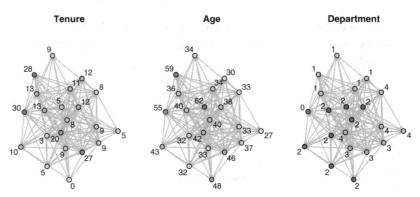

FIGURE 3.2 The Krackhardt advice network with vertices colored by tenure, age, and department, respectively.

3.2 THE EXPONENTIAL RANDOM GRAPH MODEL (ERGM)

Here, we present the mathematical definition of the ERGM. Consider the network N, composed of E edges and V vertices. For the moment, let us assume that only binary edges – those which are either present or absent but have no value – exist between any two vertices i and j. Let present edges be coded one and absent edges zero such that $N_{ij} \in \{0, 1\}$. The assumption of binary edges can be relaxed, and ERGM-style models for valued networks is the topic of Chapter 7. Let $\mathcal{N}$ denote the set of possible permutations of the network N with the same number of vertices. That is to say, $\mathcal{N}$ contains the set of every possible edge configuration of N with a constant number of vertices V, from the completely empty network (with no edges at all), to the completely connected network (where every vertex has an edge to every other vertex), and every possible configuration in-between.

To estimate a proper probability model for N, we take the maximum likelihood approach, and seek to find a model that maximizes the probability of observing the network that we *did observe*, $\mathcal{P}(N)$, with $\mathcal{N}$ being the set of possible networks that we *could have* observed. The probability (e.g., the likelihood function) of observing network N under the ERGM is

$$\mathcal{P}(N, \boldsymbol{\theta}) = \frac{\exp\{\boldsymbol{\theta}' \mathbf{h}(N)\}}{\sum_{N^* \in \mathcal{N}} \exp\{\boldsymbol{\theta}' \mathbf{h}(N^*)\}}, \tag{3.1}$$

where $\boldsymbol{\theta}$ is a vector of real-valued parameters, $\mathbf{h}(N)$ is a vector of statistics computed on N (e.g., number of edges, number of trianvges), and N^* is an element of $\mathcal{N}$. Note too that we use prime notation to indicate the vector transpose here rather than the traditional T in order to avoid confusion when we introduce temporal indices in later chapters. This defines the basic ERGM.

To understand Equation (3.1), begin by considering $\mathbf{h}(N)$. Each element of the $\mathbf{h}(N)$ vector, h, is a statistic computed on N. These statistics can reflect exogenous covariates at both the vertex and edge levels of measurement, as well as nearly any type of endogenous effect (with weak restrictions discussed in detail below). The ability of the ERGM to incorporate such a wide range of effects into a single model makes it an extremely powerful analytical tool. The numerator of the equation assigns positive weight to the observed network, while the denominator normalizes over each of the possible permutations of N in $\mathcal{N}$. Decomposed more simply,

$$\underbrace{\mathbf{h}(N)}_{\text{Net Stats}} \quad \underbrace{\theta}_{\text{Effects}} \quad \underbrace{\exp\{\theta'\mathbf{h}(N)\}}_{\text{+ Weight}} \quad \underbrace{\sum_{N^* \in \mathcal{N}} \exp\{\theta'\mathbf{h}(N^*)\}}_{\text{Normalizer}}$$

As such, we can see that the fundamental logic of the ERGM – computing the probability of the observed network given all of the networks we could have observed – is directly reflected in the mathematics of the model.

The ERGM can be used to relax the often untenable assumption that the dyads in the network – the set of all vertices which share or may share an edge – are statistically independent from one another, by treating the entire network as a single multivariate observation, rather than a large number of independent relational observations. This conceptual trick, which is essentially akin to $n = 1$ inference, affords the ERGM the ability to model nearly any type of dependence structure, but also is the root cause of some of the numerical instability problems discussed in Chapter 5.

The ERGM requires two primary assumptions. First, it requires that there be an equal probability of observing any two networks with the same values for the vector of statistics $\mathbf{h}$. Suppose two networks possess ten edges and five closed triangles each, with no additional network statistics specified. The ERGM requires that these two networks be equiprobable. Were these network not equiprobable, that would imply that some unmodeled effect is making one more likely than the other. As such, we can see that this first assumption is functionally equivalent to the assumption made in regression analysis that the model is correctly specified, without omitted variables (Bull et al. 1994). In practice, this means that we must assume that our model specification has controlled for all relevant factors, endogenous and exogenous. Otherwise, the model will be misspecified and suffer the same sort of omitted variable bias to which regression analysis is subject. It is interesting to note that while models that are not completely and correctly specified, whether regressions or ERGMs, suffer omitted variable bias, only the ERGM is capable of adjusting for endogenous effects. This reinforces the point made in Chapters 1 and 2 that conducting a regression analysis on network data using conventional estimators for both coefficients and standard errors involves the strong assumption that no endogenous dependencies are part of the data-generating process.

The second assumption required for the ERGM is that, given a set of observed network statistics **h**, the observed network exhibits the average value of those statistics over the networks that could have been observed. This assumption is necessary to identify the parameters because, recall, the network is treated as a single multivariate observation and inference is conducted on that single observation. Functionally, this is similar to the regression assumption that the average relationships in a dataset are representative of a population; an assumption that is implicit in regression models anytime inference is made from a sample to a population. This assumption should be thought of as considering the observed network to be typical of the network distribution to be inferred via ERGM.

3.3 ERGM SPECIFICATION: A BRIEF INTRODUCTION

An analyst specifying an ERGM has two primary tasks: she identifies effects that she expects to exist in the network, be they endogenous or exogenous, and she defines (selects) empirical measures of those effects (i.e., $\mathbf{h}(N)$). Following this, the software finds the set of parameters θ that approximately maximizes the likelihood of observing the data, and simulates networks so that the analyst may check model fit. We dedicate Chapter 4 to considering the specification of ERGMs in detail and Chapter 5 to the estimation of the ERGM, but here we present a brief exposition of the essential concepts in order to give the reader context and a preliminary understanding of these steps.

3.3.1 Endogenous Dependencies

The ERGM captures both endogenous and exogenous effects through the vector of network statistics $\mathbf{h}(N)$. Chapter 4 is dedicated to a detailed discussion of endogenous dependencies and their specifications. Here, we briefly introduce the concept to illustrate how both endogenous and exogenous statistics may be included in the **h** vector of Equation (3.1).

An endogenous dependency is in which the contribution of at least one edge to the network statistic value depends on the state/value of at least one other edge. For example, under the edge statistic – the count of the number of edges in the network, which is not an endogenous dependency, each edge contributes one unit to the network statistic regardless of the sates of the other edges in the network. In contrast, the tendency of two individuals who are both friends with a third to be friends with one another, called triadic closure, is an endogenous dependency. The edge between the first two friends only contributes a triangle to the network if there is at least one third node with whom both of the first two nodes are tied. The ERGM accommodates such dependencies with relative ease. The most basic and most common class of endogenous dependencies that are included in the ERGM are called Markov dependencies. Under Markov dependence, the probability of a tie between nodes i and j depends only on edges that are incident to either i or j (e.g., under Markov dependence, the tie between i and j cannot depend on the relationship between k and l). Markov dependence terms can be expressed as sums of subgraph products. Note that endogenous dependencies are somewhat more complicated than exogenous covariates because their specifications vary by the type of dependency being captured. This requires a different statistic to be created for each type of endogenous dependency and bars us from including the entire class of dependencies with a single equation as we do for exogenous covariates below.

Consider one of the most basic endogenous dependencies possible: reciprocity. Reciprocity captures the tendency of connections to be mutual, for i to consider j a friend and for j to also consider i a friend, for example. This sort of relationship is illustrated in Figure 3.3. Naturally, reciprocity is only possible in directed networks. We may create a reciprocity statistic in **h** as

$$h_R(N) = \sum_{i<j} N_{ij} N_{ji}. \tag{3.2}$$

FIGURE 3.3 Illustration of a reciprocal relationship. In a directed network, a reciprocal relationship exists in the ij dyad when $N_{ij} = 1$ and $N_{ji} = 1$.

We see that Equation (3.2) is defined on a subgraph involving the two vertices i and j. We also see that the principal quantity in the equation is a product of the N_{ij} edge by the N_{ji} edge. Notice that $N_{ij}N_{ji} = 1$ only when both N_{ij} and N_{ji} are 1, meaning that a reciprocal tie exists between i and j. Finally, the statistic in Equation (3.2) sums the subgraph product over all ij pairs in the network. We see then that this statistic increases in value every time a reciprocal edge exists. As such, the statistic merely counts the number of reciprocal edges. Yet this simple statistic captures the phenomena of interest because we would expect it to be high if ties tend to be reciprocated a lot and low if they tend not to be. Furthermore, this statistic satisfies the general definition of a Markovian statistic on the network in that the contribution of N_{ij} to the network statistic does not depend on edges that do not involve either i or j.

A large number of common and theoretically important endogenous dependencies may be captured as sums of subgraph products. Consider the concepts of popularity, sociality, and transitivity as further examples. Popularity is evidenced empirically, in directed networks, by some vertices receiving disproportionately many incoming edges, indicating that senders of ties prefer to send ties to those who already receive many ties (De la Haye et al. 2010). Popularity may be defined on the subgraph of three vertices and is written as

$$h_P(N) = \sum_{i,j,k} N_{ji}N_{ki} + N_{kj}N_{ij} + N_{ik}N_{jk}. \qquad (3.3)$$

Note that each product treats a different member of the subgraph as the focal vertex. The right panel of Figure 3.4 illustrates the popularity dynamic for vertex i. In this figure, Equation (3.3) yields a count of three in-two-stars, a structure often used to capture popularity, which we discuss in more detail below. The sociality process is just the opposite of popularity. Instead of receiving many edges, highly social vertices send many edges. The construction of the endogenous statistic is very

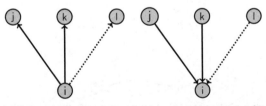

FIGURE 3.4 Illustration of sociality (left) and popularity (right). The focal vertex i either sends or receives many edges, respectively.

similar to that for popularity and requires only that the ordering of the subindices be reversed in order to indicate outgoing rather than incoming edges:

$$h_S(N) = \sum_{i,j,k} N_{ij}N_{ik} + N_{jk}N_{ji} + N_{ki}N_{kj}. \tag{3.4}$$

The sociality process is illustrated in the leftmost panel of Figure 3.4.

Finally, transitivity exists in directed networks in which a two-path from i to k through j indicates that i is likely to send a tie to j. Such a "transitive triple" exhibits a hierarchy in which $i > j > k$, and vertices send ties to those beneath them in the hierarchy. The left panel of Figure 3.5 illustrates this dynamic: vertex i has outgoing connections to j and k, while j also sends an edge to k. We can translate this dynamic into a statistic for the **h** vector as follows:

$$h_T(N) = \sum_i \sum_{j,k \neq i} N_{ij}N_{ik}N_{jk}, \tag{3.5}$$

where we see the configuration of ties directly spelled out in the subscripts. The value of the subgraph product $N_{ij}N_{ik}N_{jk}$ will only be 1 when each of the directed edges in question are 1, so Equation (3.5) literally counts the number of transitive configurations in the network that are of the type depicted in Figure 3.5.

While the entirety of the following chapter is dedicated to explicating endogenous dependencies, note the flexibility this framework affords the analyst. If one wanted to adjust for cyclical triads instead of transitive triads, depicted in the rightmost panel of Figure 3.5, one need only reverse the direction of the N_{ik} edge in Equation (3.5) to create such a statistic. A wide variety of other endogenous dependencies may be created with similar ease.

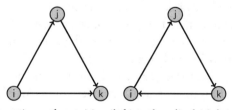

FIGURE 3.5 Illustrations of transitive (left) and cyclical (right) triads. These are distinct forms of triadic closure in directed networks that can reflect different data-generating processes.

3.3.2   Exogenous Covariates

Exogenous effects refer to network statistics in which the contribution of each edge depends on the value of information external to the network, but not on the state/value of other edges in the network. Exogenous effects constitute the independent variables that researchers are familiar with including in regression models. These are fairly straightforward to include, because their inclusion is represented with a single equation. A general statistic that captures the relationship between a covariate matrix X and the network of interest N is

$$h_D(N, X) = \sum_{ij} N_{ij} X_{ij}. \tag{3.6}$$

Note that X has the same dimensions as N. As such, X_{ij} is the covariate value corresponding to the N_{ij} dyad. The statistic described in Equation (3.6) pertains to the subgraph (i.e., sub-network) of two vertices: i and j. For this ij subgraph, the covariate value X_{ij} is multiplied by the edge indicator N_{ij}, and the resulting quantity is summed over all ij pairs in the network. It is clear then, that this statistic only increases in value for dyads for which an edge is present and that the statistic is the sum of X_{ij} values for all present edges in N. Specifying statistics in **h** as sums of subgraph products will become a theme throughout Chapter 4.

The interpretation of the statistic in Equation (3.6) is straightforward: if X has a positive effect on edge formation, then $h_X(N)$ will be higher than if the covariate values were randomly assigned to edges, controlling for the effect of the other $h(N)$s on the network configuration. The result is that the corresponding θ value in Equation (3.1) will be positive.

Notice that the covariate matrix X captures covariate values that correspond directly to the dyads of N. We see from this that Equation (3.6) most naturally accommodates dyad-level covariates; those that capture something exogenous to the network of interest about the relationship between vertices i and j. As there are many relationships that may be measured bilaterally, dyadic covariates account for a substantial percentage of the covariates that may be of interest to the analyst. Examples include indicators for having studied at the same school in studies of professional networks (Keller 2016), trade flows between countries in international networks (Duque 2018), and the number of times legislators have worked together in legislative networks (Arnold et al. 2000).

Aside from dyadic covariates, the other major class of covariates is that measured at the actor level. These covariates, rather than capturing dyadic relations between vertices, measure attributes of the vertices themselves. Examples include age or sex in friendship networks, GDP or military expenditures in international networks, and time in office or political party in legislative networks. Vertex-level covariates are easily accommodated in the ERGM but do not have the correct $n \times n$ dimensions to be included directly in Equation (3.6). Rather, vertex-level covariates must be transformed in order to be included in Equation (3.6). Consider vertex-level *sender* covariate Z, a vector of values with an entry for each vertex in the network. The $1 \times n$ vector Z can be made to conform with the $n \times n$ matrix X by populating X such that $X_{ij} = Z_i$. That is, each row of the scaled-up vertex-level covariate matrix has all the same entries, corresponding to the value of Z_i. This is akin to having each vertex have a constant relationship with every other vertex, where that constant value is the value of vertex i's value of Z, Z_i. Now, X has the same dimensions as N and Equation (3.6) may be applied directly. If Z were a receiver covariate, the transformation would be to populate $X_{ij} = Z_j$. If the network is undirected, or the researcher does not want to distinguish between a sender and receiver effect, the transformation would be to populate $X_{ij} = Z_i + Z_j$.

In some cases, a dyadic covariate is constructed through some function, besides summation, of vertex-level covariates. For example, consider terms that capture homophily effects – those designed to capture whether two vertices have identical/similar values of an exogenous predictor. Examples include same-sex indicators in friendship networks, same regime type indicators in international networks, and the absolute difference in ideology scores in legislative networks. These terms naturally take on a dyadic form even though they are based on vertex-level measures. All the same, the X matrix has the appropriate dimensions, with X_{ij} capturing whether vertices i and j are of the same type, and Equation (3.6) may be applied. Note that some software implementations allow the user to specify homophily terms directly on the vertex-level indicators. In such cases, the user is spared the construction of homophily matrices, that process being automated and invisible to the user, but not different from what is described above.

Running Example: Krackhardt's Advice Network

Here we consider how one ought to arrive at an ERGM specification. While different authors have different approaches to the specification of ERGMs, we like to start with consideration of the endogenous effects, thinking through these effects theoretically prior to adding exogenous covariates.

It is possible that reciprocity will be a generative feature of the network. This is so because it makes sense that relationships of mutual advice giving would emerge: a relationship of trust may emerge where either manager goes to the other for advice when they need it. If this reciprocal dynamic is indeed a generative feature of the network, we would expect the `mutual` term, which represents the reciprocity statistic explained in Equation (3.2), to produce a positive coefficient. While this seems plausible, it is in contrast to a mentorship dynamic in which advice-giving relationships would tend to be one-sided, the mentee receiving advice from the mentor but not the other way around. If the mentee–mentor dynamic is in place, we would expect to find a negative effect for the `mutual` term, indicating that the one-way flow of advice is a generative feature of the network. This discussion indicates that we should certainly include the `mutual` term in the model, but highlights that we do not have a clear expectation regarding the sign of the reciprocity effect. Were we developing a theory for a research article or book, we would need to flesh out this dynamic in more detail and arrive at a specific expectation for hypothesis testing.

Some individuals are likely to be especially active in advice seeking. This could be either because they enjoy such discussion with others or because they are less hesitant than others to receive advice. If we think about what a highly active advice seeker looks like in terms of network topology, this would be a vertex that sends many ties. Because such a structure can look like an out-star – a node from which many edges emanate, particularly when the number of ties is high, the statistics computed for **h** in the ERGM are called "star" statistics. But let us be more precise: a two-star exists when focal vertex i has connections to alters j and k, a three-star exists when i is connected to j, k, and l, and so on. Because this is a directed network, we must also differentiate between in-stars and out-stars, indicating stars formed by incoming and outgoing edges, respectively. For example, a structure in which a node receives ties from two other nodes is referred to an in-two-star. Lower-order stars are naturally embedded in higher-order stars. For example, a single in-three-star includes three in-two-stars. To model the advice-seeking tendencies in the Krackhardt network, we include out-two-stars and out-three-stars in the model specification. The out-two-star captures the effect of each single out-tie on the likelihood of sending a new tie. The out-three-star reflects the effect of every pair of ties sent on the likelihood of sending a new tie. Including the higher-order out-three-star term provides flexibility in modeling a threshold effect in activity (i.e., in the event of a positive coefficient, it would indicate that a node becomes more likely to send additional ties once that node has sent at least two ties) or a decay effect in activity (i.e., in the event of a negative coefficient, it would indicate that the positive activity effect would eventually drop off). We could continue adding star statistics (e.g., out-four-stars), but the need and ability of the data to differentiate star effects to fit the out-degree distribution diminish rapidly with the size of the star. The out-stars are included in the specification with the command `ostar(2:3)`, indicating that we want to include out-stars two and three. Note, since two-stars are nested in three-stars (i.e., a three-star includes three two-stars), it is important to include two-stars in the model to correctly identify the effect of three-stars.

The last endogenous term we will consider for this model accounts for clustering. It seems theoretically likely that cliques of managers seeking one another's advice may emerge from natural communities of expertise and familiarity. A useful and common way to account for clustering in directed networks is with the transitivity statistic described in Equation (3.5). This statistic essentially captures the adage that the "friend of a friend is a friend" and produces clustered topologies on the network level. However, inclusion of this statistic in the model results in the numerical instability problem known as degeneracy (see our brief discussion at the end of this chapter and our lengthy discussion in Chapter 5). This is so because the network is relatively dense and the value of the transitivity statistic increases nonlinearly as the density of the network increases; the inflated value of the statistic causes the problem. As an alternative, we include this clustering effect with a statistic called "transitive ties" (`transitiveties`). The transitive ties statistic tends to be more robust to degeneracy than transitive triads, but captures a very similar process: it counts the number of edges in the network that are embedded in at least one transitive triple. The fact that it cannot count a given edge more than once suppresses the value of the statistic relative to transitive triads, thus making it more computationally stable.

We now move on to consider the exogenous covariates we have available. Because we expect a manager to be more likely to get advice from their direct superior, we include the edge-level covariate of "reports to." This variable, as we saw above, is a $n \times n$ adjacency matrix, having the same dimensions as the outcome network. In this matrix, the i, j element of X indicates whether i reports to j. We include this in the specification as an edge covariate using the `edgecov()` command as `edgecov("reportsto")`.

Because of the interesting relationship between tenure and age that we observed visually, we include both age and tenure in the model. We include each in three ways. First, because the value of an actor's age or tenure variable may affect their tendency to receive incoming ties, we include these covariates as incoming vertex-level covariates using the `nodeicov()` command. Under the `nodeicov()` command, the i, j element of X is equivalent to vertex j's covariate value. Second, because those same values can affect the tendency of a manager to send outgoing ties, we include both as outgoing vertex-level covariates using the `nodeocov()` command. Lastly, because the difference between the values of these variables for any given pair of managers may affect the probability of edge formation, we include the absolute difference in the vertex-level covariate values with the command `absdiff()`

The final term we mention is the `edges` term – the count of the number of edges in the network. The edges term is exogenous, and is analogous to the intercept in a regression model. Indeed, if endogenous terms are excluded from the ERGM, the edges coefficient will be exactly equivalent to the intercept in a dyadic logistic regression fit to the network adjacency matrix. With our theory-driven specification of the model complete, we may now estimate the ERGM. As we are using only the basic ERGM here we will rely on the functions in the `ergm` package. The code below simply illustrates the estimation of the ERGM. Before we discuss or interpret our results, we need to assure that the model provides a suitable fit to the network. In subsequent sections of this chapter, we consider the fit of this model and the interpretation of the results.

```
1  library(ergm)
2
3  set.seed(510)
4  mod1 <- ergm(Net ~ edges + mutual + ostar(2:3) + transitiveties
5               + edgecov("reportsto")
6               + nodeicov("Tenure") + nodeocov("Tenure") +
                   absdiff("Tenure")
7               + nodeicov("Age") + nodeocov("Age") + absdiff("Age"),
8           control=control.ergm(
9               MCMC.samplesize=5000,
10              MCMC.burnin=10000,
11              MCMLE.maxit=10),
12          verbose=TRUE)
```

Note that we always set a random seed, via `set.seed()`, so that we can reproduce exactly the same results. This is essential for replicability in published work and a very good habit to form when conducting any analyses. Further note that we set MCMC burnin and sample sizes. A detailed discussion of the MCMC estimation procedure is given in Chapter 5, but suffice it to say here that larger values of each will, in expectation, lead to more accurate estimates. The trade off is that larger values mean that the model will take longer to run, and the marginal gains in accuracy diminish with the size of these arguments. With the values above, this model took over a half hour to run on a standard (as of 2016) laptop. These values may be decreased to produce faster run times for examples, but they should be increased again for models intended to appear in published works.

3.4 MODEL FIT

Evaluating model fit is an important aspect of analysis with the ERGM. After all, if the model fit is poor, meaning that the observed network is not typical of the distribution represented by the ERGM specification and estimates, why would we care what results are implied? Recall that one of the two foundational assumptions of the ERGM is that the observed network is typical of the distribution reflected by the estimated model. Furthermore, ERGMs often suffer from an estimation problem called degeneracy, which is discussed further in Chapter 5 and manifests as very poor fit. As such, we strongly encourage consideration of model fit *before* interpreting the model.

While there are many ways in which fit may be checked, a common way is through the comparison of the observed networks with networks simulated from the estimated model. Because the ERGM produces a multivariate distribution of networks, simulation from the estimated model represents a straightforward methodology for assessing what is and is not typical of networks represented by the model. The "standard" approach to fit-checking involves simulating a large number of networks from the set of parameters estimated by the ERGM and comparing the topology of the simulated networks to that of the observed network (e.g., Atouba & Shumate 2015). To do this, several descriptive measures of the network are chosen (e.g., edgewise shared partners, degree) and box plots are created based on the value of these statistics over all of the simulated networks. Then, the value of those same statistics for the observed

network is plotted over the box plots. The closer the medians of the simulated networks are to the observed values of the network statistics, the
closer the observed network is to being "typical" of the networks generated from the respective model. Furthermore, since the boxes include 50

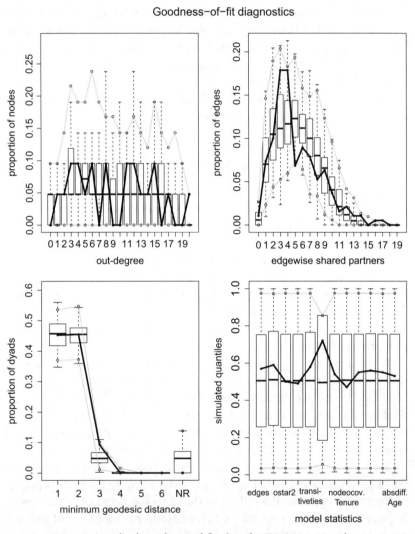

FIGURE 3.6 Standard goodness-of-fit plots for ERGMs using the `ergm`
package. The proximity of the black line to the medians of the box plots
throughout the figures is indicative of better fit.

percent of the simulated values, we want to see approximately 50 percent of the values calculated on the observed network landing within the boxes.

Krackhardt's Advice Network

Consideration of model fit is very important when working with ERGMs. Both the `ergm` and `xergm` packages have similar goodness-of-fit functionality. Note that both packages name this function `gof()`, so whichever package is loaded last will mask the function from the package loaded first. In this case, we are using the `gof()` function from the `ergm` package. The command is simple:

```
gof1 <- gof(mod1)
par(mfrow=c(2, 2))
plot(gof1)
gof1
```

The first line executes the goodness-of-fit function and creates a new object, which we have called `gof1`. The second line produces some goodness-of-fit plots from this object, and the third line examines the object itself.

To evaluate the fit, consider first the plot produced by the above code displayed in Figure 3.6. The objective in assessing the goodness-of-fit plots is to check whether the observed network is unusual with respect to the distribution implied by the model, along dimensions that are almost universally relevant in networks research (e.g., the degree distribution). Furthermore, we check the model fit based on features that ERGMs have been designed to fit well given appropriate specifications. We see in Figure 3.6 that the fit of the model varies substantially according to which statistic we consider. On the one hand, considering the minimum geodesic distance (the lower left plot of Figure 3.6), the fit appears quite good: the black line reflecting the observed values of the statistic in question intersects the medians of most box plots, and the general pattern seems to track quite well. On the other hand, if we consider the out-degree statistic in the top left of Figure 3.6, we see that the observed out-degree values are substantially more bouncy than the rather unimodal trend reflected in the simulation-based box plots. One might interpret this as bad fit because there are several prominent instances in which the observed-value line is quite far from the box plots. However, one might also think it more reasonable that a model produces a unimodal degree distribution rather than one that bounces as erratically as the observed-value line. When considering the distribution of edgewise shared partners, the upper right plot of Figure 3.6, the fit seems to fall somewhere in between that of the degree distributions and the minimum geodesic distance distribution. The trend of the simulations is nicely smooth and seems to be about right, even though some variation in the observed-value line occasionally takes it rather far from the simulated medians.

Examining the gof1 object created by the gof() function can render the enterprise of interpreting the goodness of fit somewhat more concrete. The gof1 object itself contains numeric information about each of the statistics plotted in Figure 3.6. For each fit statistic under consideration, it contains the observed number in each category, the minimum simulated, mean simulated and maximum simulated values. It also contains a *p*-value pertaining to the statistical difference between observed and simulated. This is a case in which small *p*-values indicate problems. Small *p*-values indicate poor fit because they indicate that there is a statistically significant difference between the observed value of the statistic and the simulated values, whereas good fit would have it that these values should be very similar.

```
 1  Goodness-of-fit for in-degree
 2
 3      obs min mean max MC p-value
 4  0    0    0 0.19   2      1.00
 5  1    0    0 0.15   2      1.00
 6  2    0    0 0.56   2      1.00
 7  3    0    0 0.75   2      0.86
 8  4    4    0 0.75   5      0.02
 9  5    2    0 0.75   3      0.32
10  6    0    0 1.37   6      0.48
11  7    1    0 1.74   6      0.88
12  8    3    0 2.13   6      0.70
13  9    2    0 2.51   5      0.90
14  10   3    0 2.51   7      0.94
15  11   1    0 2.09   5      0.80
16  12   0    0 1.96   8      0.20
17  13   2    0 1.52   5      0.98
18  14   0    0 1.16   5      0.58
19  15   2    0 0.56   4      0.20
20  16   0    0 0.18   2      1.00
21  17   0    0 0.08   1      1.00
22  18   1    0 0.04   1      0.08
23
```

```
24  Goodness-of-fit for out-degree
25
26       obs min mean max MC p-value
27  0     0    0 0.64   2      0.98
28  1     1    0 0.38   2      0.66
29  2     1    0 0.86   3      1.00
30  3     2    0 1.58   5      0.96
31  4     2    0 1.52   6      0.90
32  5     1    0 1.57   5      1.00
33  6     2    0 1.64   5      0.90
34  7     0    0 1.31   5      0.46
35  8     2    0 1.09   5      0.56
36  9     0    0 0.99   5      0.80
37  10    0    0 1.10   4      0.68
38  11    2    0 0.90   3      0.54
39  12    2    0 1.09   5      0.64
40  13    1    0 1.00   4      1.00
41  14    1    0 0.90   4      1.00
42  15    2    0 1.16   4      0.72
43  16    0    0 1.07   4      0.68
44  17    1    0 0.74   3      1.00
45  18    0    0 0.76   3      1.00
46  19    0    0 0.50   3      1.00
47  20    1    0 0.20   2      0.36
48
49  Goodness-of-fit for edgewise shared partner
50
51         obs min  mean max MC p-value
52  esp0    2    0  1.66   7      0.90
53  esp1    14   2 13.89  30      1.00
54  esp2    19   8 19.79  36      0.96
55  esp3    34   6 21.96  35      0.06
56  esp4    34  11 22.49  37      0.08
57  esp5    13  13 23.61  38      0.02
58  esp6    17  10 21.54  36      0.50
59  esp7    15   4 19.53  38      0.58
60  esp8    10   1 16.08  44      0.48
61  esp9    12   0 12.02  29      1.00
62  esp10   7    0  8.11  22      0.98
63  esp11   3    0  5.38  19      0.92
64  esp12   4    0  2.82  18      0.64
65  esp13   2    0  1.53  20      0.62
66  esp14   2    0  0.55  12      0.24
67  esp15   0    0  0.21   6      1.00
68  esp16   1    0  0.09   4      0.12
69  esp17   1    0  0.01   1      0.02
70
71  Goodness-of-fit for minimum geodesic distance
72
73        obs min   mean max MC p-value
```

```
74  1    190 146 191.27 254         0.92
75  2    191 147 189.97 240         1.00
76  3     39   1  21.00  46         0.10
77  4      0   0   0.95  15         1.00
78  5      0   0   0.02   1         1.00
79  Inf    0   0  16.79  58         0.90
80
81  Goodness-of-fit for model statistics
82
83                          obs  min    mean    max MC p-value
84  edges                   190  146  191.27   254        0.92
85  mutual                   45   25   46.16    78        0.96
86  ostar2                 1062  613 1070.15  1741        1.00
87  ostar3                 4322 1948 4342.97  8265        0.98
88  transitiveties          188  142  189.61   254        0.92
89  edgecov.reportsto        19   15   18.91    20        1.00
90  nodeicov.Tenure        2588 2081 2599.51  3311        0.92
91  nodeocov.Tenure        1871 1477 1879.14  2469        0.94
92  absdiff.Tenure         1401 1052 1412.03  1862        0.92
93  nodeicov.Age           7514 5772 7549.26 10016        0.88
94  nodeocov.Age           7384 5882 7407.90  9540        0.90
95  absdiff.Age            1732 1232 1735.90  2185        0.94
```

Considering these values for our model, we certainly see some small p-values, but the majority are large. Importantly, there are no patterns in the p-values (e.g., overpredicting edges between vertices with no shared partners, underpredicting large degree values), that could be easily corrected through updates to the specification. We can conclude that the observed network is not an outlier with respect to the model.

3.5   INTERPRETATION

Almost as striking as the ERGM's general flexibility is its ability to be interpreted in a meaningful way at a variety of levels, including the network, dyad, vertex, and arbitrary subgraph levels. Though ERGM results may be interpreted at each of these levels, interpretation often requires additional nontrivial transformation and/or computation. Desmarais & Cranmer (2012a) provide an in-depth discussion of the interpretation of ERGM at multiple levels. Let us consider ways to interpret ERGM results in ascending order of difficulty.

3.5.1   Network-Level Interpretation

One can interpret ERGM coefficients at the network level quite easily. ERGM coefficients reflect conditional log odds. As such, the log odds of an edge between any two vertices is the sum of the product of the coefficient and the change in the relevant statistic over all effects in the model. Equivalently, the exponent of a given coefficient, $\exp(\theta_r)$, reflects the relative likelihood of observing N^{r+} to observing N^{r-}, where N^{r+} is one unit greater than N^{r-} on statistic r (e.g., N^{r+} has one more closed triangle, one more edge), holding all other statistics constant.

3.5.2   Edge-Level Interpretation

Edge-level interpretation can be accomplished by examining the conditional probability of a particular edge existing in the network:

$$P(N_{ij} = 1 \mid N_{-ij}, \boldsymbol{\theta}) = \text{logit}^{-1}\left(\sum_{r=1}^{k} \theta_r \delta_r^{(ij)}(N)\right) \tag{3.7}$$

where N_{-ij} indicates the network excluding the dyad N_{ij}, $\delta_r^{(ij)}(N)$ is equal to the change in h_r when N_{ij} is changed from zero to one, and logit^{-1} is the inverse logistic function such that $\text{logit}^{-1}(x) = 1/(1 + \exp(-x))$. While this type of interpretation requires a bit more than the back-of-the-envelope type of calculation that network-level interpretation requires, this quantity is easily computed for any dyad in the network and provides a direct and simple interpretation in terms of the probability that any edge of interest exists. Presentation of this quantity may be difficult, though, as it will vary from dyad-to-dyad. Solutions to the presentation problem include presenting particularly high- and low-probability dyads or computing summary statistics on the set of all dyadic probabilities.

3.5.3   Block-Level Interpretation

Desmarais & Cranmer (2012a) proposed a general block Gibbs sampling framework through which the analyst can interpret ERGM results for any given subgraph. The primary inferential benefit of using the ERGM is that it can represent how ties in the network depend upon each other. The fundamental idea underlying this framework was that conditional distributions offer a unifying concept for analyzing any sort of interdependencies. For example, one might ask how expected values depend upon another, how variance in ties propagates through the network, which vertices are relatively "independent," or any variety of other questions. Furthermore, as the dependencies of interest will vary by application, such a framework offers much-needed flexibility.

This framework requires the assumption that the network under study evolves sequentially and involves partitioning the network, N, into m disjoint blocks. Such blocks can be defined as any conceivable partition of the network, such as (1) each potential tie in the network, (2) each dyad in the network, (3) blocks of outgoing ties from each vertex in the network, (4) blocks of incoming ties to each vertex in the network, and (5) subnetworks defined by within and across-group ties (e.g., those within and across political parties in a legislative network) (Desmarais & Cranmer 2012a). Assume a probabilistic updating sequence for the blocks, $S(m)$. For example, if the network consisted of only three blocks, $S(m)$ would draw sequences from $\{(1, 2, 3), (1, 3, 2), (2, 1, 3), (2, 3, 1), (3, 1, 2), (3, 2, 1)\}$. The block Gibbs sampling approach sequentially and probabilistically samples the blocks (i.e., subgraphs), conditioned on the rest of the variables (Gill 2008), to construct a full joint distribution (i.e., a full network). This is valuable because a network that has been updated many times according to $S(m)$ ERGM-based conditional distributions will have an ERGM distribution. As $S(m)$ is straightforward, we require only the ability to compute the probability of a given block conditional on the rest of the network. Denote a given block of the network N_b and the rest of the network, excluding block N_b, as N_{-b}. We can then compute the probability of a given block (N_b) conditional on the rest of the network (N_{-b}) as

$$P(N_b \mid N_{-b}) = \frac{\exp(\sum_{j=1}^{k} \theta_j h_j(N_b \cup N_{-b}))}{\sum_{N_b^* \in \mathcal{N}_b} \exp(\sum_{j=1}^{k} \theta_j h_j(N_b^* \cup N_{-b}))}, \qquad (3.8)$$

where $N_b^* \cup N_{-b}$ refers to the complete network created by holding N_{-b} constant and inserting N_b^* into the bth block of N. Equation (3.8) can articulate the probability of any given block and thus show exactly how edges depend on one another given a set of ERGM results. One can use this approach to probe nearly any conditional aspect of the network generating process, including dyad- and actor-level tendencies. This approach also applies trivially to the temporal ERGM discussed in later chapters.

Running Example: Krackhardt's Advice Network

Now that we have assured ourselves of sufficiently good model fit, we consider what the model results tell us about the generative processes that define the network. Running `summary(mod1)` prints a table that is very similar in structure to a regression summary table.

```
===========================
Summary of model fit
===========================

Formula:   Net ~ edges + mutual + ostar(2:3) + transitiveties +
    edgecov("reportsto") + nodeicov("Tenure") + nodeocov("Tenure") +
    absdiff("Tenure") + nodeicov("Age") + nodeocov("Age") +
    absdiff("Age")

Iterations:  2 out of 10

Monte Carlo MLE Results:
                    Estimate Std. Error MCMC %  p-value
edges               -3.634706  1.223426      0 0.003145 **
mutual               0.486790  0.335491      0 0.147555
ostar2               0.226068  0.099487      0 0.023586 *
ostar3               0.001935  0.010625      0 0.855588
transitiveties       1.366274  0.789701      0 0.084366 .
edgecov.reportsto    3.781289  1.134372      0 0.000936 ***
nodeicov.Tenure      0.138663  0.022853      0  < 1e-04 ***
nodeocov.Tenure     -0.022546  0.013557      0 0.097061 .
absdiff.Tenure      -0.049192  0.018612      0 0.008532 **
nodeicov.Age        -0.048106  0.019335      0 0.013244 *
nodeocov.Age         0.015160  0.008853      0 0.087573 .
absdiff.Age         -0.016775  0.014607      0 0.251479
---
Signif. codes:  0 '***' 0.001 '**' 0.01 '*' 0.05 '.' 0.1 ' ' 1

     Null Deviance: 582.2  on 420  degrees of freedom
 Residual Deviance: 415.0  on 408  degrees of freedom

AIC: 439    BIC: 487.5    (Smaller is better.)
```

We illustrate the interpretation of the results at multiple levels. First consider interpretation at the network level. We can, for example, interpret the out-two-star by exponentiating the coefficient: $exp(0.226068) = 1.253661$. Thus, holding all other effects constant, the relative likelihood of observing a network that includes one more out-two-star is 1.253661.

Let us consider this type of interpretation in more detail. To keep the algebra clean and easy to understand, we introduce an oversimplistic model with only two effects. First, the edge count statistic is specified simply as edges. This captures the number of edges in the network. It would be quite rare that we would want to specify an ERGM without an edges term.

The second term we will consider is a homophily term that will capture the effect of two actors in the network being at the same level in the company. This is accomplished through use of the nodematch() command. nodematch() accepts a qualitative vertex attribute and counts the number of cases in which any two vertices sharing an edge have that same qualitative attribute.

Our overly simple ERGM is then run with the command

```
set.seed(510)
mod0 <- ergm(Net ~ edges + nodematch("Level"),
        control=control.ergm(
            MCMC.samplesize=5000,
            MCMC.burnin=10000,
            MCMLE.maxit=10),
        verbose=TRUE)
summary(mod0)
```

and produces the following results:

```
===========================
Summary of model fit
===========================

Formula:   Net ~ edges + nodematch("Level")

Iterations:  4 out of 10

Monte Carlo MLE Results:
               Estimate Std. Error MCMC % p-value
edges            0.04763    0.15435      0  0.7578
nodematch.Level -0.40045    0.20049      0  0.0464 *
---
Signif. codes:  0 '***' 0.001 '**' 0.01 '*' 0.05 '.' 0.1 ' ' 1

    Null Deviance: 582.2  on 420  degrees of freedom
Residual Deviance: 574.4  on 418  degrees of freedom

AIC: 578.4    BIC: 586.5    (Smaller is better.)
```

The log odds of an edge in the advice network is given by the linear predictor: 0.0476 × change in the edge count + −0.4005 × change in count of same-level edges. The log odds of a tie across levels in the company is 0.04763 (the edges coefficient). Taking the inverse logistic transformation, $\text{logit}^{-1}(0.04763) = 1/(1 + \exp(-0.04763)) = 0.5119$ produces the probability of such a tie. We can produce a probability for same-level ties by computing the log odds of such a tie, $0.04763 - -0.40045 = 0.44808$ and applying the same inverse logistic transformation, $1/(1 + \exp(0.44808)) = 0.610$. So, we see that the probability of forming a within-level edge is 0.098 higher than forming an across-level edge.

The functionality of the xergm package can be used to facilitate interpretation. The interpret function takes an object of class ergm or btergm, as well as indicators for a pair of vertices and returns the probabilities associated with different types of ties. For example, we can consider the tie probabilities between actors 1 and 2 in the Krackhardt data with the command

```
library(xergm)
interpret(mod0, type="dyad", i=1, j=2)
```

which produces the following results:

```
            j->i = 0   j->i = 1
i->j = 0 0.2382370 0.2498583
i->j = 1 0.2498583 0.2620465
```

Interpretation of these dyadwise probabilities is straightforward. For instance, the probability that actor 1 (i) will have an edge to actor 2 (j) is 0.25, conditional on the states of the other relationships in the network. Considering edge probabilities for particular dyads can be interesting and illuminating if the pair is somehow representative or of particular interest. However, it can also be useful to consider these probabilities across all dyads in the network. Below, we consider a more sophisticated application of the interpret() function in the context of our theoretically driven model specification.

While the coefficients can be interpreted at the network or edge levels as above, we explore here how to use the interpret() function from the xergm package more effectively. Note that this is one of many possible ways to use the `interpret()` function and should not be taken to be a/the "standard" way; `interpret()` may be used to compute most conditional quantities of interest to the researcher and theory should drive its application. Furthermore, most of the code below involves setting up objects in which to store probabilities, and computing the probabilities of interest over a sampling of dyads in the network. Even though it would be possible in this small network to compute every dyadic probability, we illustrate a sampling strategy that is more practical for larger networks.

```
1   ## extract coefficients and create null hypothesis vector
2   null <- coef(mod1)    # estimated coefs
3   null[2] <- 0          # set mutual term = 0
4
5   ## sample 20 dyads and compute probability ratios
6   probabilities <- matrix(nrow = 9, ncol = 1)
7
8   ## nrow = 9 because three probabilities + upper and lower CIs; ncol
        = 1 because
9   ## only have one time point
10
11  d <- dim(as.matrix(Net))   # how many row and column vertices?
12  size <- d[1] * d[2]                    # size of the matrix
13  nw <- matrix(1:size, nrow = d[1], ncol = d[2])
14  nw <- nw[lower.tri(nw)]                # sample only from lower
        triangle b/c
15  samp <- sample(nw, 20)                 # dyadic probabilities are
        symmetric
16  prob.est.00 <- numeric(0)
17  prob.est.01 <- numeric(0)
18  prob.est.11 <- numeric(0)
19  prob.null.00 <- numeric(0)
20  prob.null.01 <- numeric(0)
21  prob.null.11 <- numeric(0)
22  for (k in 1:20) {
23      i <- arrayInd(samp[k], d)[1, 1]    # recover 'i's and 'j's from
            sample
24      j <- arrayInd(samp[k], d)[1, 2]
25      # run interpretation function with estimated coefs and mutual = 0:
26      int.est <- interpret(mod1, type = "dyad", i = i, j = j)
27      int.null <- interpret(mod1, coefficients = null, type = "dyad",
28          i = i, j = j)
29      prob.est.00 <- c(prob.est.00, int.est[1, 1])
30      prob.est.11 <- c(prob.est.11, int.est[2, 2])
31      mean.est.01 <- (int.est[1, 2] + int.est[2, 1]) / 2
32      prob.est.01 <- c(prob.est.01, mean.est.01)
33      prob.null.00 <- c(prob.null.00, int.null[1, 1])
34      prob.null.11 <- c(prob.null.11, int.null[2, 2])
```

```
35     mean.null.01 <- (int.null[1, 2] + int.null[2, 1]) / 2
36     prob.null.01 <- c(prob.null.01, mean.null.01)
37   }
38
39   prob.ratio.00 <- prob.est.00 / prob.null.00   # ratio of est. and
40                                                           null hyp
41   prob.ratio.01 <- prob.est.01 / prob.null.01
42   prob.ratio.11 <- prob.est.11 / prob.null.11
43   probabilities[1] <- mean(prob.ratio.00)   # mean estimated 00 tie
44                                               prob
45   probabilities[2] <- mean(prob.ratio.01)   # mean estimated 01 tie
46                                               prob
47   probabilities[3] <- mean(prob.ratio.11)   # mean estimated 11 tie
48                                               prob
49   ci.00 <- t.test(prob.ratio.00, conf.level = 0.99)$conf.int
50   ci.01 <- t.test(prob.ratio.01, conf.level = 0.99)$conf.int
51   ci.11 <- t.test(prob.ratio.11, conf.level = 0.99)$conf.int
52   probabilities[4] <- ci.00[1]              # lower 00 conf. interval
53   probabilities[5] <- ci.01[1]              # lower 01 conf. interval
54   probabilities[6] <- ci.11[1]              # lower 11 conf. interval
55   probabilities[7] <- ci.00[2]              # upper 00 conf. interval
56   probabilities[8] <- ci.01[2]              # upper 01 conf. interval
57   probabilities[9] <- ci.11[2]              # upper 11 conf. interval
58
59   ## create barplots from probability ratios and CIs
60   require("gplots")
61   bp <- barplot2(probabilities[1:3, ], beside = TRUE, plot.ci = TRUE,
62                  ci.l = probabilities[4:6, ], ci.u = probabilities[7:9,
                    ],
63                  col = c("#e5f5e0", "#a1d99b", "#31a354"), ci.col =
                    "grey40",
64                  xlab = "Dyadic tie values",
65                  ylab = "Estimated Prob./Null Prob.",
66                  cex.lab = 1.4, ci.lwd = 2)
67   mtext(1, at = bp, text = c("(0,0)", "(0,1)", "(1,1)"),
68                  line = 0.4, cex = 1.3)
```

The results are displayed in Figure 3.7 and reflect a comparison between the theoretically driven specification of our model and one in which the reciprocity effect is set to zero; this contrast is made with respect to dyadic edge probabilities (no edge, unidirectional, and reciprocal). We see that the difference is quite similar and hovers just below one for dyads with no edges and a single edge, while the value is substantially higher for reciprocal edges. Under the full model, mutual dyad is approximately 50 percent more likely to occur than it is under the null model.

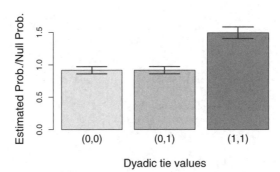

FIGURE 3.7 Example of conditional probabilities computed via block Gibbs and produced using the `xergm` package's `interpret()` function.

3.6 LIMITATIONS

While the ERGM is a powerful and flexible model for statistical inference with networks, it is has several important limitations. We dedicate subsequent chapters to each of these major limitations, but it is worth raising these points briefly here.

A major and recurrent problem with the ERGM is its tendency to be numerically unstable in estimation. This numerical instability, called degeneracy (Schweinberger 2011), occurs when all or most of the probability mass is placed on one or a few of the possible permutations of the network. Degeneracy typically occurs when the Markov chain used in the estimation process moves to the completely empty or completely connected network and is unable to move. Clearly, when this occurs, the values produced by the MCMC process do not reflect the maximum likelihood estimates and cannot be used. While the degeneracy problem is frustratingly common, it is mercifully easy to detect through goodness-of-fit checking – a degenerate model will fit *very* poorly – and built-in suites of tests in ERGM software.

Addressing the degeneracy problem is usually more difficult than identifying it. Degeneracy can be caused by poor specification of the model. A specification that is highly unlikely to have generated the data will often be degenerate. As such, adjustment of the model, particularly with respect to the endogenous dependencies, can often help. Degeneracy can also be caused by overly dense or overly sparse networks. Addressing degeneracy of this form is tricky because alternative measurements of the network (e.g., applying a higher threshold to weighted ties) are frequently required, but this changes the substantive meaning of the edges. Chapter 5 discusses estimation and degeneracy in detail.

Another limitation of the basic ERGM articulated in Equation (3.1) is that it cannot be used to model longitudinally observed networks. The basic form of the ERGM we have introduced here is specified on a single network N. The ERGM can be extended to model longitudinally observed networks in a technique known as the temporal ERGM (TERGM), though this extension complicates specification and estimation. Chapter 6 is dedicated to discussion of the TERGM.

Considering Equation (3.1), we can see that the ERGM is also unable to accommodate weighted networks, those in which the edges have numerical values instead of being on or off. One can see the problem by considering what happens to $\mathcal{N}$ if the edges in N were to have continuous values. $\mathcal{N}$ is now infinite for two reasons: because continuous edges are not bounded and because of the infinite granularity of the measure. An infinite $\mathcal{N}$ renders the normalization of the ERGM completely infeasible. In Chapter 7, we introduce the generalized ERGM (GERGM), a technique for accomplishing ERGM-like inference on weighted networks, though specification and estimation are complicated nontrivially.

One final limitation of the ERGM, which is related to the problems with degeneracy and specification, is that the researcher must have a reasonably effective theory regarding the endogenous effects that should be included in the model, as the ERGM cannot adjust for endogenous effects that are not included in the specification. This is not an overly burdensome limitation, as most researchers who study networks will be inclined to develop relevant theoretical expectations. However, for those who are new to network analysis, or just getting started with a given network application, it may not be apparent which endogenous effects should be included in the model. An alternative network modeling framework, based on latent variables, does not require a precise theory of endogenous effects. In Part III of this book, we cover this modeling framework.

3.7 WRAPPING UP

The ERGM is a powerful and popular method for conducting statistical inference on networks. It is a particularly useful tool because it is capable of simultaneously modeling both endogenous and exogenous effects, produces a set of coefficients broadly similar to those produced by regression models, and is straightforward to interpret. As such, the ERGM is a good choice for researchers interested in hypothesis testing, particularly if the hypotheses to be tested involve endogenous effects. A challenge often faced by researchers using the ERGM is that these models are prone to an estimation problem known as degeneracy, which tends to occur when a specification fits poorly, the network is very sparse, or the network is very dense. In its basic form, the ERGM is also limited in that it cannot accommodate longitudinally observed networks or networks with valued edges. In the following chapters, we provide more details on the ERGM: Chapter 4 explores ERGM specification in detail, Chapter 5 explicates estimation and degeneracy, Chapter 6 introduces the temporal ERGM for longitudinally observed networks, and Chapter 7 introduces the generalized ERGM for ERG-type modeling of networks with weighted edges.

3.8 SELF-STUDY PROBLEMS

Select a network dataset to study using ERGM, but avoid using the data from ina that was used in this chapter. Be sure that the dataset includes at least one vertex attribute. If you do not have a dataset that you would like to use for this exercise, we recommend that you use the Strike dataset from ina, which is introduced in Section 8.2. Using this dataset, complete a report that includes the following information:

1. **Description of the dataset:** What does the dataset cover? Where did it come from? Has it been used in any prior studies?
2. **Hypotheses:** Describe and test at least one hypothesis regarding a vertex attribute and at least one hypothesis regarding interdependence among the ties. Describe these hypotheses
3. **Model specification:** Identify a model specification that you believe is capable of testing your hypotheses.
4. **Estimates:** Present the estimates of the ERGM in either graphical or tabular form.
5. **Diagnostics:** Evaluate whether this ERGM fits your network adequately.
6. **Interpretation:** Substantively interpret your results. Do you find support for your hypotheses? Do you think the effects that you find are large?

4

ERGM Specification

In this chapter we cover specification of the ERGM in detail. The practical objective here is to show how ERGM specifications can be derived from theory, and driven in part by the data. As will be clear from the discussion, however, the overarching objective is to show how network theories can be developed based on expectations about vertex relations, and then operationalized into specific, theoretically motivated and valid, ERGM specifications.

Much of the chapter is dedicated to exploring and understanding the different types of effects that can be included in the ERGM's **h** vector. However, the vast, and ever-growing, set of statistics it is possible to include in **h** renders a comprehensive discussion impossible. We make an effort to always consider the substantive meaning of these specifications, and the interpretation of their respective effects on network-generating processes. In this sense, the consideration of substantive theory and ERGM effects are closely related.

Running Example: Romantic Hookups in *Grey's Anatomy*

To illustrate the statistics that can be used when specifying an ERGM, we make use of a dataset derived from populare entertainment, initially gathered by Gary Weissman and later augmented by Benjamin Lind (2012). The data capture the network of implied sexual encounters in the television show *Grey's Anatomy*. For ease of use, we will call this the "hookup" network. The vertices are characters in the show, and the undirected edges capture the occurrence of at least one implied sexual encounter between the characters. The augmented data also include vertex-level covariates on sex, race, birth year, position in the hospital, what season the character first appears and what sign the character has in the metaphysical practice of astrology. We will use these data as a running example in this chapter. Because the theory and practice of operationalization are so closely related, and because it is easier to discuss these statistics in the context of an example, we integrate the running example into the chapter text here more than in most chapters.

The analysis of the hookup network corresponds to a problem well known in epidemiology. When monitoring or modeling the spread of sexually transmitted infections, epidemiologists frequently must study sexual contact networks. So, while this is a humorous example drawn from fiction, the underlying reason for being interested in such networks stems from real-world statistical challenges.

4.1 STARTING WITH THEORY

The best way to start building a model specification for ERGM is to develop a theoretical characterization of tie formation. Various approaches to theory and specification building with ERGMs have been proposed (Lusher et al. 2013), but in our experience it is best to start with the question of how the vertices and edges are expected to relate to one another. In other words, we try to start with endogenous effects before considering covariates, though this is by no means the exclusively correct way to approach theory building and specification. In some cases this will be intuitive, and in other cases it may take more effort. While it sounds anecdotal, we often find it helpful to tell vignette/case stories about who/what the vertices are, what their preferences are, and to what incentives are they subject.

When operationalizing a theory to specify an ERGM, the primary challenge is choosing a set of statistics for the **h** vector that capture one's theoretical expectations about the network data-generating process, both endogenous and exogenous. One should also keep in mind that many statistics do similar things, but are specified differently. For example, both the `triangle` statistic and the `GWESP` statistic broadly capture the tendency for closed triads to form, but there are important differences in how they are specified that can have pronounced effects on one's models and their interpretations. Yet, as a general rule, the evaluation of a hypothesis regarding a particular dependence effect will be most effective when each dependence effect is represented by one and only one term in the model specification. If a hypothesis is represented by more than one term, the results will often be inconclusive, and subject to limited efficiency due to multicollinearity (Duxbury 2018). When approaching specification, the analyst should consider all possible statistics, whether they reasonably operationalize core theoretical concepts, and how they relate to each other. In this section, we try to cover the most useful and frequently used statistics for ERGMs, but our list is by no means exhaustive. After reading this chapter, we encourage the reader to consult Morris, Handcock, and Hunter (2008) for an extensive review of endogenous effect specification, as well as to spend some time reviewing the complete list of statistics available for the `ergm()` function in the `?ergm.terms` help page.

Running Example: Romantic Hookups in *Grey's Anatomy*

In the case of the *Grey's Anatomy* hookup network, we begin by considering endogenous structure. First, it is likely that some individuals will have notably more hookups than others. This is likely because of a combination of someone's ability to initiate hookups (e.g., relationship status on the show) and their willingness to participate when being courted (driven, e.g., by the promiscuousness associated with a character's personality). The undirected nature of our data (and indeed the definition of an edge) implies a confounding between in- and out-degree. As a result, we expect some individuals to have high degree, while most others will have smaller degree.

We also expect few closed triangles. The characters and sexual interactions depicted on *Grey's Anatomy* are overwhelmingly heterosexual (Kuorikoski 2010). A hookup network can only form triangles through the addition of same-sex edges. We expect most hookups to be heterosexual and thus for closed triangles to be few in number. Relatedly, however, sexual networks tend to be cliquish since they derive from friendship networks (Felmlee & Faris 2013). This means that the hookup network may exhibit a tendency toward closed circuits among four people; the shortest path that can form a closed structure in a heterosexual hookup network.

We now consider exogenous covariates. Many covariate effects that we should include are related to homophily in some way. For example, sociologists have found that people tend to prefer romantic partners who are similar to themselves with respect to things like age, education, income, and race (Byrne 1971, Berscheid & Hatfield 1969). Though fictional, we expect to observe similar homophilous tendencies in the *Grey's Anatomy* hookup network. With a television show, in particular, we would expect homophily with respect to the role of the character, as those who work closely together will simply have more contact time in general.

While very simple, these theoretical expectations give us something on which to go when specifying an ERGM of the hookup network. In the remainder of the chapter, we will consider different ways to operationalize these concepts, both mathematically and in terms of the effects that those decisions have on the model.

4.2   EXOGENOUS COVARIATE EFFECTS

We begin by considering exogenous covariates. We start this way primarily for pedagogical purposes: exogenous covariates are easier to explain than endogenous dependencies, most analysts will be used to thinking in terms of exogenous covariates because those are the sort of effects that are typically included in regression models, and this progression will take the chapter from material most readers familiar with regression will find more straightforward to material they will likely find more foreign. An advantage of the exogenous-first approach to model building is that covariate-only ERGMs are fundamentally logistic regression models and do not require Markov chain Monte Carlo (MCMC) techniques to estimate (see the detailed discussion of estimation in Chapter 5), making them very stable. That said, in our own research, we tend to start with the endogenous specification, primarily to identify and resolve any stability issues brought on by the endogenous dependency early in the model-building process.

Recall from Chapter 3 that we include exogenous covariates with a general statistic that captures the relationship between X and N:

$$h_D(N, X) = \sum_{ij} N_{ij} X_{ij}. \tag{4.1}$$

This statistic naturally accommodates dyad-level covariates; those that are included as their own adjacency matrices when working with software. In such cases, the statistic sums the values of the covariate X that correspond to dyads for which an edge is present in the outcome network N. Vertex-level covariates are also easily accommodated, but must be "scaled up" to the dyad level such that $X_{ij} = Z_i$ for vertex-level covariate Z. That is to say, every relationship that vertex i has with alters in the rest of the network is given a covariate value corresponding to Z_i, vertex i's individual value.

Running Example: Romantic Hookups in *Grey's Anatomy*

Table 4.1 provides an overview of the most common ways to include exogenous covariates in an ERGM. Let us consider these in the context of our *Grey's Anatomy* hookup data. The data include several vertex attributes, but no edge-level covariates. That, however, does not mean that interesting and relevant edge-level covariates are unavailable. For instance, many people have preferences for romantic pairings within their approximate age range. The absolute difference in ages between individuals may be a predictor of hookup potential: one would expect a negative coefficient because large values of absolute age should result in lower probabilities of a hookup. We can create this edge-level variable easily based on the vertex attributes we attached to our network using the absdiff() command in the ERGM specification. This saves us the trouble of coding and adding an actual matrix covariate with this information (though one could do that too). If our data had quantitative information about the edges that we did not create from vertex attributes, such as how long any two individuals in the network had been acquainted, we could include that relational matrix in the ERGM specification using the edgecov() term.

TABLE 4.1 *An overview of different ways to include exogenous covariates in an ERGM*

ERGM term	Input	Substance
edgecov()	matrix covariate	tie prediction
dyadcov()	matrix covariate	directional tie prediction
absdiff()	quantitative vertex attr.	homophily
nodecov()	quantitative vertex attr.	degree prediction
nodefactor()	qualitative vertex attr.	degree prediction
nodeicov()	quantitative vertex attr.	popularity prediciton
nodeifactor()	qualitative vertex attr.	popularity prediction
nodeocov()	quantitative vertex attr.	sociality prediction
nodeofactor()	qualitative vertex attr.	sociality prediction
nodematch()	qualitative vertex attr.	homophily
nodemix()	qualitative vertex attr.	homophily (exhaustive)

Turning our attention to the vertex attributes we have available, there are a variety of effects that are consistent with our theory. First, it may be the younger people have more hookups than older people. This supposition is consistent with results in sociology indicating that younger people tend to have more partners, whereas older people are more likely to be in stable relationships (Chandra et al. 2013). To operationalize this idea, we want to include quantitative information about how old a member of the network is. This can be accomplished using the nodecov() command. In our case we want to include information about age, so we will use the birthyear attribute of our data, making the appropriate command nodecov("birthyear"). We would expect a positive coefficient because younger people (those with higher birth years) are expected to have more hookups. It is also worth noting that we have now used the birthyear attribute twice: once to look for homophily in age pairings, and one to look for age-based differences in behavior.

Next, we consider homophily in hookup generation. The most obvious effect to consider here is with respect to sex. Less than 5 percent of the US population is homosexual or bisexual (Gates 2011), so it is reasonable to expect that most hookups will involve heterosexual pairings. We can use the nodematch() command to include an indicator for whether two vertices are of the same type. In our case nodematch("sex") will indicate the prevalence of same-sex pairings (homophily), and we would expect this effect to be negative because such pairings should be comparatively uncommon in the data. Alternatively, we could use nodemix() rather than nodematch(). The nodemix() term creates and includes factors for every type of pairing based on the variable of interest. When used with the sex attribute, nodemix() would create factors and estimate coefficients for female–male, male–male, and female–female relationships.

We can also consider race-based homophily because individuals have a tendency to form sexual partnerships within their own racial groups (Lin & Lundquist 2013). As with sex, we could use the nodematch() term to measure the extent to which people prefer same-race hookups, or we could use the nodemix() term to measure the odds of cross-racial hookups for across every racial category in the data (which in this case include white, black, and other). As with sex and race, we can examine homophilous tendencies with respect to the position of the characters within the hospital. Those who work together more regularly have greater opportunity for every form of social interaction, including hookups.

Lastly, we include another nodecov term – the season in which the character joined the show – to adjust for the amount of exposure the character had to the others in the network. We expect the coefficient on this effect to be negative, as the later the character was introduced to the show, the less opportunity that character would have had to form hookup ties with other characters.

Table 4.2 summarizes the exogenous effects we have considered for the *Grey's Anatomy* hookup data. The dataset in ina named 'Hookups' includes a network object that includes a binary network among characters as well as several vertex attributes. Using these effects and data, we can specify a preliminary ERGM as follows:

```
 1  library(ina)
 2  library(ergm
 3  data("Hookups")
 4
 5  set.seed(5)
 6  m0 <- ergm(Hookups ~ edges
 7                      # people hookup within approximate age group
 8                      + absdiff("birthyear")
 9                      # younger people are more likely to hookup
10                      + nodecov("birthyear")
11                      # people are less likely to hookup within their working
                           unit
12                      + nodematch("position")
13                      # people prefer to hookup within their racial group
14                      + nodematch("race")
15                      # people prefer to hookup with members of the opposite
                           sex
16                      # (negative effect))
17                      + nodematch("sex")
18                      # earlier characters form more ties
19                      + nodecov("season"))
20  summary(m0)
```

Note that the model runs very quickly and is completely numerically stable. This is so because we have not yet added any endogenous effects to the ERGM, and it thus is functionally doing logistic regression and does not require MCMC in the estimation process. This will change when we begin to include endogenous effects below. The results of this preliminary specification are as follows:

```
 1 Monte Carlo MLE Results:
 2                     Estimate Std. Error MCMC % z value Pr(>|z|)
 3 edges              -11.359939  49.020610      0  -0.232   0.8167
 4 absdiff.birthyear   -0.127056   0.031593      0  -4.022   <1e-04 ***
 5 nodecov.birthyear    0.002593   0.012453      0   0.208   0.8351
 6 nodematch.position   0.856905   0.351704      0   2.436   0.0148 *
 7 nodematch.race       0.835202   0.355855      0   2.347   0.0189 *
 8 nodematch.sex       -3.263679   0.731655      0  -4.461   <1e-04 ***
 9 nodecov.season      -0.139294   0.061315      0  -2.272   0.0231 *
10 ---
11 Signif. codes:  0   ***    0.001    **   0.01   *   0.05   .  0.1
             1
12
13      Null Deviance: 1311.4  on 946  degrees of freedom
14 Residual Deviance:  274.5  on 939  degrees of freedom
15
16 AIC: 288.5    BIC: 322.5    (Smaller is better.)
```

TABLE 4.2 An overview of the statistics we may want to use when modeling the *Grey's Anatomy* hookup data and the substantive meaning of those effects

ERGM term	Substance
absdiff("birthyear")	people hook up within approximate age group
nodecov("birthyear")	younger people more likely to hook up
nodematch("position")	more likely to hook up within working unit; also consider nodemix("position")
nodematch("race")	people more likely to hook up within racial group
nodematch("sex")	people more likely to hook up across sexes (negative effect)
nodecov("season")	earlier characters formed more hookup ties

Before interpreting the results, note that the "MCMC %" is always zero because MCMC is not being performed in the absence of endogenous effects. Substantively, the results indicate that larger age differences correspond to smaller hookup probabilities, hookups are more likely for pairs working in the same job at the hospital, and hookups tend to happen within the same racial group. These effects are statistically significant at or beyond the traditional 0.05 level. The node-level effect of age is not statistically significant, indicating that age does not play a significant role in the tendency of these characters to form hookup edges. Though it is not statistically significant (likely because of the very small sample/proportion), the coefficient of −3.26 – the largest magnitude effect – on same-sex relationships relative to the male-female baseline indicates that sex-based heterophily is very common in the network. We also find a negative and statistically significant coefficient on the season variable, indicating that characters introduced earlier formed more hookup ties.

4.3 ENDOGENOUS NETWORK EFFECTS

The ability to include endogenous network effects – those related to the structure of and dependence among connections in the outcome network rather than exogenous covariates, is what sets the ERGM apart from most other statistical models. Whereas the exogenous predictors considered above are not conceptually different from those in, and indeed could be included in, a standard regression, endogenous dependencies are a significant departure from what those with regression training will be used to. As such, it is worth having a detailed discussion about them for the rest of this chapter. We begin by considering the two primary types of endogenous dependencies, those related to Markov graphs and those related to curved ERGMs, and then consider vertex-based, dyadic, triadic, and higher-order dependencies both as Markov graphs and as curved ERGMs.

4.3.1 Markov Graphs and Curved ERGMs

Many endogenous dependencies can be captured as Markov graph statistics. Markov graph statistics tend to be both more intuitive, but less computationally stable than their curved counterparts for reasons we will explore in this chapter and the next, respectively. For this reason, it is common, though by no means exclusively correct, to begin the process of ERGM specification with Markov statistics and migrate those to curved specifications if the model turns out to be computationally degenerate.

Frank and Strauss (1986, p. 832) provide a definition: "A graph is said to be a Markov graph if only incident dyads can be conditionally dependent." This definition assumes that the number of vertices is fixed at V, and possible edges between disjoint pairs of vertices are independent conditional on the rest of the network. The intuition here is that a common actor must be involved for any two (or more) edges to be dependent (Snijders et al. 2006). As Snijders et al. further point out, the Markov property in an undirected network with vertices i, j, k, and ℓ means that N_{ij} and $N_{k\ell}$ are independent conditional on the rest of the network.

The original paper by Frank and Strauss (1986) considered only three Markov graph statistics: the number of edges, the k-star, and the number of triangles. Yet subsequent research has greatly expanded the set of Markov statistics used by analysts; we will consider many of them as examples throughout the remainder of this chapter. Moreover, many common statistics that can be computed as a sum of subgraph products are Markov statistics. To illustrate this concept, consider the triangles statistic proposed by Frank and Strauss,

$$h_T(N) = \sum_{i \leq < j < k \leq V} N_{ij} N_{ik} N_{jk}, \qquad (4.2)$$

and let us see that this is indeed a sum of subgraph products. The subgraph is that of three vertices, denoted i, j, and k in the equation. The product in the subgraph is among the three possible edges. Because this statistic is defined for binary (i.e., edges are on and coded 1 or off and coded 0) undirected networks, the subgraph product will equal one only when all three of the possible edges among the three vertices are present and will be zero otherwise. Lastly, we take the sum over each possible triangle in the network. This statistic very literally counts the number of closed triangles in the network. Yet we can see that this sum of subgraph products meets Frank and Strauss (1986) definition of a Markov graph, as only incident dyads are conditionally dependent. However, note that some statistics that can be calculated as simple sums of subgraph products are not Markov Graph statistics. For example, the count of the number of four-cycles in a network, which can be calculated as a sum over subgraph products, is not a Markov graph statistic.

Snijders et al. (2006) introduced a new concept in ERGM specification. They considered the possibility that θ^T might enter the ERGM, not linearly, but via a function $\eta(\theta)^T$. If this is the case, then the basic ERGM, which, recall, is written

$$P(N, \theta) = \frac{\exp(\theta^T \mathbf{h}(N))}{c(\theta)}, \qquad (4.3)$$

becomes a curved ERGM of the form

$$P(N,\boldsymbol{\theta}) = \frac{\exp(\boldsymbol{\eta}(\boldsymbol{\theta})^T \mathbf{h}(N))}{c(\boldsymbol{\theta})}, \tag{4.4}$$

where $\boldsymbol{\eta}(\boldsymbol{\theta})$ is a nonlinear function of $\boldsymbol{\theta}$.

Curved ERGM specifications tend, on the whole, to be less intuitive than Markov specifications because of their nonlinearity. Yet the family of curved ERGM specifications tends to suppress the total value of their Markov counterparts and often enhances the numerical stability of the model as a result. As such, curved specifications have become the go-to statistics of analysts whose model is suffering from degeneracy. We explore degeneracy and its remedies more fully in the following chapter, but it is worth noting that curved ERGMs are not a silver-bullet solution to this problem: in many cases they will help, but in many cases they will not.

We now consider vertex-based, dyad-based, and higher-order endogenous statistics for ERGM specification and examine both Markov and curved examples of each class.

4.3.2 Vertex-Based Network Dependencies

Many endogenous network dependencies that are interesting to include in the ERGM are centered around a particular vertex and its set of connections.

One of the most popular such statistics, and one originally proposed in the foundational Frank and Strauss (1986) paper, is the k-star. The k-star examines how other vertices connect to the focal vertex. As such, in the undirected case, this structure can be used to operationalize preferential attachment (Barabási & Albert 1999), the tendency for some vertices with many connections to receive even more connections (i.e., "the rich get richer"). Specifically, a positive coefficient associated with a two-star statistic provides evidence for preferential attachment. While preferential attachment is a dynamic process, and we have thus far limited ourselves to the consideration of single cross-sectional "snapshot" networks, k-stars can help to capture a process consistent with preferential attachment.

The k-star is actually a class of statistics that includes the one-star (equivalent to the number of edges in the network), the two-star, the three-star, and so on. The class of statistics gets the "star" in its name because of the the starlike structure that can be seen as one considers

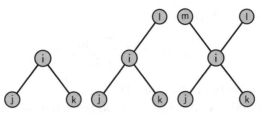

FIGURE 4.1 From left to right, a two-star, three-star, and four-star. There is no theoretical limit to the size of a star, but two- and three-stars tend to be most practical and are generally used to capture a process consistent with preferential attachment in single "snapshot" networks.

progressively higher k in the k-star: the focal vertex as a single point with many connections radiating from it. Figure 4.1 shows a few examples of k-star specifications. The k-star may be written generally as

$$h_S(N) = \sum_{i \leq j \leq n} \binom{N_{i+}}{k}, \qquad (4.5)$$

where we can see from the formula that this is a Markov statistic. To build intuition on what this statistic does, the two-star counts the number of two-stars in the network, the three-star counts the number of three-stars, and so forth.

The k-star is easily adapted to function in directed networks. One can consider in-k-stars and out-k-stars to reflect incoming and outgoing edges to the focal vertex, respectively. From a substantive perspective, the incoming ties in an in-k-star reflect popularity. For example in a social network, the tendency of others to nominate the focal vertex as a friend is likely to be subject to popularity dynamics. Out-stars can be seen to reflect the property of sociality in social networks, the tendency of an individual (the focal vertex) to form outgoing social ties. Though they may look and sound similar, in many contexts such as social networks, in-k-stars (popularity) and out-k-stars (sociality) have very different interpretations and reflect fundamentally different properties of the focal vertex. Figure 4.2 illustrates an in-three-star and an out-three-star.

Out-k-stars, in-k-stars, and undirected k-stars are included easily in R using `ostar(k)`, `istar(k)`, or `kstar(k)`, respectively, where k is the user-specified star value. For example, `ostar(3)` would be used to include out-three-stars.

The curved ERGM counterparts to stars of various degree are the geometrically weighted degree counts. As will be discussed in the following

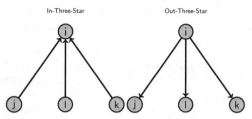

FIGURE 4.2 An in-three-star (left) and an out-three-star (right). In social networks, these may be interpreted as popularity and sociality, respectively.

chapter, the star statistics are prone to degeneracy due to the very high counts of statistics that are rapidly reached as the network grows dense. The class of curved ERGMs aims to down-weight such structures, thus suppressing the higher values of these statistics. Geometrically weighted degree counts is one way that this can be accomplished.

Snijders et al. (2006) describe the geometrically weighted degree as

$$h_\alpha^{(d)}(N) = \sum_{k=0}^{n-1} e^{-\alpha k} d_k(N) = \sum_{i=1}^{n} e^{-\alpha N_{i+}}, \tag{4.6}$$

with $\alpha > 0$ and the number of vertices with degree k given by $d_k(N)$. α is an important parameter in this statistic because it is the geometric penalty. As α approaches zero, increasing weight is placed on the high-degree networks. For intuition, the geometrically weighted degree aims to capture the same basic structure as the Markov star statistics considered above, but applies a nonlinear penalty to the degree. It should be clear from this discussion, and worth emphasizing, that the value of α – whether estimated or set by the user – has a substantial impact on the value of the coefficient associated with the geometrically weighted degree and its interpretation (Levy 2016).

While geometrically weighted degree is the most popular curved alternative to star counts, it is worth briefly mentioning the alternating-k-star as it sees frequent usage by practitioners. Snijders et al. (2006) proposed the alternating-k-star as

$$h_\lambda^{(s)}(N) = S_2 - \frac{S_3}{\lambda} + \frac{S_4}{\lambda^2} - \ldots + (-1)^{n-2}\frac{S_{n-1}}{\lambda^{n-3}} \tag{4.7}$$

$$= \sum_{k=2}^{n-1} (-1)^k \frac{S_k}{\lambda^{k-2}}$$

TABLE 4.3 *Common vertex-based endogenous dependencies*

ERGM term	Statistic	Substance
ostar(k)	# k out-stars	sociality
istar(k)	# k in-stars	popularity
kstar(k)	# k stars	preferential attachment
gwidegree	geom w'ted in-degree	popularity
gwodegree	geom w'ted out-degree	sociality
gwdegree	geom w'ted degree	preferential attachment
altkstar	geom w'ted stars	preferential attachment

Note. The first column gives their implementation in R (with the value of k chosen by the user), the second gives a brief technical description of the statistic, and the third column gives the statistic's substantive interpretation. Terms presented in red are prone to degeneracy.

where "S_k indicates the degree of the star and $\lambda = e^{\alpha}/(e^{\alpha} - 1) \geq 1$, α and λ are decreasing functions of each other. Moreover, as $\alpha \to \infty$, $\lambda \to 1$ and the above approaches $d_o(N)$" (Snijders et al. 2006). Because the weights for each increment in k have alternating signs, the alternating positive and negative terms balance one another out. Note that the geometrically weighted degree and alternating k-star statistics measure equivalent mathematical properties of a network (Hunter 2007) and therefore should not be included together in a single model.

Table 4.3 summarizes the vertex-based endogenous dependencies we have discussed here and presents their R implementation and substantive meaning.

4.3.3 Dyad-Based Endogenous Effects

Not all endogenous effects are centered around a focal vertex. Many important endogenous processes center around a focal dyad, or pair of vertices. Table 4.4 summarizes some common dyad-based network dependencies and their corresponding R commands. The formula for Markov statistics centered on the dyad will be familiar; they are specified as sums of subgraph products.

To see an example of this, consider what is probably the most prominent dyad-based effect: reciprocity. Reciprocity exists in directed networks when vertex i sends an edge to vertex j and vertex j also sends an edge to vertex i. This process is illustrated in Figure 4.3. The concept of reciprocity is critical in cooperation theory (Axelrod 1984) and contribution theory (Axelrod 2006), so it is not surprising that this

TABLE 4.4 *Common dyad-based network dependencies*

ERGM term	Statistic	Substance
mutual	# mutual dyads	reciprocity
asymmetric	# asymmetric dyads	antireciprocity
degcor	ρ between tied dyads	degree homophily

FIGURE 4.3 Reciprocity. In directed networks, i sends an edge to j, and that edge is reciprocated by j to i.

dependency arrises in some form in nearly every study of directed human or institutional networks (Molm 2010). Its operationalization as a sum of subgraph products is straightforward: the subgraph includes two vertices, i and j, and the product of their directed ties is summed across the network. The formula for reciprocity is written as

$$h_R(N) = \sum_{i<j} N_{ij} N_{ji}. \tag{4.8}$$

To build intuition about this statistic, consider that, because the networks under consideration are binary and directed, the only time the subgraph product $N_{ij} N_{ji}$ will be equal to 1 is when i and j each send an edge to the other; this subgraph product will be 0 in all other conditions. Thus, the statistic in (6.7) literally counts the number of reciprocal edges in the network.

It is worth noting that network dependencies of this sort are simple to expand or create. This is important because the operationalization of the model should match theory as closely as possible, and the situation may arise where none of the statistics implemented in the software match the researcher's theory appropriately. In such situations, the researcher will want to create a custom endogenous effect. Let us illustrate this process by extending reciprocity to what we will call mutuality. Perhaps we are examining a small social network in which everyone can reasonably be assumed to know everyone else, for example a small company or classroom. In such a setting, people *not* nominating one another as friends is meaningful. Thus, we want a statistic that will also capture the situation in which neither i nor j consider each other friends, but we also want to capture reciprocity as discussed above. What we want is a statistic that captures when a dyadic relationship is mutually on (standard reciprocity) or mutually off. Begin by considering reciprocity as presented in Equation (4.8): $\sum_{i<j} N_{ij} N_{ji}$. We could change this to capture relationships that are mutually off by subtracting each of the edge values from 1, as in $(1 - N_{ij})(1 - N_{ji})$. Because edges are either 0 or 1, $(1 - N_{ij})(1 - N_{ji})$ will only equal 1 when no edges exist between i and j. We can complete our mutuality statistic by adding this "mutually off" component to the equation for reciprocity:

$$h_M(N) = \sum_{i<j} N_{ij} N_{ji} + (1 - N_{ij})(1 - N_{ji}), \qquad (4.9)$$

where the subgraph product $N_{ij} N_{ji} + (1 - N_{ij})(1 - N_{ji}) = 1$ if the relationship between i and j is either mutually on or mutually off. This mutuality statistic is not provided by the software, though we have seen that it is simple to develop such statistics on one's own.[1]

In networks where reciprocity is especially prevalent, situations of nonreciprocity may be more interesting than reciprocity itself. Antireciprocity, or asymmetric dyads, occur when i sends an edge to j, but j does not send an edge to i. Naturally then, we can write the statistic as a modification of the reciprocity equation,

$$h_A(N) = \sum_{i<j} N_{ij}(1 - N_{ji}), \qquad (4.10)$$

such that the subgraph product is equal to 1 only when j does not return i's edge.

Reciprocity and asymmetry tend to dominate the landscape of dyadic endogenous effects, but other options exist as well. One worth mentioning is the inclusion of the correlation between the degrees of the two vertices incident to each edge as an endogenous effect. This term captures degree-homophily – the tendency for two vertices that have similar numbers of connections to be connected with one another (Morris & Kretzschmar 1995).

4.3.4   Triadic and Higher-Order Endogenous Effects

Perhaps the most compelling feature of the ERGM is its ability to directly model higher-order dependencies. Such higher-order effects are specified on subgraphs of three or more vertices. A comprehensive review of all

---

[1] For clarity, be aware that the ergm package uses the term mutual to indicate reciprocity of the form shown in Equation (4.8), not our Equation (4.9).

higher-order dependencies is not feasible, but in this subsection, we will discuss several of the more commonly used higher-order dependencies.

The simplest higher-order endogenous effect, as well as the most prominent, is the triangle. A triangle occurs in a network when vertex i is connected to vertices j and k, and those vertices (j and k) are connected to one another. The leftmost cell of Figure 4.4 illustrates this configuration in an undirected network. Closed triangles operationalize the concept that "the friend of a friend is a friend" and tend to be very common in positively valanced networks. More nuance is added to the triadic configuration when the network is directed. The middle and rightmost cells of Figure 4.4 show two possible closed-triadic configurations in directed networks. A cyclic triple occurs when i sends an edge to j, which sends an edge to k, which sends an edge to i. In a cyclic configuration, the triad can be interpreted as having a reciprocal process that goes through an intermediary (e.g., the return of an edge happens through a third vertex). The transitive configuration is shown in the far rightmost cell of the figure when vertex i sends edges to j and k while j also sends an edge to k. This configuration can be interpreted as i co-supporting j and k, or as k being co-supported by i and j.

The undirected closed triad or directed transitivity may be written as

$$h_T(N) = \sum_{i<j<h} N_{ij} N_{ik} N_{jk},\tag{4.11}$$

where the ordering of the subscripts does not matter when dealing with an undirected network, and the transitive configuration could be shifted to be cyclical by changing $N_{ij}N_{ik}N_{jk}$ to $N_{ij}N_{jk}N_{ki}$.

Triangles, whether directed or undirected, suffer from the same degeneracy problems that affect the star statistics. To remedy this problem, Snijders et al. (2006) proposed two geometrically weighted variants of the the triangle – the geometric weight suppressing the value of the statistic and thus helping to reduce the tendency of models specified in

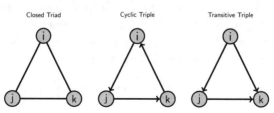

FIGURE 4.4 Closed triangles on the subgraph of three vertices, i, j, and k. Each vertex shares an edge with the other two.

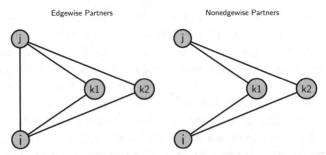

FIGURE 4.5 An illustration of geometrically weighted edgewise shared partners (GWESP) and geometrically weighted nonedgewise shared partners (GWNSP) with four vertices.

this way to be degenerate. The most commonly used such statistics are the geometrically weighted edgewise shared partners (GWESP) and geometrically weighted nonedgewise shared partners (GWNSP) statistics. GWESP and GWNSP are illustrated in the left and right cells of Figure 4.5. Both statistics are based around the idea of k-triads, that a focal dyad ij may share many mutual connections with other vertices generically denoted k. If we consider the case of GWESP, the edgewise shared partners are the vertices with whom the members of the focal ij edge are connected. If i and j are individuals in a friendship network, they may have several friends in common. The geometric weight down-weights the number of partners that i and j have in common. A useful intuitive interpretation of the weighting in GWESP holds that the first shared partner contributes more to the likelihood of a tie between i and j, than does the second shared partner, and the tenth shared partner contributes much less than the first or the second shared partner. In our *Grey's Anatomy* hookup network, we expect GWESP to be attributed with a negative coefficient, indicating a low likelihood of interaction between nodes with shared partners. We have already seen that very few triads exist in this network.

Both statistics are specified in a similar fashion. Note first, though, that the specification of a statistic with a geometric weight implies the need to choose a weight, denoted λ. Consider the parameters $\phi_T = \log \lambda_T$ for edgewise partners and $\phi_P = \log \lambda_P$ for dyadic partners. The GWESP and GWNSP statistics are then specified as follows:

$$\text{GWESP}(N, \phi_T) = e^{\phi_T} \sum_{i=1}^{n-2} \left\{ 1 - \left(1 - e^{-\phi_T} \right)^i \right\} EP_i(N), \qquad (4.12)$$

$$\text{GWNSP}(N, \phi_P) = e^{\phi_P} \sum_{i=1}^{n-2} \left\{ 1 - \left(1 - e^{-\phi_P} \right)^i \right\} DP_i(N), \qquad (4.13)$$

TABLE 4.5 *Common endogenous statistics specified on the subgraph of three vertices*

ERGM term	Statistic	Substance
triangles	# of triangles	transitivity
ttriple	# of transitive triads	transitivity
ctriple	# of 3-cycles	indirect reciprocity
gwesp	geom w'ted edgewise sp	transitivity
gwnsp	geom w'ted nonedge sp	antitransitivity

Note. Those statistics shown in boldface are prone to degeneracy.

where EP refers to edgewise partners and DP refers to dyadwise partners. We can see from the formula that both these statistics involve the direct down-weighting of the number of shared partners on either the edge or the nonedgewise dyad. Because they have relatively straightforward interpretations and often help prevent degeneracy in a given model, these statistics have seen widespread application.

Table 4.5 displays the R commands and brief interpretations of some of the most common statistics on the subgraph of three vertices. However, this should not be taken to suggest that these are the only useful statistics that can be specified on triadic structures, or that three vertices is the largest meaningful subgraph. For example, a four-path exists when i has an edge with j, which has an edge with k, which has an edge with ℓ, which has an edge with a fifth vertex. A four-cycle exists when that last edge does not go to a fifth vertex, but instead connects back to i, creating a square structure of edges.

The ergm package has a wide array of endogenous statistics that can be used in an ERGM (nearly 100 as of this writing), far more than it is sensible to try to review here. We have tried to focus on some of the most theoretically useful and empirically common statistics while also giving the reader a sense for what they mean and how they can be used. We encourage the novice ERGM analyst to spend some time studying the help page at ?ergm.terms to get a better sense of what the range of specification options looks like.

Running Example: Romantic Hookups in *Grey's Anatomy*

We can see some examples of these endogenous structures in the plot of our *Grey's Anatomy* hookup network, presented in Figure 4.6. This is an undirected network, so in- and out-stars are not meaningful. We

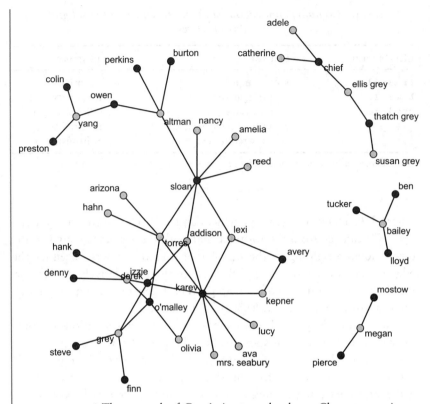

FIGURE 4.6 The network of *Grey's Anatomy* hookups. Character sex is represented by vertex color, dark shade for males and light shade for females.

see a two-star with Megan connecting with Mostow and Pierce. We can also see an easy example of a three-star with Bailey as the focal vertex: she connects with Tucker, Ben, and Lloyd. Note, however, that Bailey's three-star also includes three two-stars with Bailey as the focal vertex: Tucker–Bailey–Lloyd, Tucker–Bailey–Ben, and Ben–Bailey–Lloyd. So, just among this small subgraph centered around Bailey that is not connected to the network, the three-star count is one while the two-star count is three. The star structure with Altman as the focal vertex is an example of a four-star. She is connected to Owen, Perkins, Burton, and Sloan. Sloan, for his sake, is the center of a seven-star, and Karev has the highest degree at nine – each of these are composed of multiple two-stars, three-stars, and so forth.

```
1  set.seed(5)
2  plot(hookups, vertex.col=c("blue", "pink")[
3                1+(get.vertex.attribute(hookups, "sex")=="F")],
4     label=get.vertex.attribute(hookups, "name"), label.cex=.75)
```

For the case of the *Grey's Anatomy* hookup network, there is not much we can do theoretically or empirically with dyad-based dependencies because the network is undirected. As a consequence, dyad-based endogenous effects will not be important.

We do not see much triadic closure in our *Grey's Anatomy* hookup network. This is unsurprising because most individuals featured in the show are heterosexual. We do see a triad emerge however between Torres, Karev, and Derek, the Karev–Derek edge being the homosexual one. Because closed triads are so rare in a predominantly heterosexual network, we would expect a negative effect for a triangles term, when included in an ERGM of this network.

We see four-cycles in the *Grey's Anatomy* network for example between Karev, Kepner, Avery, and Lexi, and again between Karev, Lexi, Sloan, and Torres.

In light of the above discussion, we can add some endogenous dependencies to our ERGM of the *Grey's Anatomy* network (Figure 4.7). To capture a tendency for monogamy, we include the term degree(1), which evaluates the tendency for vertices to have degrees of one (monogamy). We also captured the tendency for triads not to form by including the term gwdsp(1, fixed=TRUE), where the arguments mean we are fixing the weight parameter to be one:

```
1   set.seed(510)
2   m1 <- ergm(Hookups ~ edges
3               # people hookup within approximate age group
4               + absdiff("birthyear")
5               # younger people are more likely to hookup
6               + nodecov("birthyear")
7               # people are less likely to hookup within their working
                  unit
8               + nodematch("position")
9               # people prefer to hookup within their racial group
10              + nodematch("race")
11              # people prefer to hookup with members of the opposite sex
12              # (negative effect))
13              + nodematch("sex")
14              # earlier characters form more ties
15              + nodecov("season")
16              # tendency for monogamy
```

```
17        + degree(1)
18        # tendency for cliquishness; also works well with
19        # gwesp(1, fixed=TRUE)
20        + gwdsp(1, fixed=TRUE),
21     control=control.ergm(
22        MCMC.samplesize=5000,
23        MCMC.burnin=5000,
24        MCMLE.maxit=10))
25  summary(m1)
26  g1 <- gof(m1)
27  par(mfrow=c(2, 2))
28  plot(g1)
```

The results are as follows, with goodness of fit diagnostics plotted in Figure 4.7.

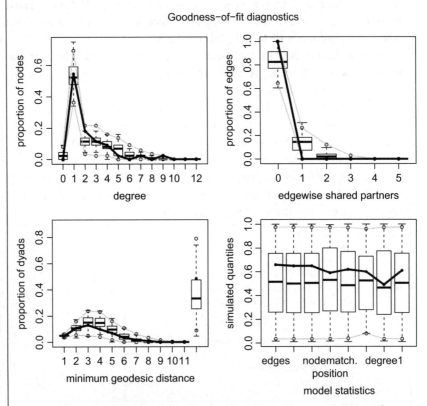

FIGURE 4.7 Goodness of fit plots for the *Grey's Anatomy* ERGM. The proximity of the black lines to the medians of the box plots throughout the figures is indicative of better fit.

```
Monte Carlo MLE Results:
                      Estimate Std. Error MCMC %   z value  Pr(>|z|)
edges               -3.824e+01 4.777e-01     100   -80.047  <1e-04  ***
absdiff.birthyear   -1.280e-01 3.118e-02       0    -4.104  <1e-04  ***
nodecov.birthyear    9.579e-03 2.212e-04      16    43.314  <1e-04  ***
nodematch.position   8.716e-01 3.328e-03      58   261.938  <1e-04  ***
nodematch.race       8.305e-01 5.858e-03      15   141.771  <1e-04  ***
nodematch.sex       -3.283e+00 5.751e-03      59  -570.932  <1e-04  ***
nodecov.season      -1.434e-01 6.642e-02       0    -2.159  0.0309  *
degree1              1.882e+00 9.175e-03       7   205.110  <1e-04  ***
gwdsp.fixed.1       -1.118e-02 1.035e-01       0    -0.108  0.9139
---
Signif. codes:  0   ***   0.001    **    0.01    *    0.05  .  0.1
                1

    Null Deviance: 1311.4  on 946  degrees of freedom
Residual Deviance:  251.1  on 937  degrees of freedom

AIC: 269.1    BIC: 312.8    (Smaller is better.)
```

The signs of the covariate effects are consistent with those from the model without endogenous effects. However, in the updated model, birth year is statistically significantly positively associated with degree – a finding that differs from the nonsignificant effect under the model with no endogenous terms. The degree1 coefficient is statistically significantly positive, and substantial in magnitude. This indicates that exclusive sexual partnerships are prominent throughout the network. Note that many terms one might expect to be interesting, such as four-cycles and two-stars, produce degenerate specifications, the diagnosis and remedy of which is the subject of the following chapter. The interested reader can look at, and attempt to run, the full set of specifications we considered for this network by consulting this book's accompanying R code.

4.4 CREATING NEW STATISTICS

Despite the wide range of statistics available in the ergm package, a situation may arise in which the researcher does not have an operationalization of her endogenous process of interest precoded in the software. This is usually not a major challenge, as creating and coding new statistics is relatively easy via what are called *change statistics* (see Goodreau et al. 2008 for a detailed discussion).

To understand how change statistics are created and coded, consider the following. Let us denote a generic endogenous effect computed in this way as h_d. Second, note that we can express the ERGM as a conditional probability of the ij edge existing,

$$\pi_{ij}(\boldsymbol{\theta}) = P(N_{ij} = 1 \mid N_{-ij}, \boldsymbol{\theta}) = \text{logit}^{-1}\left(\sum_{d=1}^{D} \theta_d \delta_d^{(ij)}(N)\right), \qquad (4.14)$$

which is equivalent to the ERGM as we had written it in Equation (3.1). In Equation (4.14), N_{-ij} denotes the network absent the ij edge, so the equation captures the probability of the ij edge existing conditional upon the rest of the network not involved in ij. The subscript d continues to denote a generic dependency included in **h**, and the term $\delta_d^{(ij)}(N)$ captures the change in the value of h_d that would occur if the edge N_{ij} were changed from off (zero) to on (one). Finally, $\text{logit}^{-1}(x) = 1/(1+\exp(-x))$, is the inverse logistic transformation commonly used in binary response models.

The intuition behind change statistics can be difficult to grasp. If we denote the value of h_d with the N_{ij} edge turned off – regardless of whether it is off or on in the actual network – as $h_d(N_{ij}^-)$ and the value of h_d with N_{ij} turned on as $h_d(N_{ij}^+)$, then the change statistic is the difference between those two values: $\delta_d^{(ij)}(N) = h_d(N_{ij}^+) - h_d(N_{ij}^-)$. For example, if we were coding reciprocity as a change statistic, the value of $\delta_r^{(ij)}(N)$ would be either 0 or 1 depending on whether or not toggling the N_{ij} edge from off to on completes a reciprocal edge or not. Under one particular estimation method, termed maximum pseudolikelihood, a matrix of change statistics can be included as a predictor in an ERGM exactly the way we include exogenous predictors (Equation 4.1). The fact that the values for present edges are summed in Equation (4.1) means that including a change statistic as such is functionally equivalent to any of the endogenous statistics for **h** that we discussed above. As such, we can rather easily code and include any endogenous effect we like as a change statistic, regardless of whether it is preimplemented in the ergm package. If the researcher wants to add a term to the ergm package to, to be estimated using Monte Carlo maximum likelihood (i.e., the default/MCMC approach), new terms can be added using the ergmuserterms package (Morris et al. 2008).

4.5 BIPARTITE ERGMS

Thus far, all of the networks we have considered in this book have been unipartite (aka single-mode) networks, meaning that all of the vertices are the same type, and they can all form connections with each other.

Yet many interesting networks are bipartite, meaning that there are two different types of vertices in the network, and ties can only be formed between nodes of two different types. Bipartite structures often emerge when, for example, individuals form edges to organizations or events. For a more concrete example, bipartite networks occur in the study of international politics when countries (one type of vertex, or *mode*) form edges connecting them to international treaties (a different type of vertex or mode). In a treaty-signing network, two vertices of the same type are not able to form edges with each other directly. One solution for modeling bipartite networks is to project them into unipartite networks. For example, if two countries both have edges to the same treaty in the bipartite network, the unipartite projection drops vertices of the treaty type and counts the two countries in question as sharing an edge between them. However, projecting bipartite networks into unipartite networks requires assumptions about the nature of edges that will be unsatisfactory in some situations, and it will be better to model the network directly in its bipartite form. Thankfully, the ERGM is easily constrained to bipartite structures and there is a suite of endogenous statistics designed specifically to be used with bipartite networks.

Much like for the unipartite networks considered above, the set of potential endogenous effects is too large to examine in detail here (as before, the reader is referred to the ergm.terms help file). We can consider a few examples, however, that will help to illustrate how bipartite terms are different from unipartite terms and how they can be used to specify a bipartite ERGM.

To begin, consider bipartite degree. This statistic is very similar to unipartite degree, except that the degree is calculated for only one type of vertex, the first or the second mode. The user specifies whether they want first or second mode degree by using the term b1degree or b2degree, respectively. Star-type statistics are also easily computed in bipartite networks. We can include a statistic that counts the number of k-stars based around the first mode using b1star(k) and around the second mode using b2star(k), where k is the star value desired (e.g., $k = 2$ is a two-star). Bipartite two-stars for each mode are illustrated in Figure 4.8.

One can also consider more complicated dependencies for bipartite networks. Above, we examined the geometrically weighted edgewise and nonedgewise shared partners statistics for unipartite networks. A variation of these dependencies exists for bipartite networks as well. In bipartite networks, two vertices of the same type cannot share an edge, but can only form edges with vertices of different types – making the nonedgewise shared partners dependency particularly useful. The

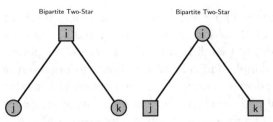

FIGURE 4.8 Illustrations of bipartite two-stars for the first (leftmost) and second (rightmost) modes of the network. Note that these structures are both bipartite two-stars, though the type of the focal vertex changes between them.

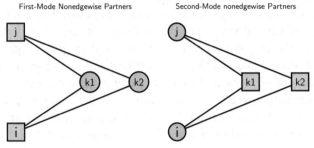

FIGURE 4.9 An illustration of bipartite nonedgewise shared partners (BNSP) with only two common ties for the first and second modes, respectively.

statistic is computed in much the same way as for unipartite networks, except for the fact that it only counts partners of a different vertex type shared by two unconnected vertices if the opposite type. The nonedgewise shared partners statistic may be computed for either mode of the bipartite network and can also be modified to take a geometric weight, making it less prone to degeneracy. These dependencies are illustrated in Figure 4.9.

Beyond the difference in the endogenous dependencies, the ERGM itself works the same way as with unipartite networks: the software command is the same, the model is checked the same way, and interpreted the same way.

Running Example: Water Policy in the San Francisco Bay Area

To illustrate the bipartite ERGM, we consider a new example since our *Grey's Anatomy* network cannot reasonably be projected to a bipartite network. Instead, we replicate part of the analysis by Lubell and Robbins (2017) examining how government agencies in the San Francisco Bay Area coordinate policy in order to adapt to the rise in sea levels associated with climate change. In this network, a variety of local and regional governments collaborate on plans, projects, and and reports around this issue, making the network naturally bipartite (agencies serve as mode one and form edges to projects/policies/reports that serve as mode two). Here, we present a semireplication of Lubell and Robbins analysis to illustrate the use of the bipartite ERGM. This is not a true replication of Lubell and Robbins because we do not parse the data into different time slices and compare results as they do. Rather, we apply their model specification to their entire dataset.

Lubell and Robbins (2017) use the following model specification:

```
mod.4.4 <- ergm(net~edges +
                gwb1degree(.4, fixed = TRUE) +
                gwb2degree(.4, fixed = TRUE) +
                b1factor("regLocVen", base = c(1:2)) +
                b2factor("regLocVen", base = 1) +
                b2star(c(2:3), "countyRegVen") +
                gwb1nsp(.1, fixed=TRUE) +
                gwb2nsp(.1, fixed=TRUE),
                constraints = ~ edges + bd(minout=netDegrees,
                                            minin=netDegrees))
```

This specification includes the geometrically weighted degree for both the first (agency) and second (project/policy/report) modes, an exogenous "regional location" factor for both the first and second modes, two- and three-stars for the second mode only, and geometrically weighted nonedgewise shared partners for both the first and second modes.

This model specification produces the following results, which can be interpreted in any way discussed in Chapter 3 (note, readers interested in how data for bipartite ERGMs are prepared and manipulated are referred to our accompanying extended R code). To note one structural finding, the negative nonedgewise shared partner effects indicate that agencies and projects are thoroughly mixed – that we do not observe similar sets of agencies focusing on all of the same projects.

```
Monte Carlo MLE Results:
                      Estimate Std. Error MCMC % z value Pr(>|z|)
edges                0.000e+00  0.000e+00     0      NA       NA
gwb1deg.fixed.0.4   -9.758e+00  4.213e-01     0 -23.161  < 1e-04 ***
gwb2deg.fixed.0.4   -1.061e+01  1.084e+00     0  -9.791  < 1e-04 ***
```

```
 6  b1factor.regLocVen.RegActor   -6.761e-03  4.283e-02   1  -0.158 0.874562
 7  b2factor.regLocVen.RegVenue   -3.008e-01  7.345e-02   0  -4.095 < 1e-04 ***
 8  b2star2.countyRegVen           1.294e-01  1.117e-02   0  11.576 < 1e-04 ***
 9  b2star3.countyRegVen          -6.887e-03  7.207e-04   1  -9.556 < 1e-04 ***
10  gwb1nsp.fixed.0.1             -1.498e-02  4.371e-02   1  -3.426 0.000613 ***
11  gwb2nsp.fixed.0.1             -2.155e-02  2.071e-02   0  -1.041 0.298065
12  ---
13  Signif. codes:  0 '***' 0.001 '**' 0.01 '*' 0.05 '.' 0.1 ' ' 1
14
15      Null Deviance:      0  on 66641  degrees of freedom
16  Residual Deviance: -1019  on 66632  degrees of freedom
17
18  Note that the null model likelihood and deviance are defined to be 0. This
        means that all likelihood-based inference (LRT, Analysis of Deviance,
        AIC, BIC, etc.) is only valid between models with the same reference
        distribution and constraints.
19
20  AIC: -1001    BIC: -919.1    (Smaller is better.)
```

The model also fits reasonably well without showing signs of degeneracy, as seen in the below R output and in the GOF statistics plotted in Figure 4.10.

```
 1  > gof_m4.4
 2
 3  Goodness-of-fit for degree
 4
 5       obs min  mean max MC p-value
 6  1      6   5 10.16  16     0.08
 7  2     10   0  1.49   6     0.00
 8  3      8   0  1.36   5     0.00
 9  4      7   0  1.96   6     0.00
10  5      6   0  3.44   9     0.20
11  6      6   1  5.19  11     0.84
12  7      4   2  7.33  15     0.22
13  8      2   1  8.16  14     0.06
14  9      4   2  8.70  14     0.14
15  10     4   2  8.36  17     0.14
16  11     6   1  7.46  14     0.76
17  12     4   2  6.87  15     0.38
18  13     2   0  5.05  11     0.26
19  14     3   1  3.99  13     0.86
20  15     2   0  3.20   8     0.68
21  16     0   0  2.46   6     0.06
22  17     3   0  1.81   5     0.56
23  18     1   0  1.04   5     1.00
24  19     3   0  0.73   2     0.00
25  20     1   0  0.56   3     0.88
26  21     1   0  0.34   2     0.62
27  22     1   0  0.16   1     0.32
28  23     1   0  0.10   2     0.18
29  24     1   0  0.01   1     0.02
30  25     2   0  0.04   1     0.00
31  26     1   0  0.02   1     0.04
32  27     0   0  0.01   1     1.00
33  29     1   0  0.00   0     0.00
34  32     2   0  1.41   2     1.00
35  33     1   0  1.19   3     1.00
36  34     0   0  0.29   2     1.00
37  35     1   0  0.81   2     1.00
```

38	36	0	0	0.23	1	1.00
39	37	1	0	0.91	2	1.00
40	38	0	0	0.13	1	1.00
41	39	0	0	0.02	1	1.00
42	40	2	1	1.85	3	1.00
43	41	1	0	0.99	2	1.00
44	42	0	0	0.16	1	1.00
45	43	0	0	0.01	1	1.00
46	44	1	0	0.89	1	1.00
47	45	0	0	0.11	1	1.00
48	58	1	0	0.96	1	1.00
49	59	0	0	0.04	1	1.00
50	102	1	0	0.97	1	1.00
51	103	0	0	0.03	1	1.00
52	112	1	1	1.00	1	1.00
53	126	1	1	1.00	1	1.00

54

55 Goodness—of—fit for edgewise shared partner

56

57   obs   min   mean   max MC p—value

58   1549   1549   1549   1549   1

59

60 Goodness—of—fit for minimum geodesic distance

61

62   obs   min   mean   max MC p—value

63	1	1549	1549	1549.00	1549	1.00
64	2	28988	28511	29207.65	29956	0.30
65	3	44398	43170	44886.71	46839	0.46
66	4	159147	154491	160149.71	164376	0.58
67	5	19347	15430	17684.53	19969	0.06
68	6	24521	18196	22327.55	28377	0.38
69	7	599	9	147.25	621	0.02
70	8	830	0	29.43	484	0.00
71	9	0	0	0.12	5	1.00
72	Inf	1496	0	4893.05	10388	0.20

73

74 Goodness—of—fit for model statistics

75

76		obs	min	mean	max
77	edges	1549.0000	1549.0000	1549.0000	1549.0000
78	gwb1deg.fixed.0.4	746.3804	739.4539	746.8541	754.1068
79	gwb2deg.fixed.0.4	148.4848	145.4973	148.2750	150.9282
80	b1factor.regLocVen.RegionalActor	735.0000	703.0000	744.7500	796.0000
81	b2factor.regLocVen.RegionalVenue	859.0000	806.0000	853.5800	893.0000
82	b2star2.countyRegVen	5444.0000	4888.0000	5533.4500	6094.0000
83	b2star3.countyRegVen	50886.0000	42814.0000	52196.3500	62371.0000
84	gwb1nsp.fixed.0.1	27220.2781	26817.7181	27409.6819	28148.4570
85	gwb2nsp.fixed.0.1	2191.2355	2052.7253	2188.3256	2325.9141

86		MC p—value
87	edges	1.00
88	gwb1deg.fixed.0.4	0.86
89	gwb2deg.fixed.0.4	0.96
90	b1factor.regLocVen.RegionalActor	0.78
91	b2factor.regLocVen.RegionalVenue	0.88
92	b2star2.countyRegVen	0.76
93	b2star3.countyRegVen	0.82
94	gwb1nsp.fixed.0.1	0.46
95	gwb2nsp.fixed.0.1	0.98

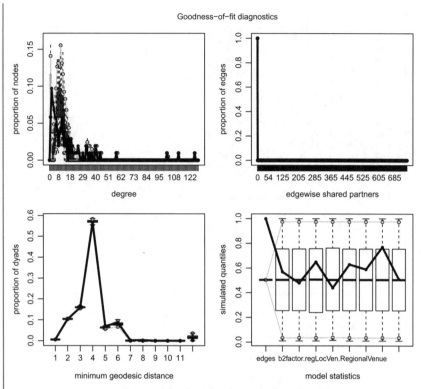

FIGURE 4.10 Goodness of fit plots for the *Lubell and Robbins* bipartite ERGM.

4.6 WRAPPING UP

Perhaps the most powerful and flexible feature of the ERGM is its ability to accommodate a broad set of effects – endogenous and exogenous – at the vertex, edge, and subgraph levels. Not only can the ERGM include the sort of exogenous effects that researchers familiar with regression models will be used to, but it opens up a new horizon of endogenous structures about which the researcher may theorize and conduct precise hypothesis tests. Though the set of endogenous effects existing ERGM software includes is extensive, it is also possible for the researcher to create her own endogenous dependencies based on change statistics if the dependency of interest is not already included in software. That said, the extreme flexibility of the dependencies the model can accommodate places an increased burden on the researcher: she must develop theoretical expectations about the endogenous effects and operationalize them appropriately or the model will be misspecified.

4.7 SELF-STUDY PROBLEMS

Select a network dataset to study using ERGM, but avoid using the data from ina that were used in this chapter. Be sure that the dataset includes at least one vertex attribute. If you do not have a dataset that you would like to use for this exercise, we recommend that you use the estuaries dataset from ina – looking at one of the estuaries from the first time period, which is introduced in Section 6.7. Using this dataset, complete a report that includes the following information:

1. **Description of the dataset:** What does the dataset cover? Where did it come from? Has it been used in any prior studies?
2. **Hypotheses:** Describe and test at least one hypothesis regarding a vertex attribute, at least one dyadic interdependence hypothesis, and one triadic or higher-order interdependence hypothesis. Describe these hypotheses.
3. **Model specification:** Identify a model that is capable of testing each hypothesis. Estimate this model, evaluate fit, and update the model if there are shortcomings in fit.
4. **Estimates:** Present the estimates of the ERGM in either graphical or tabular form.
5. **Diagnostics:** Demonstrate that the model fits the network adequately.
6. **Interpretation:** Substantively interpret your results. Do you find support for your hypotheses? Do you think the effects that you find are large?

5

Estimation and Degeneracy

5.1 METHODS FOR ESTIMATING ERGM

Any user of ERGMs will quickly realize that the methods by which parameters are estimated are more computationally intensive than estimation methods used for conventional models used in the social sciences. Relatedly, the flexibility and complexity reflected in the functional form of the ERGM can give rise to very odd behavior in terms of model fit, which can also manifest as an estimation problem. Maximum likelihood estimation (MLE) is highly attractive in the case of ERGMs. The ERGM has a canonical exponential family form, which implies several ideal properties of MLE. First, as long as the MLE exists, the likelihood function is convex (Geyer 1990), which means that there is no risk of arriving at a local maximum in the likelihood (i.e., the estimate is guaranteed to be the best possible estimate given the model). Second, the statistics used to parameterize the model, $\mathbf{h}$, are by definition sufficient statistics for θ (Geyer 1990), which means we do not need any information besides $\mathbf{h}$ to estimate θ. Third, the MLE, if it exists, is asymptotically normally distributed (Hedayati & Bartlett 2012).

Unfortunately, MLE is infeasible for all but the smallest networks. To calculate the MLE, we need to calculate the denominator of the log-likelihood $\sum_{N^* \in \mathcal{N}} \exp\{\theta' \mathbf{h}(N^*)\}$. The denominator, or normalizing constant poses an insurmountable computational challenge in all but trivial cases. Table 5.1 gives the number of networks involved in the normalizing constant, based on the number of vertices in the network. In what follows we discuss the two most common methods of estimation for ERGM.

TABLE 5.1 *Number of unique undirected dichotomous networks*

Vertices	Unique undirected networks
5	1,024
10	35,184,370,000,000
15	40,564,820,000,000,000,000,000,000,000,000

5.1.1 Monte Carlo MLE

The literature offers two prominent approaches to approximating the MLE for ERGMs. The first approach to approximation, which is considered the state of the art in the literature, is termed Markov chain Monte Carlo maximum likelihood estimation (MCMC-MLE), or just Monte Carlo MLE (MC-MLE) (Geyer & Thompson 1992; Snijders 2002). In this method, a sample of networks taken from the ERGM defined by the parameter values discovered in the previous iteration of estimation is used to approximate the normalizing constant. Given starting values for the parameters, each iteration of MC-MLE proceeds by using the current estimate of the parameters to draw a sample of networks, and then updating estimates to maximize the stochastically approximated likelihood function. When there is no significant change from one iteration to the next, the estimates have converged. Hanneke et al. (2010) extended this algorithm to the context of a time series of networks, whereby each iteration involves taking samples of networks at each point of time represented in the dataset.

We present Pseudo-code for MC-MLE estimation of the ERGM in Figure 5.1. The parameter s gives the number of networks that are to be sampled in each iteration to approximate the likelihood function. This number is typically set to at least several thousand. The initial parameter values, $\theta^{[0]}$, are calculated using either maximum pseudolikelihood estimation, as reviewed in the next section, or the more recently developed methods proposed by Krivitsky (2017). Ideally, estimation will be run until convergence, that is, until the parameter values and likelihood do not change significantly from one iteration of estimation to the next. In practice, the researcher sets a maximum number of iterations. The default number in the `ergm` package is 20. Within each estimation iteration, $\tilde{N}$, the sample of s networks, is taken using a Metropolis-Hastings algorithm in which one element of the adjacency matrix is proposed to be changed in the respective sample (i.e., either an edge is toggled to a

---

s is the MCMC sample size (typically several thousand)
N_o is the observed network
n is the number of vertices in the network
$\theta^{[0]}$ = starting value for θ
$u = 0$
repeat
  $u = u + 1$
  draw $\tilde{N} \sim ERGM(N, \theta^{[u-1]})$ by MCMC, s networks with n vertices
  $\widehat{C(\theta)} = \ln \left(\sum_{v=1}^{s} \exp \left[(\theta - \theta^{[u-1]})' \mathbf{h}(\tilde{N}_v) \right] \right)$
  $\theta^{[u]} = \arg\max_\theta \left[\theta' \mathbf{h}(N_o) - \widehat{C(\theta)} \right]$
until convergence $(\theta^{[u]} \approx \theta^{[u-1]})$

FIGURE 5.1 Estimation by MC-MLE.

nonedge or a nonedge is toggled to an edge). This means that, in each iteration of the sampling, the network changes by at most one toggle to the adjacency matrix. This introduces substantial autocorrelation to the network sampling, such that it is often advisable to discard some number of iterations in the sampler between drawing new networks. For example, one could set the sampler to draw a new network on each tenth iteration of the Markov chain, meaning it would take 50,000 Markov chain iterations to draw 5,000 networks. In each iteration, the new estimates of θ are calculated by $\arg\max_\theta \left[\theta' \mathbf{h}(N_o) - \widehat{C(\theta)} \right]$ using Newton–Raphson (Haberman 1988) iterations.

From a practical perspective, there are three related challenges to estimation with MC-MLE. First, if starting values are poor, it will take many iterations for MC-MLE to converge, or MC-MLE may not be feasible due to the poor sample of networks generated in the initial iterations of MC-MLE. Second, the sample size s may be too small for the sample of networks to accurately reflect the distribution of networks under a given vector of parameter values. Third, it may require many iterations until the estimates converge. Thankfully, as we review below, it is possible to assess convergence of the estimates for a given application, and increase the MCMC sample size, and/or maximum number of MC-MLE iterations as necessary.

5.1.2 Maximum Pseudolikelihood

The second method used to approximate the MLE is maximum pseudolikelihood estimation (MPLE) (Besag 1974). We assume that N is the adjacency matrix, such that $N_{ij} = 1$ if vertex i sends a tie to vertex j

and o otherwise. If N is undirected, it is an indicator of i and j being tied. In MPLE, the likelihood is not approximated directly as part of the estimation routine. Rather, in MPLE the joint likelihood is replaced by the product over the conditional probability of each element of the adjacency matrix given the rest of the network. The conditional probability of a tie in the ij^{th} element of the adjacency matrix is

$$\pi_{ij}(\theta) = Pr(N_{ij} = 1 \mid N_{-ij}, \theta) = 1/\left[1 + \exp\{-\theta'\delta_{ij}(x(N))\}\right], \quad (5.1)$$

where N_{-ij} indicates the network except element ij, and $\delta_{ij}(x(N))$ is the vector of change statistics – the changes in the network statistics $x(N)$ when N_{ij} is toggled from o to 1, holding the rest of N at the observed values (Strauss and Ikeda 1990). A hill-climbing algorithm is used to maximize the pseudolikelihood:

$$\arg\max_{\theta} \sum_{\langle ij \rangle} \ln\left[\left(\pi_{ij}(\theta)\right)^{N_{ij}} \left(1 - \pi_{ij}(\theta)\right)^{1-N_{ij}}\right], \quad (5.2)$$

where $\langle ij \rangle$ denotes all pairs of vertices – unordered pairs in an undirected network and ordered pairs in a directed network. The calculation of the MPLE does not require any sort of simulation. The MPLE has been shown to be consistent, meaning that it approaches the MLE in distribution as the size of the network increases (Strauss and Ikeda 1990, Hyvärinen 2006).

5.1.3 Comparing MC-MLE and MPLE

MC-MLE is the default method in software for estimating ERGMs, and is generally seen in the literature as preferable to MPLE. There are three major advantages to MC-MLE. First, the MC-MLE converges to the MLE as the number of simulated networks used in estimation increases. As such, the researcher can always increase the accuracy of the MC-MLE by increasing m. Second, relatedly, in a simulation study, MC-MLE, when implemented with a sufficiently large m, was shown to be more efficient (i.e., lower variance) than MPLE (van Duijn et al. 2009). Indeed, MCMC-MLE has been favored in recent work with ERGMs, though not without exception (see, e.g., Faust & Skvoretz 2002, Saul & Filkov 2007). Third, van Duijn et al. (2009) find that the confidence intervals used with MC-MLE exhibit much better coverage properties than those that are used by default with MPLE. However, Schmid and Desmarais (2017) show how the parametric bootstrap can be used to construct valid confidence intervals for MPLE with ERGM.

MPLE does offer some advantages when compared to MC-MLE. First, the researcher does not know whether the number of simulated networks used in the approximation of the likelihood is large enough to make MC-MLE more efficient than MPLE. Second, to achieve efficiency gains over MPLE, MC-MLE requires an amount of simulation effort that grows on an order greater than n^2, where n is the number of nodes in the network. Since MPLE grows more efficient as the size of the network increases, MC-MLE requires more simulation, as the network grows, to out-perform MPLE. As the size of the network increases, each simulation used in MC-MLE is more computationally expensive (i.e., more simulation effort is required as the size of the network(s) increases, approximately on the order of n^2). This is because, due to its consistency, the performance of the MPLE improves with the size of the network. For very large networks, and probably only for large networks, MPLE may be preferable to MC-MLE.

Running Example: Cosponsorship among Senate Ideologues

In this chapter we will, as we did in Chapter 2, use cosponsorship among US senators as our running example. In this case, however, we will not look at the entire Senate. Rather, we will study the subnetwork that includes the five most liberal and five most conservative senators. We focus on this smaller network in the interest of presenting empirical examples that run relatively quickly. The dataset in the `ina` package named 'Senate' includes these data. `Senate` is a network object with ideology and vertex name attributes, as well as a 10×10 matrix-valued network attribute that gives the straight-line distance between senators' state capitals. The ideology scores are calculated based on senators' roll call voting records. See the running example in Chapter 2 for more detailed discussion of this example. We subset to ten senators to assure that the reader can run the example on their own in a timely manner. In this network, an edge from senator i to senator j indicates that i cosponsored at least two bills that were sponsored (i.e., introduced) by j during the 108th congress. The code below presents code to read these data in using the `ina` package and produces a plot of the network.

```
1  library(ina)
2  data(Senate)
3
4  ## Read in ERGM library
5  library(ergm)
6  library(network)
```

```
 7
 8  ## Simple Plot
 9  ## Nice package for creating color spectra
10  library(colorRamps)
11
12  ## replicable plot
13  set.seed(2345)
14
15  ## write outside the line
16  ## define colors
17  cols <- blue2red(10)[rank(get.vertex.attribute(Senate,"ideol"))]
18  plot(Senate, displaylabels=TRUE, vertex.col=cols,
19       edge.col="grey50", xpd=TRUE)
```

This network plot is relatively simple but illustrates that the structure is ideological in nature. That is, the senators who are tied through cosponsorship edges are likely to be similar to each other.

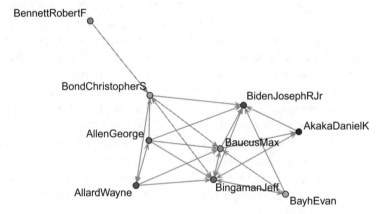

5.2 PROBLEM OF DEGENERACY

In the context of the ERGM, a substantial literature has arisen around how to best formulate network statistics to represent important generative processes such as transitivity, balance, and preferential attachment (Wasserman & Pattison 1996; Park & Newman 2004a; Snijders et al.

2006; Hunter et al. 2008). The initial development of specifications for the ERGM focused on intuitive local subgraph counts, such as the number of two-stars and triangles, that implied straightforward conditional distributions for each tie given the rest of the network (i.e., Markov graphs; see Strauss and Ikeda Strauss:1990). Intermediate extensions of the standard suite of network statistics used in the ERGM focused on more advanced or higher-order subgraph counts (Pattison & Robins 2002), reflecting longer paths and clique-like structures among vertex sets.

Unfortunately, intuitive specifications lead to empirically implausible models due to the problem of degeneracy. This became apparent with the Markov chain Monte Carlo simulations, both for exploring ERG distributions and estimating ERGM parameters, as presented by Snijders (2002). Degeneracy is a condition under which only a few network configurations – usually very sparse and very dense networks – have high-probability mass. When specifying an ERGM using counts of higher-order subgraphs, each edge contributes to many potential subgraph configurations. When a parameter associated with a higher-order configuration increases (e.g., in the iterative estimation process), this combinatorial property of simple subgraph statistics results in a distributional preference for many more ties, due to each edge's multiplicative impact on the number of subgraph configurations. To improve the behavior of ERG specifications, scholars have developed network statistics that correspond closely to the subgraph configurations used to specify Markov graphs but exhibit a decreasing marginal return to the number of underlying subgraph configurations in the network (Snijders et al. 2006; Hunter et al. 2008).

Snijders et al. (2006) and Hunter et al. (2008) propose the use of geometrically decreasing weights in the calculation of statistics for transitivity, as well as the in- and out-degree distributions. These geometrically weighted specifications avoid degeneracy with much greater success than models specified with simple local subgraph counts. Consider the measure of transitivity, or triangle closure, developed within the geometrically weighted framework. Early applications of ERGMs used counts of the number of triangles in a network to model triangle closure. One way to count triangles is through an edgewise algorithm whereby for each edge, the number of shared partners between the two vertices incident to the edge is tallied and added to the sum. Since each triangle would contribute three to such an edgewise count, the final summation would be divided by three to give the number of triangles in the network. From an edgewise perspective, a simple triangle count treats the first shared partner between two vertices as contributing the same weight to the transitivity measure as the third or tenth shared partner. This is computationally problematic since adding an edge to the network can cause combinatorial jumps in the calculation of the transitivity statistic that are as high as $n - 2$. The geometrically weighted analogue to the triangle count is the geometrically weighted edgewise shared partners (GWESP) statistic (Hunter et al. 2008), the formula for which is

$$\text{GWESP}(v) = e^v \sum_{i=1}^{n-2} \left[1 - \left(1 - e^{-v} \right)^i \right] E P_i(N),$$

where v is a positive scalar that controls the rate at which the weights attributed to edges change with the number of shared partners. In using GWESP to model transitivity, the weight contributed by an edge always increases with the number of shared partners between the vertices incident to the edges, but the increase in the weight is decreasing (i.e., the second derivative of the weight function with respect to the number of shared partners is negative as long as $v > 0$).

In Figure 5.2, we illustrate what happens to an ERG distribution when it reaches parameter values that exhibit degeneracy. The plots in this figure depict the distribution of edges and triangles in a model parameterized with both of those statistics. Once the parameter estimate for the number of triangles reaches 0.5, the model is degenerate, the fully connected graph accounts for most of the probability distribution, and it will be the only network simulated when conducting MCMC-MLE. The changes in the distribution show just how sensitive ERGM parameterization and estimation can be due to the issue of degeneracy.

To further asses the potential for degeneracy in a model, Snijders et al. (2006) propose a "hysteresis" visualization. Starting with a sparse network and holding all other parameter estimates at their observed values, a hysteresis plot is created by varying each structural parameter estimate (both in ascent and descent) from several standard deviations below the estimate value to several standard deviations above. Plotting the mean network density at each parameter value reveals whether the model is likely subject to instability due to degeneracy. Extreme jumps in the density of the networks that result from small changes in parameter values indicate an underlying issue with model degeneracy. Hysteresis analysis is intuitively similar to the analysis of the model in Figure 5.2, in which

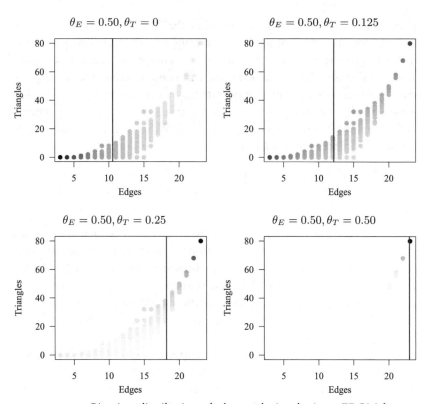

FIGURE 5.2 Bivariate distribution of edges and triangles in an ERGM for a directed network with five vertices, parameterized with edges and triangles. Darker points occur with higher probability. The vertical black bar is drawn at the average number of edges in networks generated under the respective distribution.

parameter values are varied within a small range to observe how the distribution of networks responds to changes in parameter values.

5.3 ADJUSTING SPECIFICATIONS TO CORRECT DEGENERACY AND IMPROVE MODEL FIT

Prior to concluding that ERGM results are ready to interpret and provide insight into the substantive process under study, there are three related empirical questions that are prudent to ask. First, if MC-MLE was used to estimate the model, was the sample of networks used to approximate the likelihood function large enough? Second, do the results exhibit signs of degeneracy? Third – a question that is advisable to ask whenever generative model fitting is used to draw inferences from data – are the data outliers with respect to the distribution represented by the fitted model? If one or more of these checks fails, the number of simulated networks, the model specification, or both, need to be changed.

Tests for sample size convergence and degeneracy are conducted using straightforward and highly revealing numerical measures that are built into the software for estimating ERGMs. We review those measures below in the application section. Evaluating goodness of fit for the ERGM, on the other hand, is a more nuanced process. In assessing and adjusting models based on fit, we must be careful not to overfit the data, and risk drawing inferences based on spurious patterns in the data.

To avoid overfitting, the approach to evaluating model fit in the ERGM literature is focused on assessing whether the observed network represents an outlier with respect to the distribution of networks implied by the ERGM fit. This is in contrast to the standard approach to fit evaluation in statistical modeling, which is focused primarily on point predictions. The box plot is the central visualization tool used in assessing ERGM fit. To review the content conveyed in a box plot, we present Figure 5.3. The box contains the interquartile range (i.e., the 25th percentile to the 75th percentile). The horizontal lines span 1.5 times the interquartile range, and observations outside of the bars are considered extreme outliers.

In evaluating ERGM fit we ask two related questions. First, does the observed network appear to be an outlier with respect to the

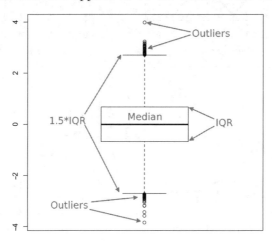

FIGURE 5.3 Annotated box plot.

distribution of networks simulated from the ERGM and depicted in the box plots? Second, if the answer to the first question is yes, does the anomalous behavior follow a pattern that could be adjusted through the modification of the ERGM specification? If the answer to both of these questions is yes, the model should be respecified to improve fit. Goodness of fit (GOF) plots for ERGMs are depicted in Figures 5.4 and 5.5. For each plot, a vertex or dyad/edgewise statistic value is depicted on the *x*-axis (e.g., the number of vertices with in-degree 5, the number of edges formed between vertices with two shared partners). A box plot is drawn for each statistic value, using 100 networks simulated from the ERGM fit. The solid black line gives the values from the observed network. The model used for Figure 5.4 does not include any dependence terms and exhibits a poor fit to both the in-degree and edgewise shared partner distributions. Figure 5.5 shows how the fit improves when in-two-stars and GWESP are added to the model.

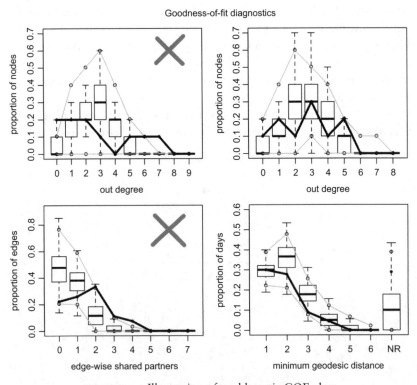

FIGURE 5.4 Illustration of problematic GOF plots.

Goodness-of-fit diagnostics

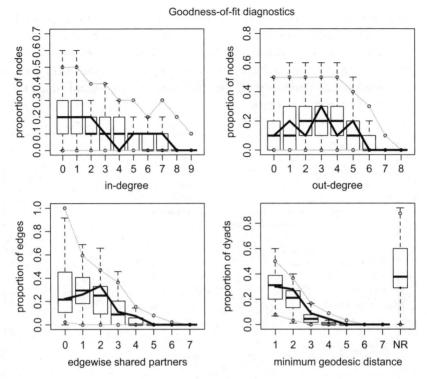

FIGURE 5.5 Illustration of improved GOF plots.

Running Example: Cosponsorship among Senate Ideologues

The code to run the ERGMs on the cosponsorship data is provided below. Running the first ERGM, and the associated diagnostics functions, we see no evidence of degeneracy, but we do see evidence of nonconvergence and evidence of poor model fit. Figure 5.4 reflects the fit of the first ERGM from the code below. Running `summary(gf.degeneracy)` produces a table of Monte Carlo *p*-values – analogous to that printed below – to test whether the observed network statistics used in the ERGM are different from those simulated from the ERGM. The MC *p*-values are all very high, indicating that the observed statistics are near the centers of the distributions of simulated statistics. Though estimation often fails when the model is degenerate, this check reassures us that the model is not close to degenerate. When we run `mcmc.diagnostics()`, the results of which are also provided below, we see that the joint *p*-value returned from the Geweke test – the last element of the output – is statistically significant at the 0.05 level. This simply indicates that we may want to use a larger sample size in approximating the likelihood for MC-MLE. When we look at model fit via `plot(gf2)`, we see that the black line misses all of the boxes in the edgewise shared partners plot. This indicates that we should adjust the model to account for transitivity.

```
set.seed(45)
## edges for density
## absdiff to model ideological homophily
## edgecov to model effect of geographic distance between states
## istar(2), in-two-stars, to model popularity
est2 <- ergm(Senate ~ edges + absdiff("ideol") +
                    edgecov("dist") + istar(2))

## See if the MCMLE Converged
mcmc.diagnostics(est2)

## See if it's degenerate
gf.degeneracy <- gof(est2, GOF=~model)
summary(gf.degeneracy)

## How does it fit?
gf2 <- gof(est2)

## Make a panel of four plots
par(mfrow=c(2, 2))

## plot goodness of fit results
plot(gf2)

## Check out results
summary(est2)

## add transitivity
## increase mcmc.samplesize to improve Geweke results
set.seed(45)
est4 <- ergm(Senate ~ edges + absdiff("ideol") + edgecov("dist") +
                 istar(2) + triangle,
             control=control.ergm(MCMC.samplesize=10000))
## Ends due to degeneracy

## try GWESP
set.seed(45)
est5 <- ergm(Senate ~ edges + absdiff("ideol") + edgecov("dist") +
                 istar(2) + gwesp(0),
             control=control.ergm(MCMC.samplesize=10000))
```

```
42 ## See if the MCMLE Converged
43 mcmc.diagnostics(est5)
44
45 ## See if it's degenerate
46 gf.degeneracy <- gof(est5, GOF=~model)
47 summary(gf.degeneracy)
48
49 ## How does it fit?
50 gf5 <- gof(est5)
51
52 ## Make a panel of four plots
53 par(mfrow=c(2,2))
54
55 ## plot goodness of fit results
56 plot(gf5)
57
58 ## Check out results
59 summary(est5)
```

The classic approach to modeling transitivity in ERGMs is with the count of the number of triangles in the network. When we add this, as in the second ERGM specification, the model does not complete estimation via MCMLE as it is a degenerate specification. In the final ERGM we run, we instead add GWESP to account for transitivity. We start the value of the GWESP exponent at 0, in which case GWESP reduces to the count of the number of edges formed between vertices with at least one shared partner. As an independent exercise, we encourage the reader to experiment with the GWESP exponent, as setting it to large starting values will result in a degenerate model. Note that we have also increased the MCMC sample size from the default (1,024) to 10,000 due to the significant Geweke convergence test in the initial iteration. Analyzing the results from this model, we see no evidence of degeneracy – the results of the degeneracy test are printed below – or nonconvergence, and we see that this model adequately fits the edgewise shared partner distribution, as depicted in Figure 5.5. This model is sufficient in terms of the estimation and fit diagnostics.

```
1 Sample statistics summary:
2
3 Iterations = 16384:4209664
4 Thinning interval = 1024
5 Number of chains = 1
6 Sample size per chain = 4096
```

```
1. Empirical mean and standard deviation for each variable,
   plus standard error of the mean:

                    Mean      SD Naive SE Time-series SE
edges         -0.08105   6.973  0.10895        0.11462
absdiff.ideol -0.05751   2.428  0.03794        0.03949
edgecov.dist   6.73315 197.710  3.08922        3.19941
istar2        -0.36890  24.332  0.38019        0.40463

2. Quantiles for each variable:

                 2.5%      25%     50%     75%    97.5%
edges         -13.000   -5.000   0.000   5.000  14.000
absdiff.ideol  -4.342   -1.782  -0.222   1.481   5.139
edgecov.dist -351.250 -136.000  -3.000 143.250 398.625
istar2        -40.000  -18.000  -3.000  15.000  54.000


Sample statistics cross-correlations:
                  edges absdiff.ideol edgecov.dist     istar2
edges         1.0000000     0.9297126    0.8829221  0.9214529
absdiff.ideol 0.9297126     1.0000000    0.7994335  0.9040151
edgecov.dist  0.8829221     0.7994335    1.0000000  0.7852842
istar2        0.9214529     0.9040151    0.7852842  1.0000000

Sample statistics auto-correlation:
Chain 1
                  edges absdiff.ideol edgecov.dist       istar2
Lag 0        1.000000000   1.000000000   1.00000000  1.000000000
Lag 1024     0.050582828   0.039766847   0.02746508  0.062077978
Lag 2048     0.023148943   0.020154279   0.03387112  0.024620615
Lag 3072    -0.002761167  -0.001864999  -0.01088563  0.005989632
Lag 4096     0.015563961   0.023345268   0.01520540  0.031709942
Lag 5120     0.016239139   0.017886353   0.01154254  0.007227798

Sample statistics burn-in diagnostic (Geweke):
Chain 1

Fraction in 1st window = 0.1
Fraction in 2nd window = 0.5

        edges absdiff.ideol edgecov.dist     istar2
       0.2165        1.1916      -0.3122     0.9604

Individual P-values (lower = worse):
        edges absdiff.ideol edgecov.dist     istar2
    0.8286042     0.2334117    0.7549221  0.3368782
Joint P-value (lower = worse):  0.03162851 .
```

```
 1 Goodness-of-fit for model statistics
 2
 3                    obs       min       mean       max MC p-value
 4 edges           27.000     3.000   25.16000    56.000      0.96
 5 absdiff.ideol    7.321     0.718    6.57483    17.021      0.84
 6 edgecov.dist   689.000   100.000  660.13000  1494.000      0.92
 7 istar2          51.000     0.000   45.03000   159.000      0.76
 8 esp#1            7.000     0.000    7.84000    20.000      0.94
 9 esp#2            9.000     0.000    6.39000    20.000      0.76
10 esp#3            3.000     0.000    3.29000    23.000      0.76
11 esp#4            2.000     0.000    1.17000    18.000      0.40
12 esp#5            0.000     0.000    0.24000    10.000      1.00
13 esp#6            0.000     0.000    0.05000     4.000      1.00
14 esp#7            0.000     0.000    0.02000     2.000      1.00
```

Given that the estimation has converged, and there are no discernible shortcomings in the fit of the model, we are ready to look at the results of the estimation. Despite this being a small and unrepresentative sub-sample of senators, we walk through the interpretation of the results for the purpose of illustration. The results of the final ERGM specification are printed below. The results indicate a strong tendency toward ideological homophily. An increase of 1 (approximately the difference between Daniel Akaka and Wayne Allard) in the ideological distance between two senators lowers the log odds of a tie between them by approximately 3 – a substantial effect. The positive value and statistical significance of the istar2 coefficient indicates a tendency toward popularity in the network – if senator i sends a tie to senator j, the log odds of senator k sending a tie to senator k increases by 0.32. The positive GWESP coefficient also indicates a tendency toward triangle closure through tie formation. The GWESP coefficient is not statistically significant at conventional levels, but the GOF analysis indicated that including the GWESP term improved the fit of the model.

```
 1 ==========================
 2 Summary of model fit
 3 ==========================
 4
 5 Formula:   senate_network ~ edges + absdiff("ideol") +
      edgecov("dist") +
 6    istar(2) + gwesp(0)
 7
 8 Iterations:  2 out of 20
 9
```

```
10  Monte Carlo MLE Results:
11                  Estimate Std. Error MCMC % p-value
12  edges           -1.510136  0.685393      0 0.03031 *
13  absdiff.ideol   -2.894751  1.084387      0 0.00912 **
14  edgecov.dist    -0.004116  0.009767      0 0.67455
15  istar2           0.322112  0.158666      0 0.04551 *
16  gwesp            0.564342  0.368577      0 0.12949
17  gwesp.decay      0.506824  0.383150      0 0.18950
18  ---
19  Signif. codes:  0 '***' 0.001 '**' 0.01 '*' 0.05 '.' 0.1 ' ' 1
20
21      Null Deviance: 124.77  on 90  degrees of freedom
22   Residual Deviance:  86.64  on 84  degrees of freedom
23
24  AIC: 98.64    BIC: 113.6    (Smaller is better.)
```

5.4   OTHER ESTIMATION METHODS FOR ERGMs

The methods for estimation of ERGMs that we have reviewed and illustrated in the current chapter represent the most commonly used methods, and those that are implemented in standard software for estimating ERGMs. However, there are a number of recent innovations in estimation for ERGMs that we should mention in brief. First, the estimation methods we have considered in this chapter were developed within the context of measuring and analyzing the complete network. In many contexts, researchers work with a sample from the network, and do not have access to a complete census of the network. Handcock and Gile (2010) present a method for estimating ERGMs with incomplete, or sampled, data on the network under analysis. Second, for researchers who are interested in working within the framework of Bayesian inference, Caimo and Friel (2011) develop methods for Bayesian inference with ERGM, and implement those methods in the bergm package for R (Caimo & Friel 2014). Third, even MPLE can be computationally prohibitive with very large networks. He and Zheng (2013) develop methods of estimation based on asymptotic approximations of the distributions of network statistics to facilitate estimation of ERGMs with very large networks (e.g., tens of thousands of nodes). These three innovations do not represent the entirety of the recent methods literature on ERGM estimation, but address a few particularly notable problems and/or interests that researchers may encounter in working with ERGMs.

5.5 WRAPPING UP

The flexibility of the ERGM comes at the price of complexity in both specification and estimation. The likelihood function requires approximation with all but the smallest of networks. Furthermore, the combinatorics involved in the subgraph structures that are typically used in specifying an ERGM can interact to make seemingly intuitive models inappropriate for real-world networks. Statistical modeling often involves some degree of specification search. In the use of the ERGM, there is a dominant tradition of evaluating the model specification based on the structural fit to the observed network. If the model is degenerate, adjustment to the specification is a necessary process.

5.6 SELF-STUDY PROBLEMS

Select a network dataset to study using ERGM, but avoid using the data from `ina` that was used in this chapter. Be sure that the dataset includes at least one vertex attribute. If you do not have a dataset that you would like to use for this exercise, we recommend that you use the `cosponsorship` dataset from `ina`, which is introduced in the beginning of Chapter 2. Using this dataset, complete a report that includes the following information:

1. **Description of the dataset:** What does the dataset cover? Where did it come from? Has it been used in any prior studies?
2. **Hypotheses:** Describe and test at least one hypothesis regarding a vertex attribute, at least one dyadic interdependence hypothesis, and one triadic or higher-order interdependence hypothesis. Describe these hypotheses.
3. **Model specification:** Identify a model that is capable of testing each hypothesis. Estimate this model, assuring that the model fits well and that the MCMC has converged.
4. **Break the model:** Add higher-order terms to the model (e.g., *k*-stars with high *k*) to see if you can find a model that is degenerate. Note the specification that resulted in degeneracy.
5. **Estimates:** Present the estimates of the ERGM in either graphical or tabular form.
6. **Diagnostics:** Demonstrate that the model fits the network adequately and that the MCMC has converged.
7. **Interpretation:** Substantively interpret your results. Do you find support for your hypotheses? Do you think the effects that you find are large?

6

ERG Type Models for Longitudinally Observed Networks

6.1 INTRODUCTION

Chapters 3–5 described how the ERGM is fit and applied to individual networks. However, many interesting networks are not observed in single, cross-sectional snapshots, but are instead observed longitudinally, over many time points. For example, the sort of advice giving, romantic, and cosponsorship networks we have considered as running examples in the preceding chapters are not static. Interpersonal relationships change, and so do the structures of the networks that they comprise.

A key element of modeling networks that change over time is developing theoretical expectations about how the networks change. Practitioners must confront questions such as: What is the tendency of new edges to be created between time periods? How likely are existing edges to dissolve? How might the endogenous process we have considered be specified over time (e.g., do new edges reciprocate past edges)? Throughout this chapter, we will address each of these questions, and present the statistical techniques that can help an analyst answer them.

This chapter focuses on an extension to the ERGM, called the temporal exponential random graph model, or TERGM. This model is designed to accomplish the sort of ERG-type modeling with which we are now familiar in cases where the network is observed as a series of snapshots over time. While the extension of the ERGM to the TERGM is relatively simple in terms of the mathematical structure of the model, the TERGM requires additional work of the analyst; specifically, the temporal nature of the effects in the TERGM represents an additional dimension of complexity in the model specification process. The analyst must also consider the question of whether a single model is appropriate for the period of observation, raising the question of whether temporal pooling, temporal separation, or some middle-ground solution should be used (e.g., should models for international networks be separated into the pre- and post–Cold War periods). Finally, we will also briefly discuss an alternative to the TERGM – an actor-centric longitudinal model called the stochastic actor oriented model (SAOM) which, with some important differences, shares some similarities to the TERGM.

6.2 DATA CONSIDERATIONS

Before considering models for longitudinally observed network data, we must distinguish between two fundamentally different types of such data.

The first type of temporal network data, and the most common in the literature, is called *discrete temporal network data*. In the case of discrete temporal data, one observes the network in a series of discrete and instantaneous snapshots. In other words, at time t, where $t = 1 \ldots T$, one observes the entire network. Because each observed network is recorded as an $n \times n$ adjacency matrix, one can think of the series of temporally observed networks as an array or as a temporally ordered list of adjacency matrices. For intuition, consider the adjacency matrix of each observed network as a playing card. The discrete temporal network data object is then a deck of cards in which each adjacency matrix, ordered from oldest to most recent, is placed.

This type of temporal network data is often produced when surveys are used to gather the data. For example, consider the task of gathering data on friendships in a school over time. If the students in question are surveyed about their friendships at a specific and regular point in time, say the last day of each school year, the result will be a series of snapshots of the complete network, one for every year in the period of observation. Longitudinal data, such as this series of snapshots, are exciting because they generally tell us much more about the process of interest than is possible from a single snapshot.

Discrete temporal data have some important limitations, however, that one must keep in mind. First, the time attribute of the data is *discrete*, meaning that we do not know what happened in the network between each snapshot. In the case of the friendship network sampled every year, we might observe a change in the ij dyad from unconnected at $t - 1$ to connected at t. The implication is that the friendship formed between observations, but we would be unable to say when during this period the friendship formed. Moreover, the ij tie might have formed and dissolved any number of times between observations, with us happening to catch it when it is off at $t - 1$ and on at t. The same is true for dyads that are stable between snapshots. For example, the lack of an edge at two consecutive time points could indicate that no tie was formed, or it could be that an edge formed and dissolved between observations, maybe more than once! When working with discrete temporal data, it is important to keep this limitation of the data structure in mind.

The second limitation of discrete temporal data is related to the first: one's modeling approach and results may be sensitive to the frequency and regularity by which the data are collected. While a lengthy discussion of data-gathering strategies and practices is not the objective of this chapter, discrete temporal data should ideally be gathered at regular intervals. The process of modeling these data will be substantially complicated if the intervals at which the data are gathered are not regular. Moreover, the frequency with which the networks are sampled should be wide enough that interesting variation is observed from snapshot to snapshot, but tight enough that the volatility in the network (e.g., the amount of change in relationships and vertex composition) is not dramatic. Finding the frequency of sampling that achieves this balance requires assumptions and knowledge of how the network changes over time and may not be straightforward.

The second type of temporal network data is called *continuous temporal network data*. As the name implies, such data are observed continuously. This means that any and all changes in network structure (e.g., the formation or dissolution of an edge) and changes in network composition (e.g., a vertex enters or exits the network) are observed with precise time stamps. For example, digital trace data – records of electronic interactions – constitute dynamic network data change with continuous time stamps (Falzon, McCurrie & Dunn 2017). Continuous temporal data will often be structured as a list of edge and vertex changes with corresponding time points.

Continuous network data are typically generated when a network is monitored, as opposed to the sampling strategy employed to create discrete network data. While monitoring a system like a friendship network might be difficult or impossible, monitoring other systems may be straightforward. For example, in the study of international politics, the network of interstate wars is substantively important (Faber 1987). As the start and end dates for wars are typically easy to measure, as is the entry and exit of countries from the international system, gathering data on all wars is equivalent to monitoring the international conflict network and the result is a network whose evolution is measured in continuous time. While continuously measured network data clearly contain much more information than discretely measured network data, they also tend to pose modeling challenges, as most statistical methods for network analysis are designed for discrete temporal data.

Researchers often treat networks as discrete temporal networks even though they are actually continuous. This is sometimes related to the statistical difficulties of modeling continuous network data and the lack of easy-to-use models for doing so. However, treating continuous-time networks as discrete is also often related to the way researchers conceive of the problem or theoretical process they are seeking to address. For example, there is a rich literature in political science examining how legislators in the US Congress cosponsor legislation (Bratton & Rouse 2011; Rocca & Gordon 2010, Box-Steffensmeier, Arnold & Zorn 1997). Because the date at which a particular legislator cosponsors a particular piece of legislation is recorded by the Congress, the data are of the continuous temporal variety. However, congressional terms last for two years and most scholars in this area have chosen to examine the network by pooling cosponsorships over each two-year congressional term and measuring edges as one or more functions of the number of times legislator i cosponsors legislator j during this period. As such, continuous temporal data are transformed into discrete temporal data (Fowler 2006, Tam Cho & Fowler 2010). The appropriateness of this practice will vary from application to application, but our point here is (1) that it is often possible to transform continuous data to discrete data, but not the other way around, and (2) the skeptical reader should consider for herself whether such a transformation is appropriate when reading research in which such a transformation is used. One key difference between continuous temporal network data that have been transformed to discrete data and discrete network data measured as such is that, for transformed continuous data, there are no missing data on ties that were formed and/or dissolved between time points.

Running Example: Film Co-appearances during the Golden Age of Hollywood

For our running analysis in the first part of this chapter – the part focused on TERGM, we reanalyze data originally gathered by Taylor et al. (2017) on the network of co-appearances among fifty-five prominent actors during the so-called Golden Age of Hollywood. In this network, each vertex is a prominent actor who appeared in Hollywood films during the period 1930–1959. The network is directed, with the direction of a tie indicating when one actor played a supporting role to another based on the order in which the actors were billed. Unlike the original Taylor et al. (2017) article, however, we treat the network as unweighted. Taylor et al. had created an edge weight based on differences in billing order, with orders 1 and 2 considered to be equal in order to account for the fact that men were generally billed above women during this period of time. We maintain the tie status of first and second billed in order to try to correct for sexism in billing status, but we drop the edge weighting scheme of the original data and focus only on co-appearances. We also extended the data to include the sex of the actor as a vertex-level attribute.

The dataset, stored in the `ina` package as `gaoh`, includes seven network objects (n1–n7), each covering a different time period, and a node attribute data frame named `attributes`. We restrict our analysis to the six networks that make up the time span 1920–1979. To prepare this time series for analysis, we create a list object called `hga`, which concatenates these networks in order of oldest to newest. This is the format of the outcome object required for TERGM analysis in the `xergm` package.

```
1  library(network)
2  library(ina)
3  data(gaoh)
4
5  ## create list from oldest to newest. This will be the outcome object
        for
6  ## TERGM analysis
7  hga <- list(n1, n2, n3, n4, n5, n6)
```

We then begin our analysis by visualizing the six networks under study in Figure 6.1.

```
1  set.seed(5)
2  par(mfrow = c(3, 2))
3  hgat <- c("20's", "30's", "40's", "50's", "60's", "70's")
4  for (i in 1:length(hga)) {
5      plot(hga[[i]], displaylabels=FALSE,
          label=network.vertex.names(n1),
6          vertex.cex=2, label.cex=1,
```

```
7     edge.col=rgb(150, 150, 150, 100, maxColorValue=255),
          label.pos=5,
8     vertex.col=c("lightblue", "pink")[
9         get.vertex.attribute(n1, "female") + 1],
10    main=hgat[[i]])
11  }
```

These data may prove challenging to model because the structure and density of the network changes so much over the observed time period. It is clear to see that the heyday of this network was in the 1930s and 1940s, with the network noticeably thinning by the 1950s, and more so for the 1960s, whereas in the 1970s the network bears little resemblance to its former structure. It is unclear at the outset if it makes sense

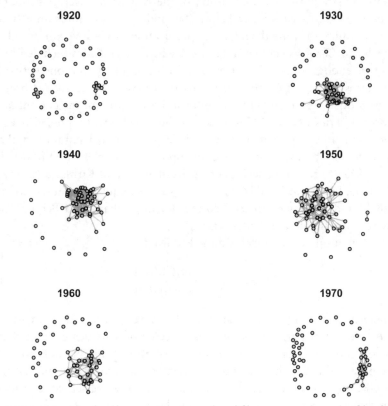

FIGURE 6.1 Six decade-spanning networks of film co-appearance by fifty-five prominent actors during Hollywood's Golden Age. Directed ties indicate that the sender played a supporting role to the receiver.

to treat all of these networks as coming from the same data-generating process. Specifically, it may not make sense to include the 1920s and 1970s in the series. The thinning of the network in the 1950s and 1960s may also be an issue, but likely less problematic.

6.3 THE TEMPORAL EXPONENTIAL RANDOM GRAPH MODEL (TERGM)

The temporal exponential random graph model (TERGM) – originally proposed by Hanneke et al. (2010), based on Robins and Pattison (2001), with extensions and additional estimation routines developed by Cranmer and Desmarais (2011) and Desmarais and Cranmer (2012b) – is a relatively straightforward extension of the ERGM to discrete temporal network data. As we will see below, the model itself is simply an ERGM that accounts for time through the specification of the **h** vector. In other words, an ERGM becomes a TERGM when the statistics included in **h** capture endogenous and exogenous effects not just within one network but across some set of previously observed networks. As such, features of previously observed networks inform the structure of the current network. A series of these TERGMs can (but need not) be pooled over a period of observation to return a single set of model parameters that apply to that period. For some contemporary examples of TERGMs in social science research, see Cranmer, Desmarais, and Kirkland (2012a), Cranmer, Desmarais, and Menninga (2012a), Almquist and Butts (2013), Leifeld and Cranmer (2014), Yeo (2018), Li, Ziebart, and Berger-Wolf (2018), and Ingold and Leifeld (2014).

In Equation (3.1), we defined the ERGM as

$$\mathcal{P}(N,\boldsymbol{\theta}) = \frac{\exp\{\boldsymbol{\theta}'\mathbf{h}(N)\}}{\sum_{N^* \in \mathcal{N}} \exp\{\boldsymbol{\theta}'\mathbf{h}(N^*)\}}, \tag{6.1}$$

where N is the adjacency matrix of the (single, observed) network, $\boldsymbol{\theta}$ is the vector of parameters, $\mathbf{h}(N)$ is a vector of statistics computed on the observed network, and $\mathcal{N}$ is the set of all possible permutations of the observed network with the same number of vertices. Recall that the ERGM estimates the probability of the network we observed, considering the entire set of networks we could have observed. As before, $\mathbf{h}(N)$ captures endogenous and exogenous dependencies in the network. Also as before, we use prime notation to indicate the vector transpose to avoid confusion with the temporal indices the TERGM will require.

To prevent TERGM notation from looking more complicated than it is, we start by rewriting the cross-sectional ERGM equation to reflect the fact that the denominator is a normalizing constant that is only a variable function of θ:

$$P(N,\theta) = \frac{\exp\{\theta'\mathbf{h}(N)\}}{c(\theta)}, \qquad (6.2)$$

This equation is identical to Equation (3.1), where $c(\theta) = \sum_{N^* \in \mathcal{N}} \exp\{\theta'\mathbf{h}(N^*)\}$. A detailed discussion of the cross-sectional ERGM can be found in Chapter 3 as well as Goodreau et al. (2008), Hunter et al. (2008), Cranmer and Desmarais (2011), Cranmer et al. (2017), and Lusher et al. (2013).

Denote the network at some discrete time point t as N^t. We can specify a TERGM for N^t by including the dependencies this network has on previous observations of the network. Specifically, the researcher must specify the order of the temporal dependence (i.e., the number of previously observed networks to condition upon). The order of the temporal dependence can be written as $K \in \{0, 1, \ldots, t-1\}$. K must be chosen such that it *fully encompasses* the dependence of N^t on previously observed networks. We will discuss how to choose K later in this chapter. For now, assume it is known and specified appropriately. Dependencies on the K previously observed networks are included in the $\mathbf{h}$ vector, implying that the TERGM for N^t is written as

$$P(N^t \mid N^{t-K}, \ldots, N^{t-1}, \theta) = \frac{\exp\{\theta'\mathbf{h}(N^t, N^{t-1}, \ldots, N^{t-K})\}}{c(\theta, N^{t-K}, \ldots, N^{t-1})}. \qquad (6.3)$$

Equation (6.3) is called a TERGM because temporal dependencies, the dependency of N^t on $N^{t-1}, \ldots, N^{t-K}$, are key components of its specification. We can make a few observations about the TERGM in Equation (6.3). First, note that, as long as K is specified correctly, it is a complete probability model for N^t. This implies that $P(N^t \mid N^{t-K}, \ldots, N^{t-1}, \theta)$ is conditionally independent of any previous network in the series.

Second, Equation (6.3) is a TERGM for a single observed time point. This may be dissatisfying if we wanted a single set of coefficients to describe the network over a longer period of time. If we apply the same model to all discrete time points in our period of observation, we can create a joint likelihood over a set of temporal observations of the network by taking the product over each of the TERGMs as specified in Equation (6.3). This is a proper joint likelihood of all the networks because of the conditional independence property discussed in the above paragraph. That joint likelihood of observing networks $K + 1$ through T, which we call a *pooled TERGM*, is written as

$$P(N^{K+1}, \ldots, N^T \mid N^1, \ldots, N^K, \boldsymbol{\theta}) = \prod_{t=K+1}^{T} P(N^t \mid N^{t-K}, \ldots, N^{t-1}, \boldsymbol{\theta}).$$

(6.4)

A pooled TERGM can be an appropriate and useful way to apply a single model to a time span. The researcher should keep in mind however that a pooled TERGM caries with it the assumption that the same coefficients apply to all observations of the network equally well. In other words, the pooled TERGM assumes that the network is in a temporally stable process. We revisit this assumption and alternative ways of specifying TERGMs to allow for temporal heterogeneity in effects below in Section 6.5.

Third, Equation (6.3) shows that the TERGM for N^t depends on some number K of previously observed networks, but it does not say much about *how* N^t depends on its predecessors. That is the subject we consider in detail in the following section.

6.4   TERGM SPECIFICATION

The terms included in the specification of **h** for the TERGM can be separated into two classes of effects: those that function more or less the same way as the ERGM effects discussed at length in Chapter 4 and those designed to capture the dependence of N^t on the K previously observed networks. We begin with the selection of K and then discuss the first class because they represent a nearly trivial extension of the ERGM dependencies with which we are already familiar, though these statistics can also be extended to reflect intertemporal dependencies.

6.4.1   Selection of K

Often, the first choice the researcher must make when specifying a TERGM is the selection of the order of the temporal dependence of N^t on previous networks, denoted K. This is an important choice because selecting an inappropriately small K – one that does not fully encompass the temporal dependencies at work in the data – can produce model misspecification, resulting in bias and poor fit. Selecting too large a K – one that encompasses irrelevant time periods – produces an unparsimonious specification that can result in overfitting and even degeneracy.

An appropriate choice of K is also important because it will inform the choice of temporal dependencies included in the model, as discussed in the next subsection.

A principal means by which researchers select K is through theory. Often, researchers will have a principled expectation, based on theory, about how the network forms from one period to the next. For example, in their study of the international alliance network, Cranmer, Desmarais, and Kirkland (2012a) expected that states would work to close two-stars into triangles in order to realize synergy gains from reinforcing alliance commitments. The implication is that the process of closing a triad (e.g., forming the final edge) is qualitatively different from, and temporally subsequent to, the formation of the two-star that constitutes the first two edges of the triangle. They expected a delay between the formation of the two-star and the closing of the triangle, so it makes sense theoretically to specify the temporal processes of interest over at least two time periods. The specifics of theory will vary substantially from application to application, but our point is that theory can often be a useful and defensible way to select K when undertaking a TERGM analysis.

In some cases, however, it will not be possible to select an appropriate K based on theory. This can occur either because the theory being tested is not sufficiently specific or because the researcher is intentionally avoiding theoretical claims, as in an application with prediction as its goal. In the case of an unspecific theory, one might generally be advised to develop the theory further, but let us assume the researcher has a good reason not to do this. One can often learn K inductively in one of two ways: directly from the data and/or by examining model performance under alternative choices for K. To give this process some context, consider Desmarais & Cranmer's (2013) study of transnational terrorism. In this study, the vertices are (mostly) countries and directed edges are created when a citizen of a given country participates in a transnational terrorist attack in a different country. Examining the raw data prior to their TERGM analysis, Desmarais & Cranmer found that more than half of the countries that received terrorist edges in a given year had received an edge from the same sender in the previous ten years, and most of those in the previous five. This provided some basic expectations about how long a memory process was at work in the data. Next, Desmarais & Cranmer trained their models on one-, five-, and ten-year intervals of data and examined the performance of the models in terms of out-of-sample prediction. They found that the predictive gains made from going from a one-year to a five-year process were large, while there was actually a small predictive loss when going from five to ten. In other words, the best predicting models were specified on the five-year training interval. While it might have been possible to experiment in this way with other plausible values of K (e.g., four or six years), Desmarais & Cranmer arrived at well-fitting and powerfully predicting specifications. This is an example of how researchers can use the data they have available to inductively find an appropriate specification for K. We discuss and illustrate out-of-sample prediction with the TERGM in the running example below.

6.4.2   Exogenous and Endogenous Dependencies

At its core, the TERGM is an ERGM for a single network N^t that also conditions on K previously observed networks. As such, the TERGM can include any dependencies, exogenous or endogenous, that can be included in the cross-sectional ERGM. Endogenous and exogenous dependencies for the TERGM are included through the **h** vector in precisely the same way that they are in the ERGM, we need only to adjust our notation to reflect the fact that multiple networks are under consideration. Here, we consider a few examples of ERGM dependencies in the TERGM context for illustration, but note that any of the dependencies considered in Chapter 4 could also be included in this way.

Consider first the case of an exogenous covariate X, where X is an $n \times n$ matrix of dyadic covariate values with identical dimensions and order as N (just as was the case in our discussion of ERGM covariates in Chapters 3 and 4. To include X in the model specification without temporal effects – meaning that current values of X are thought to predict current values of N – one need only to add temporal indices to the covariate equation (3.6):

$$h_X(N^t, X^t) = \sum_{i \neq j} N_{ij}^t X_{ij}^t. \tag{6.5}$$

Just as before, this statistic sums the values of X_{ij} for those dyads where $N_{ij} = 1$. Now that we have multiple networks to consider, one could just as easily include a lagged value of X to predict current values of N. For the case of a one-period lag, the lagged exogenous covariate effect is written

$$h_X(N^t, X^t) = \sum_{i \neq j} N_{ij}^t X_{ij}^{t-1}, \tag{6.6}$$

which only requires that N and X have the same dimensions and that the order in which the vertices are reflected in the rows and columns of these matrices be the same. This lagged covariate, however, is a simple example of the second class of TERGM statistics that capture temporal dependencies.

Endogenous dependencies can be specified in a TERGM in a nearly identical manner to an ERGM. If the endogenous dependency is not intertemporal, one need only to add the temporal indices to the statistic, reflecting the fact that we now have more than one network that can be considered. A dependence term is intertemporal if the contribution of any one edge depends in part on the value of an edge formed (or not formed) at a previous time point. For example, the reciprocity statistic that we have seen previously as $h_r(N) = \sum_{ji} N_{ij} N_{ji}$ is now written as

$$h_r(N^t) = \sum_{ji} N_{ij}^t N_{ji}^t. \tag{6.7}$$

Like before, this statistic counts reciprocal edges in the current network. Yet it is simple to modify this statistic to include intertemporal dependencies. One might have a theoretical reason to think that reciprocity will not occur within a time period but rather occurs across two time periods (e.g., Song, Nyhuis & Boomgaarden 2019). That is, if j forms an edge to i in period $t - 1$, i is likely to reciprocate by forming an edge to j in period t. This single-period delayed reciprocity statistic may be written as

$$h_r(N^t, N^{t-1}) = \sum_{ji} N_{ij}^t N_{ji}^{t-1}, \tag{6.8}$$

where the statistic is now computed across two networks rather than one.

The two examples we have just seen involve extending cross-sectional ERGM statistics to reflect dependencies across consecutive time periods in a TERGM. Recall that the TERGM can model dependencies on K previous networks. $K = 1$ may often be a reasonable specification, but the model is by no means restricted to first-order dependencies. For example, transitive closure could be specified across three periods, with a new edge of the triangle forming in each. Likewise, a four-path could be specified across four periods. One could just as easily extend any ERGM dependency to occur across an arbitrary number of time periods, though one would naturally need a theoretical justification for the specification.

6.4.3 Memory Terms

"Memory" terms represent a special class of endogenous dependencies for TERGMs. Unlike the temporal extensions to ERGM dependencies we considered above, memory terms aim to capture temporal dependencies without capturing additional network structure. In other words, they do not capture characteristics of the network, such as reciprocity or transitivity, but instead capture only the degree to which the current network reflects previous networks.

Here, we consider the most commonly used memory terms as described by Leifeld, Cranmer, and Desmarais (2019): positive autoregression, dyadic stability, and edge innovation/loss. Note, however, that many other memory terms are possible, such as the "two-timing" term proposed by Krivitsky (2012). It is generally straightforward to compute memory terms as change statistics and include them in the TERGM that way (see the discussion of change statistics in Chapter 4). As such, the analyst should not feel restricted to those most commonly used memory terms that are implemented in R packages such as xergm.

Positive Autoregression (Lagged Outcome Network). Positive autoregression is equivalent to including a lagged outcome network as a predictor in the TERGM. Positive autoregression is specified as

$$h_a = \sum N_{ij}^t N_{ij}^{t-1}. \tag{6.9}$$

If one were to substitute $N^{t-1} = X^t$, one would recover the equation for an exogenous covariate from (6.6). As such, we can see the equivalence between positive autocorrelation and the inclusion of a lagged outcome network as a predictor. From the equation, we can see that this memory term results in a count of the edges that persist from $t - 1$ to t. We then interpret its coefficient in terms of the log-odds of edge formation increasing as more edges persist from one period to the next. Note that the focus of this statistic is on edges that exist at $t - 1$ continuing to exist at t. The implication is that edge persistence is of interest to the researcher, but the persistence of nonedges is not. For this reason, positive autoregression is often a useful effect to include when modeling sparsely connected networks, though its use and import is certainly not restricted to such cases.

Dyadic Stability. The researcher finding positive autoregression's focus on edges that exist overly restrictive may prefer a memory term that treats the period-to-period persistence of both edges and nonedges equivalently. The dyadic stability term does precisely that. The statistic is written as

$$h_s = \sum_{ij} N_{ij}^t N_{ij}^{t-1} + (1 - N_{ij}^t)(1 - N_{ij}^{t-1}). \tag{6.10}$$

Note that the $N_{ij}^t N_{ij}^{t-1}$ part of the equation is equivalent to positive autoregression. Because $N_{ij}^t = 1$ when i and j share an edge and 0 otherwise, the $(1 - N_{ij}^t)(1 - N_{ij}^{t-1})$ part of the equation counts the number of edges that are off at $t-1$ and remain off at t. So, this statistic adds to the positive autoregression statistic the number of edges that are persistently off between periods. The result is the count of dyadic relationships that are stable (e.g., always on or always off) between two periods. The coefficient produced by the dyadic stability term will be larger the more stable are the period-to-period dyadic relationships. Note that one may include either positive autoregression or dyadic stability in a model, but not both as one of them should be omitted as a baseline. Further note that dyadic stability is the opposite of network volatility, the tendency of dyadic relationships to change their status from one period to the next. A volatility term could be included instead of stability and would be helpful in modeling very stable networks. From a practical perspective, volatility can be coded using its change statistic – coded 1 any time a dyadic relationship changes and 0 otherwise – and included as an edge level covariate.

Edge Innovation and Edge Loss. Finally, some theories will make predictions about the rate at which new edges are formed and existing edges dissolve (e.g., Bartal, Pliskin & Ravid 2019). Indeed, the separable TERGM (STERGM), introduced by Krivitsky and Handcock (2014) and implemented in the tergm R package (Krivitsky & Handcock 2019), includes separate equations that govern edge creation and edge loss. Edge innovation and loss can be measured as

$$h_e = \sum_{ij} N_{ij}^t (1 - N_{ij}^{t-1}) \tag{6.11}$$

and

$$h_\ell = \sum_{ij} (1 - N_{ij}^t) N_{ij}^{t-1}, \tag{6.12}$$

respectively. Intuitively, these statistics count the number of new edges and lost edges between $t-1$ and t, respectively. Alternatively, edge innovation could be included as a covariate via its change statistic, which would be coded 1 if $N_{ij}^{t-1} = 0$ and 0 if $N_{ij}^{t-1} = 1$. Likewise, edge loss could be included as a change statistic coded -1 if $N_{ij}^{t-1} = 1$ and 0 if $N_{ij}^{t-1} = 0$. Because edge innovation (loss) is counting the number of newly created (dissolved) edges from one period to the next, the coefficient for this effect will be higher the more common it is that edges are created (dissolved).

To close the discussion of memory terms, notice that each of these alternative formulations, functionally, is only using a different categorical baseline. So, we could switch between alternative memory terms to make interpretation easier, and the fit of the model will not be affected, conditional on some function of N_{ij}^{t-1} and the intercept (i.e., edge count).

Running Example: Film Co-appearances during the Golden Age of Hollywood

We can now begin the process of model building with our example data. We will discuss the effects we considered employing but did not, along with the ones that we ultimately did include.

Consider the vertex-level covariate `female` (coded 1 if female and 0 otherwise). We include a term to examine whether there is a preference to pair male actors with female actors. This tendency for heterophily can be operationalized quite simply using `absdiff("female")`, which sums the difference between the values of the two vertices for any edges that are present and thus adds 1 any time a male and female actor are paired together. In addition to the heterophily effect, we include `nodefactor("female")` in order to account for the fact that men and women might receive ties at different rates.

We can begin our endogenous specification with the simplest effect: reciprocity. If two actors work well together, it is reasonable to think that they might appear in multiple films together, possibly with reversed leading and supporting roles. This configuration would result in reciprocity in our directed network. As such, we include both `mutual` and the memory term `delrecip` to capture reciprocity within one decade, and delayed reciprocity across two decades.

Next, we turn our attention to vertex-level endogenous effects. A popular actor who tends to be the star of films will draw multiple other actors to work with him/her. So, one would expect a preferential attachment effect to be at work in the data-generating process. But how to operationalize this? Reasonable choices would be the inclusion of in-two-stars (`istar(2)`), a measure of the in-degree (e.g., `idegree` or `gwidegree`), or a measure of in-degree based popularity (e.g., receiver or indegreepopularity). All of the above possibilities are consistent with our hypothesis, though they represent different operationalizations. After some experimentation, we came to the conclusion that the model fit best when we used indegreepopularity, which is a transformation of the indegree in which the sum over the actors of each actor's in-degree is multiplied by its square root (Snijders, Van de Bunt & Steglich 2010), so that is the effect we include in our final model.

We faced a similar choice among multiple possible operationalizations for triadic effects. As the network is positively valanced and seems to display some clustering, it is reasonable to hypothesize a tendency toward triadic closure in the network. That is, two actors who co-appeared with a third also tend to co-appear with one another. One could consider using the ttriple statistic or the closely related transitivities to capture this effect. An alternative would be to use the gwesp statistic, which puts a geometric weight on the number of shared partners as discussed in Chapter 4. Ultimately, we found that gwesp(0.5, fixed=TRUE) produced the best fit. It is worth noting that we experimented with several values of the gwesp weight parameter and let fit be our guide, because our theory is insufficiently detailed to suggest a particular value of the weight parameter.

To round out our endogenous specification, we include an effect for the stability of ties in the network: the tendency of edges to persist from one period to the next and for nonedges also to persist from one period to the next. This is accomplished by memory(type="stability").

6.5 TO POOL OR NOT TO POOL? TEMPORAL STABILITY OF EFFECTS

Earlier in this chapter, we touched on the question of whether it is appropriate to assume that a single TERGM – including a set of terms and parameter values – adequately reflects the entire period of observation. In this section, we examine this question in detail.

A longitudinally observed network necessarily changes over time. A key question the analyst must consider is whether that change is driven by a single underlying network generating process (i.e., one that can be captured with a single TERGM), or whether the process itself changes over time. The prior situation implies that the θ are stable over time, whereas the later implies temporal variation in θ.

Either situation can be modeled with the TERGM – the single-TERGM situation with the application of Equation (6.4) across the period of observation and the dynamic θ situation with techniques we discuss below. Researchers have many options when it comes to diagnosing and representing temporal variation in the specification and/or parameter values.

Theory often plays an important role in determining whether a pooled TERGM makes sense. For illustration, suppose we wanted to model the network of transnational wars. International conflict scholars in political science and international relations often use a dataset called the Correlates of War (COW) (Sarkees & Schafer 2000). These data include all transnational wars beginning in 1816 and running through the present day. Let us assume, following Campbell, Cranmer, and Desmarais (2018), that we are primarily interested in the a-transitivity of the network; that is, the tendency of two states at war with a third not to be at war with each other. If this endogenous process is part of the data-generating process, the result will be very few closed triangles in the network over time. The logic that two states fighting a third should not fight each other is straightforward – such behavior would interfere with their ability to defeat the common foe and fighting two wars at one time multiplies logistical and strategic challenges. States should go to great lengths to avoid closing a conflict triangle. It also makes sense that this strategic dynamic should apply over time. That is, there is no reason to think that the process would be fundamentally different in 1816 than in 2016. But does this logic apply *evenly* over time? Is the θ associated with this effect the same, or close enough that it could reasonably be treated as the same, in every year between 1816 and 2016? That is less clear. Periods of high polarization, such as the Cold War period, might see higher levels of atransitivity than periods of quickly changing alliances, such as the period preceding the First World War (Miller & Kagan 1997). So, in this case, we see that theory can shed light on whether temporal pooling is appropriate or not, or at least lead us to question the assumption that all of the time periods should be pooled.

Thankfully, choosing a temporally pooled model over one without or with less temporal pooling is something that we can learn inductively. A clear symptom of temporal heterogeneity in θ is that the set of coefficients derived from a pooled model will produce substantially different fit when applied to different periods. The diagnostic process is straightforward: apply the pooled results to each observed time point over the period of observation and look for nontrivial changes in the fit measures described in earlier chapters. If fit differs substantially across time, a pooling model usually cannot be justified.

One strategy for dealing with temporal heterogeneity in θ is to drop pooling completely. An un-pooled TERGM can take a few forms. First, local pooling might be justified if periods of stability in the coefficients can be identified. In the hypothetical example of the conflict network from above, we said that the Cold War period might see stable effects because the overall polarization of the international system was more or less constant during that time span, though this is an assumption that we would want to validate empirically before assuming that period was stable. In the published literature, Cranmer, Desmarais, and Kirkland (2012a) found several periods of stability in their analysis of the international alliance network. They described the stability of the system as one of "punctuated equilibrium," periods of stability followed by periods of rapid and dramatic change. In data-generating processes with such periods of stability, a series of pooled TERGMs over restricted time spans can be an appropriate modeling strategy.

Second, a completely unpooled TERGM – that is, one in which there is no temporal pooling at all – can be specified. Such a TERGM applies Equation (6.3) to each time point and never pools over even two periods, though that is not to say that the statistics entering **h** in Equation (6.3) must be specified on a single period. The result is a time series of coefficients and standard errors/confidence intervals, one for every time point in the period of observation. This is the strategy taken by Schmid et al. (2019), and it is interesting because it can often reveal nuanced differences in effects across even small periods of time, as it did in that article.

A middle ground between a completely unpooled and completely pooled model is to smooth the effects of individual statistics in **h**. This approach was developed by Leifeld and Cranmer (2014), and involves interacting the elements of **h** with smooth functions of time. Leifeld et al. (2019) point out that such effects may be written generally as

$$h_t = \sum_{ij} N_{ij}^t f(t), \tag{6.13}$$

where $f(t)$ is a function of time. Intuitive forms of the $f(t)$ function include a "linear time trend $f(t) = t$, a quadratic trend $f(t) = t^2$, arbitrary polynomial functions of the form $f(t) = a + bt + ct^2$, geometric decay $f(t) = \sqrt{t}$, or stepwise functions of the form $f(t) = 1$ if $a < t < b$ and 0 otherwise, with user-defined a and b which capture exogenous events" (Leifeld et al. 2019, pp. 6–7), though certainly not an exhaustive list. Leifeld et al. (2019) further note that such functions of time, $f(t)$ can also be interacted with exogenous covariates:

$$h_{tcov} = \sum_{ij} N^t_{ij} X^t_{ij} f(t). \tag{6.14}$$

Interactions of this form will model the extent to which the effect of an exogenous covariate X varies with time, be it linearly, quadratically, polynomially, geometrically, or otherwise. The result of applying such functions of time to the **h** vector is a single set of network statistics, but one whose effects change dynamically over time.

6.6 ESTIMATION

TERGMs may be estimated in one of two ways, both of which were discussed in Chapter 5, so we will not discuss them at length here. The first means by which TERGMs can be estimated is via MC-MLE as developed in the original TERGM paper by Hanneke et al. (2010). The Monte Carlo–based procedure is subject to the same advantages and limitations as described in Chapter 5, most importantly that it is unbiased if the sample of networks used in approximating the likelihood is both large and converged, it requires the analyst to check that the chains mixed appropriately through the target distribution and becomes computationally more demanding as the size of the network increases.

An alternative to MC-MLE is the bootstrap-corrected maximum pseudolikelihood estimate (MPLE) proposed by Desmarais and Cranmer (2010). The MPLE is defined in Equation (5.2), and has the advantages of being a consistent estimator (i.e., approaches the MLE as the size of the network increases) and is computationally fast. It also performs better as the network gets larger, whereas MC-MLE will become computationally more demanding as the network grows. The conventional standard errors calculated with the uncorrected MPLE are biased downward (i.e., the resulting confidence intervals exhibit low coverage probabilities), as found by van Duijn et al. (2009). This problem can be corrected via bootstrapping, as described in successive works by Desmarais and Cranmer (2010), (2012c) and Schmid and Desmarais (2017).

Running Example: Film Co-appearances during the Golden Age of Hollywood

We now run our model using the `btergm` function for TERGM estimation via bootstrap maximum pseudolikelihoood estimation, which is part of the `xergm` package (Leifeld, Cranmer & Desmarais 2018). We specify that the model should be estimated with R=100 bootstrap iterations so the model will run quickly. Note that for modest increases in computational time, we could run many more iterations (and should run at least 500 for publication-quality results).

```
library(xergm)
set.seed(12345)

m1 <- btergm(hga ~ edges + mutual + gwesp(0.5, fixed=TRUE) +
    idegree1.5 +
    absdiff("female") + nodefactor("female") + delrecip +
    memory(type="stability"), R=100)

summary(m1)

gof1 <- gof(m1, statistics = c(esp, dsp, geodesic,deg,
    triad.undirected,
            walktrap.modularity))
plot(gof1)
```

The in-sample goodness of fit plots are presented in Figure 6.2 and the model results are

```
Estimates and 95% confidence intervals:
                    Estimate    2.5%     97.5%
edges              -6.423693 -6.9039  -5.8881
mutual              6.007808  5.0848   6.9930
gwesp.fixed.0.5     0.617819  0.4137   1.0876
idegree1.5          0.299247  0.1291   0.3549
absdiff.female      0.120250 -0.1419   0.2300
nodefactor.female.1 -0.056032 -0.1571  0.0478
edgecov.delrecip[[i]] 0.671244 0.0914  1.4734
edgecov.memory[[i]]  -0.201031 -0.5874  0.0745
```

We can see from Figure 6.2 that the model produces quite good in-sample fit to the data: all the major features of the network's topology seem to be reproduced by the GOF simulations. The table of results show us that all of our endogenous effects except for stability have statistically significant effects (i.e., zero not included in the 95 percent confidence interval) and that neither of our exogenous effects are statistically significant. In other words, we can interpret the table to mean that the networks display a positive tendency for reciprocal edge formation (within period as well as delayed one period), a positive tendency for triadic closure, and a positive popularity effect. Interestingly, we do not find support for the ideas that male and female actors are preferentially cast together or that they are cast at different rates.

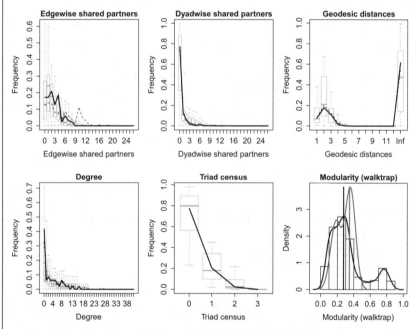

FIGURE 6.2 Goodness of fit (in-sample) for the TERGM of co-appearance in films during Hollywood's Golden Age.

One of the advantages of using longitudinal data, as compared to a single network observation, is that it is straightforward to estimate parameters and evaluate fit using separate parts of the data – separate network observations. Evaluating model fit out-of-sample helps to avoid overfitting, and provides a general assessment of the model's ability to generalize beyond the data (Cranmer and Desmarais 2017). Out-of-sample prediction is also particularly important if part of the objective of the study is to create a model that can forecast new data. That criterion is less applicable here, but, for example, was a major consideration in Desmarais and Cranmer's (2011) work on forecasting transnational terrorist edges. Out-of-sample prediction can be accomplished easily by specifying which network periods to use in estimating the model (test set) in the btergm function and which networks we wish to predict (training set) in the gof function. The prior can be done very simply in btergm by indicating the training data in brackets behind the network outcome list, and the latter can be done using the target option to the gof command. In our case, we will train on the second through fourth periods (39s through 50s) and then predict out-of-sample to the fifth period (60s).

```
set.seed(12345)
mloos <- btergm(hga[2:4] ~ edges + mutual + gwesp(0.5, fixed=TRUE) +
    idegree1.5 +
    absdiff("female") + nodefactor("female") + delrecip +
    memory(type="stability"), R=100)

gofloos <- gof(mloos, target=hga[[5]],
               statistics=c(esp, dsp, geodesic, deg, triad.undirected,
                            walktrap.modularity))
plot(gofloos)
```

The goodness of fit results are presented in Figure 6.3. We see that the fit is somewhat poorer than in the in-sample fit, and this is expected when moving to an out-of-sample scheme. Still, the major features of the data seem to be approximately reflected in the simulations. We may conclude that the out-of-sample fit is sufficient, though not spectacular. This also functions as something of a test of our pooling assumption: rather than assume that the same coefficients apply to all time periods, we pooled over the second, third, and fourth periods in order to predict the fifth. The fact that the data-generating process does not seem to have changed in any major ways between the periods included in this fit evaluation exercise lends credibility to our choice to pool over all time periods when producing results for interpretation. Were it the case that the pooling assumption were inappropriate, out-of-sample fit here would likely be quite poor.

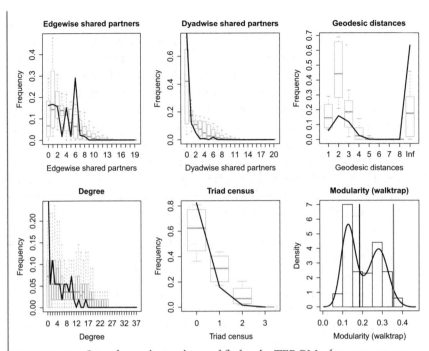

FIGURE 6.3 Out-of-sample goodness of fit for the TERGM of co-appearance in films during Hollywood's Golden Age. The model is trained on the second through fourth periods (39s through 50s) and used to predict (test) the fifth period (60s).

6.7 THE STOCHASTIC ACTOR–ORIENTED MODEL (SAOM)

The stochastic actor oriented model (SAOM) was originally developed by Snijders (1996) and further refined by Snijders (2001) and Snijders et al. (2010) and thus predates the TERGM. Implemented in the package *RSiena* (Canty & Ripley 2017), and often referred to colloquially as Siena after its software package, the SAOM follows a stochastic updating process designed to mimic the continuous time evolution of the network between discrete observed network snapshots, thus focusing on the dynamics of the network over time. While our goal here is not a detailed comparison of the TERGM and the SAOM (see works by Lerner et al. 2013, Desmarais & Cranmer 2012a, Block, Stadtfeld & Snijders 2019, Block, Koskinen 2018, Leifeld and Cranmer, 2014, for such comparisons), Leifeld and Cranmer (2014) describe the difference between the two models as follows: "While the TERGM is primarily a joint model of network states at multiple time points and is usually parameterized in a way that builds dynamics across time points into the model as an explanatory factor, the SAOM models the changes that take place between time points, rather than the outcomes of these processes as in the TERGM." On the surface, the TERGM and SAOM appear very similar because, in both, the researcher models a temporal series of discrete network snapshots using a combination of endogenous and exogenous effects that are specified in a nearly identical manner as sums of subgraph products. Yet the models differ substantially in their basic assumptions, and these differences have consequences worth exploring.

The SAOM begins with some basic assumptions that the TERGM does not share explicitly. First, the vertices in the network are assumed to have agency. Vertices are seen as actors that want to improve their position in the network to maximize parameter-weighted combinations of the endogenous and exogenous statistics included in the model specification. The SAOM also makes the assumption that network change is a first-order Markov process. In other words, it assumes that actors consider the current network structure – not structural features of past network observations – in deciding how to change their ties, making the structure of the network at time t dependent only upon the network at time $t - 1$ (as well as exogenous features included in the model specification). The SAOM is dynamic in a way that the TERGM is not because it breaks down the time between two consecutively observed network snapshots (e.g., $t - 1$ and t) into a large – possibly infinite – number of "mini-steps" in which the network incrementally evolves. Another important difference between SAOM and TERGM is that the SAOM includes a component for modeling a temporal node attribute as endogenous to the network, that is, as node "behavior" that responds to the network structure, and also potentially influences network structure.

A mini-step is an instantaneous period between observed snapshots in which a vertex (actor) is selected according to actor-specific *rate-of-change functions* to change either their outgoing ties or behavior, and selects stochastically among a set of states that include the current state – of either the network or behavior, and all states that can be achieved by one tie state or increasing/decreasing behavior by one unit. The formula governing the selection of network and behavior states is referred to as the *objective function*. The first part of a given mini-step involves the rate-of-change function, whose software default and modal form in the literature is

$$\forall i : \quad \lambda_i(N^t) = \rho_t, \tag{6.15}$$

selecting a vertex that will have an opportunity to change its edge structure or behavior. The default rate function in Equation (6.15) gives each vertex a uniform probability of being selected in each mini-step via a Poisson process. It is possible to specify alternative rate-of-change functions – see Snijders et al. (2010), Amati (2011), and Snijders and van Duijn (1997) for details. After selection by the rate-of-change function to consider a change to its outgoing ties, the selected vertex uses the objective function to add an edge, remove an edge, or leave its sent-edge profile unchanged. The change the focal (e.g., ego) vertex i makes to its edge profile is governed by

$$f_i(\boldsymbol{\theta}, N) = \sum_k \theta_k \mathbf{h}_{ik}(N), \tag{6.16}$$

where k is a potential other (e.g., alter) vertex, and $\mathbf{h}$ is a vector of statistics on the network very similar to that used in the TERGM.

An important difference between the TERGM and SAOM is that the SAOM statistics included in the $\mathbf{h}$ vector are computed from the perspective of a given focal vertex (the ego). Leifeld and Cranmer (2014) illustrate this with the example of reciprocity. Reciprocity in a TERGM is computed from the "perspective" of a focal *dyad*, ij,

$$\mathbf{h}_{\text{reciprocity\_tergm}} = \sum_{i \neq j} N_{ij} N_{ji}, \tag{6.17}$$

and reciprocity in a SAOM is computed from the perspective of the focal vertex i:

$$\mathbf{h}_{\text{reciprocity\_saom}}(i) = \sum_j N_{ij} N_{ji}. \tag{6.18}$$

While this difference in perspective between the two models is important, we also see a similarity in that both statistics are computed as sums of subgraph products, as discussed extensively in Chapter 4.

In order to determine which dyad to change and how, the SAOM uses the objective function of Equation (6.16). Intuitively, "the probability that an actor makes a specific change is proportional to the exponential transformation of the objective function of the new network, that would be obtained as the consequence of making this change" (Snijders et al. 2010, p. 58), which may be written as

$$Pr(N_{ij}) = \frac{\exp(f_i(\boldsymbol{\theta}, N))}{\sum_{N^* \in \mathcal{N}} \exp(f_i(\boldsymbol{\theta}, N^*))}. \tag{6.19}$$

While this form looks rather similar to the ERGM, there are important differences: the statistics included in **h** are constructed from the perspective of a focal (ego) vertex and $\mathcal{N}$ contains potential networks that are achievable by vertex i changing its edge profile rather than the set of all possible networks with the same number of vertices as in the ERGM. If an actor is selected to change its behavior, the probabilities of behavior states are formed in a way that is analogous to the formulation in Equation (6.19), except (1) the statistics measure the ways in which behavior depends upon other node attributes and the network structure and (2) the sates considered include the node's current behavior level (e.g., a student's grades in school), a one-unit increase in behavior, and a one-unit decrease in behavior. Default estimation is accomplished by simulated generalized method of moments using a modified version of the Robbins-Monro algorithm (Snijders 2001, Amati, Schönenberger & Snijders 2015), but an MLE routine is also available (Snijders 2017).

Running Example: Organizational Networks Surrounding Estuaries in the United States

To illustrate the use of the SAOM, we consider a different data example. Before we describe the new example, we discuss why we cannot use the Golden Age of Hollywood network. The Golden Age of Holywood network is continuous-time data, on which we have complete information about the ties between nodes. The SAOM is intended to use with truly discrete snapsot data. That is, network data in which the networks are measured in a sequence of discrete instantaneous time points, and the state of the network is not observed between snapshots. The simulated micro-steps used in the formulation and estimation of the SAOM, are intended to model the process of tie formation that occurred between snapshots. Due to this mismatch between the structure of the SAOM and the measurement of the Golden Age of Hollywood network, we change to a new data example – a network of information sharing between organizations that are engaged in the management of estuaries in the United States.

These data were originally collected and analyzed by Schneider et al. (2003) and was also analyzed by both Berardo and Scholz (2010) and Desmarais & Cranmer (2012a). The data were collected via survey at two periods in time. A tie from vertex i to vertex j indicates that the representative from organization i listed organization j as an organization with which organization i works. There are ten separate estuary networks included in the data, with a total of 194 nodes. The attribute data include a government actor variable in which a 0 indicates a nongovernmental organization and 1 indicates a governmental organization, a pro-development variable in which higher values indicate that the respondent is more supportive of economic development, and an attribute variable that was gathered in each wave that measures the degree to which the organization has trust for the other organizations in the network. The data are stored in the `estuaries` dataset in the `ina` package. The network data are stored as two matrix objects, `nets1` and `nets2`, corresponding to the two survey waves, respectively. The dataset also includes three vertex-level matrices that store attribute data – `govact`, `prodev`, and `trust`.

In our illustrative example, we present a model that is specified to nearly match the model used in Berardo and Scholz (2010). We model the network, and also treat the trust attribute as endogenous behavior. We include terms that capture the sender effects, receiver effects, and homophily with respect to the government actor, pro development, and trust variables. In terms of network effects, we also include terms that capture reciprocity, transitivity, and popularity effects. The model also includes rates that govern the frequencies with which nodes consider changing their ties and behaviors, and an out-degree term that controls the density of the network. In the behavior equation for trust, we include effects that capture the trend in the wave-to-wave change in trust, the tendency for nodes to change their trust values to match those of their neighbors in the network, and the effects of government actor and pro development on trust. The `estuaries` data are included in the `ina` package, and the code used to run the analysis in `RSiena` is given below.

```
1  library(ina)
2  library(RSiena)
3  data(estuaries)
4
5  ## Create Siena Model
6  ## Model Object
7  ## Phase 1, estimate derivatives for Robins-Monro stepping
```

```
 8  ## Phase 2, Iterative simulation of observed networks and adjustment
 9  ##    of parameter estimates to improve fit. Subphases determines the
10  ##    of iterative adjustments
11  ## Phase 3, Estimation of the covariance matrix (i.e., SEs)
12  policyModel <- sienaModelCreate(fn=simstats0c, nsub=7,
13                                  n3=6000, seed=12345)
14
15  ## Create the network object
16  policyNet <- sienaNet(array(c(nets1, nets2),
17                        dim=c(nrow(nets1), nrow(nets1), 2)))
18
19  ## Convert trust into a 'behavior' variable
20  ## This is a node attribute that will be modeled
21  trust_net <- sienaNet(trust, type="behavior")
22
23  ## Lagged value of trust, for behavior model
24  tr1 <- c(trust[,1])
25
26  ## Convert it to a constant node covariate
27  trust99 <- coCovar(tr1)
28
29  ## Prodevelopment Beliefs constant node covariate
30  prodev_cov <- coCovar(c(prodev))
31
32  ## Government Actor constant node covariate
33  govac_cov <- coCovar(c(govact))
34
35  ## Combine it all into a SIENA data object
36  policyData <- sienaDataCreate(policyNet, trust_net, prodev_cov,
37                                trust99,govac_cov)
38
39  ## Effects object, used to specify the model
40  policyEff <- getEffects(policyData)
41
42  ## Names of all effects that can be included in the model
43  effNames <- policyEff$effectName
44
45  ## Character vector of desired effects
46  ## First look at effNames, then the RSiena Manual
47  ## to define which ones to include in the model
48  incl_effs <- c("basic rate parameter policyNet", "outdegree
        (density)",
49                 "indegree - popularity", "reciprocity",
50                 "transitive triplets", "prodev_cov ego", "prodev_cov
                    alter",
51                 "prodev_cov similarity", "govac_cov ego", "govac_cov
                    alter",
52                 "govac_cov similarity", "trust_net ego", "trust_net
                    alter",
53                 "trust_net similarity", "rate trust_net period 1",
54                 "trust_net linear shape",
```

```
55                "trust_net: effect from prodev_cov",
56                "trust_net: effect from govac_cov",
57                "trust_net average similarity")
58
59  ## Find the locations of desired effects in the vector
60  ## of possible effects
61  effs <- match(incl_effs, effNames)
62
63  ## Set all effects to FALSE
64  ## The $include element of the effects objects
65  ## controls what gets into the model specification
66  policyEff$include <- rep(FALSE, length(policyEff$include))
67
68  ## turn desired effects on
69  policyEff$include[effs] <- TRUE
70
71  ## Estimate the model
72  est_siena <- siena07(policyModel, data=policyData, effects=policyEff,
73                       batch=TRUE, returnDeps=TRUE)
74
75  ## t-ratios should be less than 0.10 in magnitude to indicate
        convergence
76  ## z-statistics can be calculated as estimate/SE
77  ## overall ratio should be below 0.25
78  est_siena
```

A summary table for the SAOM is produced by printing the result of running `siena07`. Since SAOMs model the network through a series of sequential changes, there is no concern about degeneracy with the SAOM. However, since simulations are used to tune parameter estimates and fit the networks, the researcher still needs to check whether the estimates have converged. Convergence can be assessed using the "Convergence t-ratio" column in the summary table, and the "Overall maximum convergence ratio" printed at the end of the table. These statistics measure differences between the observed networks and the networks simulated during the fitting of the SAOM. For the model to be considered "converged," the `RSiena` documentation directs the user to look for convergence t-ratios that are all less than 0.10 in magnitude, and an overall ratio that is less than 0.25. If the model is not converged, the researcher can re-run the `siena07` command, setting the `prevAns` argument equal to the previously returned result from `siena07`. Doing so will restart the estimation where the previous run left off. This continued estimation can be repeated until the model converges.

```
 1  > est_siena
 2  Estimates, standard errors and convergence t-ratios
 3
 4                                         Estimate   Standard
                                                   Convergence
 5                                                     Error      t-ratio
 6  Network Dynamics
 7     1. rate basic rate parameter policyNet   4.8647  ( 0.4925  )   -0.0188
 8     2. eval outdegree (density)             -2.2411  ( 0.1328  )    0.0097
 9     3. eval reciprocity                      0.7360  ( 0.2335  )    0.0242
10     4. eval transitive triplets             0.1722  ( 0.0950  )    0.0172
11     5. eval indegree - popularity           0.2108  ( 0.0226  )    0.0187
12     6. eval prodev_cov alter                0.0326  ( 0.0453  )    0.0101
13     7. eval prodev_cov ego                  0.0477  ( 0.0579  )    0.0003
14     8. eval prodev_cov similarity           0.2118  ( 0.5148  )   -0.0078
15     9. eval govac_cov alter                 0.2173  ( 0.1142  )    0.0074
16    10. eval govac_cov ego                   0.0215  ( 0.1436  )    0.0176
17    11. eval govac_cov similarity            0.1831  ( 0.1260  )    0.0188
18    12. eval trust_net alter                 0.0068  ( 0.0377  )   -0.0116
19    13. eval trust_net ego                  -0.0315  ( 0.0541  )    0.0126
20    14. eval trust_net similarity            0.2717  ( 0.7222  )    0.0108
21
22  Behavior Dynamics
23    15. rate rate trust_net period 1         6.7842  ( 1.2682  )   -0.0084
24    16. eval trust_net linear shape          0.0419  ( 0.0503  )    0.0052
25    17. eval trust_net average similarity    4.3642  ( 1.3053  )   -0.0161
26    18. eval trust_net: effect from prodev_cov -0.0246 ( 0.0425 )    0.0079
27    19. eval trust_net: effect from govac_cov  0.1062 ( 0.1014 )   -0.0081
28
29  Overall maximum convergence ratio:    0.0625
30
31
32  Total of 35039 iteration steps.
```

The results indicate that the estuary networks are governed by high levels of network dependence – reciprocity, transitivity, and popularity are all positive and statistically significant. The coefficients can be interpreted on the log-odds scale (e.g., the log odds that i decides to send a tie to j increases by 0.736 if j has a current tie to i). The covariate effects on tie formation are, for the most part, not statistically significantly different from zero. The one covariate effect that is statistically significant is the effect of government actor on in-degree, which is positive. When it comes to the model for behavior, we find evidence, via the "average similarity" term, that nodes exhibit a tendency to make behavior changes that increase the similarity between their behaviors and the other nodes to which they are tied in the network. We pause here to note that we have presented a powerful inference – separating between homophily and influence with respect to the trust variable. The SAOM represents what is arguably the most popular framework for simultaneously modeling the effects of a node attribute on tie formation (i.e., selection), and the effects of network structure on the node attribute (i.e., influence). We think it is important to note that there is a broader methodological debate regarding the validity of this sort of inference with observational network data (see, e.g., Shalizi & Thomas 2011, Lyons 2011).

6.8 WRAPPING UP

Because many interesting networks are observed longitudinally, the extension of the ERGM to longitudinal networks via the TERGM (and the related SAOM) relaxes one of the major practical limitations of the basic ERGM. Considering networks over time adds complexity to the analyst's jobs in several ways: she must consider what order of temporal dependence is most appropriate, consider endogenous dependencies – including memory terms – that span multiple time periods, and make a decision as to whether the data-generating process during the period of observation is sufficiently stable that pooling results over that period of observation is reasonable. In this chapter, we have aimed to provide analysts with the tools they need to make those decisions when applying two popular statistical models used to study longitudinally observed networks.

6.9 SELF-STUDY PROBLEMS

Select a longitudinal network dataset to study using TERGM and SAOM, but avoid using the data from ina that was used in this chapter. Be sure that the dataset includes at least one vertex attribute. If you do not have a dataset that you would like to use for this exercise, we recommend that you use the ScottishSchool dataset from ina, which is introduced in Section 10.1. Using this dataset, complete a report that includes the following information:

1. **Description of the dataset:** What does the dataset cover? Where did it come from? Has it been used in any prior studies?
2. **Hypotheses:** Describe and test at least one hypothesis regarding a vertex attribute's effect on the network, at least one interdependence hypothesis, and one hypothesis regarding an endogenous vertex attribute (i.e., "behavior" in SAOM terminology). Describe these hypotheses.
3. **Model specification:** Identify TERGM and SAOM specifications that are both capable of testing your hypotheses regarding exogenous vertex attributes and interdependence. Expand the SAOM specification to incorporate your behavior hypothesis.

4.   **Estimates:** After assuring that the estimates have converged for each model, present the estimates of the ERGM in either graphical or tabular form.

5.   **Fit:** Evaluate the fit of both the TERGM and the SAOM.

6.   **Interpretation:** Substantively interpret your results. Do you find support for your hypotheses? Do you think the effects that you find are large? Are the results regarding the first two hypotheses consistent across both the TERGM and SAOM?

7

Valued-Edge ERGMs: The Generalized ERGM (GERGM)

As noted in previous chapters, exponential family random graph models (ERGMs) are a popular, powerful, and flexible tool for statistical inference with network data (Holland & Leinhardt 1981; Wasserman & Pattison 1996; Snijders et al. 2006). However, one major limitation of the formulation and implementation of the early versions of ERGMs is that they can only be applied to networks with dichotomous edges. In many networks, the edges are annotated with important weight or strength information (e.g., financial exchange, migration, and correlation networks are, by their nature, weighted). In recent years, researchers have tried to address this limitation in the original ERGM specification by developing variants of ERGMs for weighted networks (Wyatt et al. 2010; Desmarais and Cranmer 2012b; Krivitsky 2012). For instance, the model developed by Wyatt et al. (2010) is applicable to networks in which edges are weighted on a discrete and finite scale (e.g., 1, 2, ..., 10), while the model developed by Krivitsky (2012) is applicable to count-weighted edges.

In this chapter, we provide detailed coverage of the model termed the generalized exponential random graph model (GERGM), which is an ERGM-style model for weighted networks in which the edges have continuous valued weights (either bounded, bounded on one side, or unbounded) (Desmarais and Cranmer 2012b; Wilson et al. 2017). We do not cover the model by Wyatt et al. (2010) in detail because there is, as of this writing, no publicly available software implementation. We do not cover the count ERGM by Krivitsky (2012), because its formulation and software application are very similar to those used with binary ERGMs, and it is currently only applicable to count-weighted networks. We do, however, encourage the reader to consider the count ERGM, implemented in the R package ergm.count (Krivitsky 2016), for applications with count-weighted networks. The dependencies that can be modeled in weighted networks using the GERGM provide seamless analogues to the network processes that are commonly modeled with dichotomous and count ERGMs. In this chapter, we present the GERGM, review methods of estimation, and provide an empirical example using the GERGM package in R (Denny et al. 2017).

Like the ERGM, in order to specify the GERGM the researcher incorporates network statistics representing processes hypothesized to characterize the network under analysis. Also like with the ERGM, Monte Carlo maximum likelihood estimation (MC-MLE) (Geyer & Thompson 1992; Snijders 2002) is the most promising approach to estimation. The GERGM departs from the ERGM in that the former comprises a two-equation structure: the first equation representing the effects of covariates on, and marginal distributional properties of, the edges (e.g., the expected values of the edges given the values of edge covariates, the variance of the edges, the bounds applied to the possible range of edge values), while the second equation represents the relationships among the edges (e.g., through processes such as reciprocity and popularity). We will present some simulated networks to assist in interpreting the structure of the GERGM. We will also describe GERGM estimation, while addressing the effects of degeneracy in the GERGM, and outline the general purpose method of adjusting GERGM specifications to avoid degeneracy.

Running Example: ACC Basketball Scoring Network

In this chapter, we demonstrate the application of the GERGM with an application to the network of scoring in National Collegiate Athletic Association (NCAA) men's basketball, specifically looking at fifteen teams in the Atlantic Coast Conference during the 2016 regular season. In this network, the edge from i to j is the number of points i scored on j during all games played in the regular season. This network is embedded in the ina R package as the dataset ACCBasketball. The dataset includes three objects – a weighted matrix in which the i, j element gives the total number of regular season points cored by team i against team j, a vertex attribute data frame named covariateData, and a weighted symmetric matrix object in which the i, j element gives the number of games played between teams i and j during the season.

The code snippet below presents code to load the data from the package and create a simple plot using the `plot_network()` function from the GERGM R package.

```
1  ## Read in R package for GERGM
2  library(GERGM)
3  library(ina)
4
5  ## Load data objects
6  ## data covers NCAA ACC Men's basketball from the 2016 season
7  ## adjacencyMatrix is the number of points i scored on j during 2016
8  ##    season (in 100s)
9  ## nGames is the number of games played between i and j during the
10 ##    2016 season
11 ## covariateData contains team name and school enrollment (in
       thousands)
12 data(ACCBasketball)
13
14 set.seed(1234)
15 plot_network(adjacencyMatrix, white_background=TRUE,
       show_legend=FALSE)
```

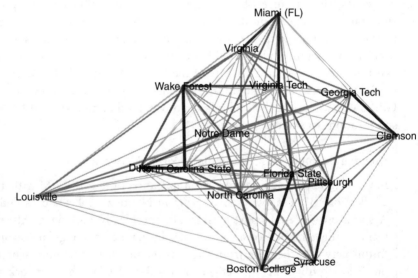

7.1 GERGM DEFINITION

Consider a network defined on a set of vertices $[n] = \{1, 2, \ldots, n\}$, where $m = n(n - 1)$ denotes the number of adjacency matrix elements that reflect the ties between these vertices. Let the weighted ties be represented by a collection of weights $(y_{i,j} : i \neq j \in [n]) \in \mathbb{R}^m$ (e.g., the amount of goods exported in dollars, the amount of time it takes to travel between places). The GERGM is a family of probability distributions that can be used to generate random edges that exhibit the distributional properties of the weights, as they are observed, and are dependent upon each other in ways that are common in networks. The probability distribution is specified by a joint probability density function (pdf) $f_Y(y, \theta, \gamma)$ that is conditional on real-valued parameters θ and γ.

A GERGM formulation is best understood as a two-step process of (1) data generation in a space of edge value quantiles – where a quantile of a value is the proportion of values from the same distribution that are less than or equal to the respective value (e.g., the quantile of the value -1.96 in the standard normal distribution is approximately 0.025) – and (2) data transformation onto the range, location, and shape of the observed edges. First, a joint distribution that captures the structure and interdependence of Y is defined on a restricted (i.e., quantile) network configuration, $X \in [0, 1]^m$. Next, the restricted network X is transformed onto the support of Y through an appropriate transformation function. We note that in the current chapter we depart from the common usage of N to denote the adjacency matrix, as the variable encoding relations in the GERGM (Y) is always a fully connected network and is modeled as a two-step transformation of another fully connected network (X). The two steps in defining the GERGM are closely related to the specification of joint distributions via copula functions (Genest & MacKay 1986). We now describe the two steps in specifying a GERGM in more detail.

In the first specification step, a function of network dependence statistics (e.g., reciprocity, popularity, transitivity) $\mathbf{h} : [0, 1]^m \rightarrow \mathbb{R}^p$ is formulated to represent the ways in which the edge values in the network are related to each other. The random vector X is modeled with a distribution that looks very similar in structure to the ERGM, and is parameterized with $\theta \in \mathbb{R}^p$ as

$$f_X(x \mid \theta) = \frac{\exp\left(\theta' \mathbf{h}(x)\right)}{\int_{[0,1]^m} \exp\left(\theta' \mathbf{h}(z)\right) dz}, \quad x \in [0, 1]^m. \tag{7.1}$$

The model component represented in Equation (7.1) – the numerator of which looks equivalent to that of the binary ERGM's likelihood function – provides a flexible specification of interdependence. For example, networks generated by a highly reciprocal process are likely to exhibit high values of the dyadwise product of the two edges in the dyad (i.e., $\sum_{i<j} x_{i,j} x_{j,i}$), and those for which there is a high variance in

the popularity of vertices (e.g., preferential attachment) are likely to exhibit high values of the "two-stars" statistic, which is calculated as the summed product of pairs of edges that are incident to a single vertex (i.e., $\sum_i \sum_{j,k \neq i} x_{ji} x_{ki}$) (Park & Newman 2004b). Furthermore, when the statistics $\mathbf{h}(X)$ play no role in the structure of X, then the joint distribution of $\{X_{i,j}\}$ reduces to a set of independent uniform random variables on the unit interval. That is, when $\boldsymbol{\theta} = 0$ the function $f_X(x, \boldsymbol{\theta})$, the distribution defined in Equation (7.1). This is a helpful property, on which we elaborate below.

If defined solely through Equation (7.1), the GERGM would be an inadequate general model for weighted networks. Most weighted networks will be measured with ranges that are not bounded between 0 and 1. Furthermore, the model represented in Equation (7.1) does not include parameters that model marginal features of continuous distributions, such as mean, variance, and other shape characteristics. The GERGM includes a transformation formula that integrates the dependence model with a realistic edgewise model of continuous edges. In the second specification step, a one-to-one function $T^{-1} : [0, 1]^m \rightarrow \mathbb{R}^m$ is formulated to model the transformation of the restricted network X onto the support of Y. Specifically, for each pair of distinct vertices $i, j \in [n]$, we model $Y_{i,j} = T_{i,j}^{-1}(X \mid \boldsymbol{\gamma})$, where $\boldsymbol{\gamma} \in \mathbb{R}^p$ parameterizes the transformation so as to capture the marginal features of Y. This transformation function can now be integrated into the GERGM, to give its complete distributional form:

$$f_Y(y \mid \boldsymbol{\theta}, \boldsymbol{\gamma}) = \frac{\exp\left(\boldsymbol{\theta}'\mathbf{h}(T(y \mid \boldsymbol{\gamma}))\right)}{\int_{[0,1]^m} \exp\left(\boldsymbol{\theta}'\mathbf{h}(z)\right) dz} \prod_{i,j} t_{i,j}(y_{i,j} \mid \boldsymbol{\gamma}), \quad y \in \mathbb{R}^m. \quad (7.2)$$

where $t_{i,j}(y \mid \boldsymbol{\gamma}) = dT_{i,j}(y \mid \boldsymbol{\gamma})/dy_{i,j}$. T^{-1} is specified such that $T_{i,j}^{-1}$ is an inverse cumulative distribution function (CDF) (e.g., if the researcher wants each edge to have a normal distribution conditional on the other edges, T^{-1} is specified to be the inverse cumulative distribution function of the normal distribution). First, when T^{-1} is an inverse CDF, $t_{i,j}$ is precisely a marginal PDF. Furthermore, when there are no network dependencies in Y, that is, when $\boldsymbol{\theta} = 0$, then $f_Y(y, \boldsymbol{\theta}, \boldsymbol{\gamma})$ reduces to a product of PDFs $\{t_{i,j}\}$. An important example includes taking T^{-1} as the inverse of a Gaussian CDF. In this special case, if Y contains no network dependencies, then (7.2) reduces to a model for conditionally independent Gaussian observations. Again, in the case of $\boldsymbol{\theta} = 0$, and T^{-1} specified as the Gaussian CDF, if the edgewise mean is given by a linear regression on edge covariates, then the GERGM reduces to a model that can be fit using ordinary least squares.

Using the GERGM is similar to using the ERGM – the researcher selects the set of dependencies and covariate effects to incorporate into the model. The differences between the GERGM and the ERGM are (1) that the researcher also needs to select a distribution (i.e., T^{-1}) that accurately represents the shape of the edgewise distribution and (2) that dependencies and covariate effects are modeled through two separate equations: (7.1) and (7.2), respectively. Like with the ERGM, the normalizing constant of the GERGM is intractable. As such, estimation is computationally intensive and accomplished using MC-MLE methods described in Desmarais and Cranmer (2012b); Wilson et al. (2017).

7.2 SPECIFYING PROCESSES ON WEIGHTED NETWORKS

The dependence modeled by the ERGM and GERGM are specified by selecting **h**. For the dichotomous ERGM, a substantial literature has arisen around how to best formulate **h** to represent important generative processes such as transitivity and preferential attachment (Wasserman & Pattison 1996, Park & Newman 2004a, Snijders et al. 2006). The initial development of specifications for the ERGM focused on intuitive local subgraph counts, such as the number of two-stars and triangles, that implied straightforward conditional distributions (Strauss and Ikeda 1990). Intermediate extensions focused on more advanced or higher-order subgraph counts (Pattison & Robins 2002). Unfortunately, many of these intuitive specifications lead to empirically implausible models due to the problem of degeneracy. When an ERG-style distribution is degenerate, most of the probability reflected in the probability mass or probability density function is assigned to one network, typically the completely empty or completely full network. When specifying an ERGM using counts of higher-order subgraphs (i.e., subgraphs that involve three or more edges), each edge contributes to many potential subgraph configurations. Thus, in order to dampen the probability mass attributed to extremely dense networks, which have a lot of subgraph configurations, Snijders et al. (2006) propose assigning decreasing weight to increasing numbers of subgraphs involving the same vertices or edges. For example, the geometrically weighted edgewise shared partner (GWESP) term assigns less weight to the second shared partner between two vertices than to the first shared partner, as compared to the triangle statistic, which assigns equal weight to each shared partner. These geometrically weighted specifications avoid degeneracy with much greater success than models specified with simple local subgraph counts.

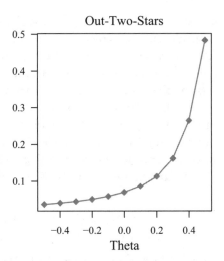

FIGURE 7.1 Activity dependence in a twenty-five-vertex network Y. The y-axis is the variance in the out-degrees across vertices. The out-two-star statistic is computed as $Out2Star = \sum_{ij} \sum_k x_{ki} x_{kj} + (1 - x_{ki})(1 - x_{kj})$.

Like the ERGM, terms for the the GERGM specification can be developed using the simple sums of subgraph products, with the product over edges in the subgraph constituting the measure of subgraph intensity (e.g., $y_{i,j} \times y_{j,i}$ to measure the strength of mutuality). We illustrate the form of one of these statistics in Figure 7.1. The model illustrated in Figure 7.1 depicts the joint distribution of continuous, unbounded edges in a network Y with **h** parameterized by a measure of out-two-stars, while T^{-1} is specified as a standard normal PDF. The x-axis gives the value of the two-stars parameter, and the y-axis gives the variance of out-degrees across vertices in the network. For each parameter value, we depict the mean over 1,000 simulated networks. We see that, as the out-two-stars parameter increases, the variance in out-degrees across vertices also increases. This models activity heterogeneity in the network – that some vertices send very low-value ties, and some send very high-value ties, when the out-two-star parameter is high, and when it is low, most vertices send similar-valued ties.

7.3   AVOIDING DEGENERACY IN THE GERGM

In the GERGM framework, we specify statistics that correspond to the subgraph configurations that have proven fruitful in specifying binary-valued ERGMs. As with binary ERGMs, GERGM specifications can exhibit degeneracy. In this section we review a flexible, two-pronged weighting scheme that dampens the extreme values that can arise through the use of summed subgraph products that lead to degeneracy. Wyatt et al. (2010) specifies subgraph statistics as the geographic mean within the subgraph, rather than the product. This exponentially dampens the potential extreme values in the subgraph product by raising the subgraph product to the inverse of the number of edges involved in the subgraph. The first of two approaches to dampening the extreme values of subgraph products in the weighted GERGM specifications can be considered a generalization of the subgraph geometric mean. That is, each subgraph is raised to an exponent ($\alpha \in (0, 1]$) before summing over all subgraphs. This is what is referred to as α-inside weighting. The second approach represents an extension of the triangle model specification in Lubetzky and Zhao (2015). For a purpose that is not directly related to addressing degeneracy, Lubetzky and Zhao proposed specifying an ERGM by raising the triangle density (i.e., the proportion of closed triangles out of all possible triangles in the network) to an exponent greater than zero, but less than 2/3. This is referred to as the α-outside approach to avoiding degeneracy with GERGM. Under the α-outside weighting, the sum over subgraphs is raised to an exponent ($\alpha \in (0, 1]$) (i.e., the exponent is outside the sum over subgraphs).

Aside from providing a different fit to the network, the α-outside approach induces to a different pattern of dependence among the ties, as under the α-outside specification all ties in the network are dependen dependent upon each other, to a degree. The α-inside specification leads to the local dependence in conventional ERGMs, in which the change statistics applied to the edge from i to j can be calculated using only those edges that are embedded in the same subgraphs as the edge from i to j (e.g., with the mutuality term, the edge from j to i is the only one needed to calculate the change statistic for edge i/j). The α-outside approach leads to global dependence, such that the change statistics depend upon the edges that are in the same subgraphs, as well as the global network statistic values. We can see this by calculating the derivative of a network statistic calculated using the α-outside specification with respect to a change in X_{ij}. Let $h_\alpha(X) = h(X)^\alpha$; then

$$\frac{dh_\alpha}{dX_{ij}} = \frac{\alpha}{h^{1-\alpha}} \frac{dh}{dX_{ij}}.$$

The change statistic for a given network statistic with respect to an edge value increases with the values of the other edges that are within the same subgraph as the respective edge (i.e., $\frac{dh}{dX_{ij}}$), but decreases with the value of the network statistic calculated on the entire network (i.e., $h^{1-\alpha}$). The decrease in the value of the change statistic as the total network statistic value increases represents a dampening effect. The interpretation of this dampening effect is that the increase in the network statistic that would lead to the formation of dense subgraphs is negatively related to the density of the other subgraphs in the network of that same type. Another way to think about this relationship is that, if the other subgraphs are dense, the amount of edge weight that needs to be added to an edge to notably increase the value of the network statistic will be high relative to a scenario in which the other subgraphs were sparse. The network statistics that have been developed for use with GERGM, and implemented in the R package GERGM, are very similar to those that have been used for the ERGM. However, the α-weighting options are, as of this writing, unique to GERGM specification. Wilson et al. (2017) illustrate α-outside specification using the statistics described in Table 7.1.

7.4 PARAMETER ESTIMATION

Due to the intractability of the normalizing constant (i.e., the denominator) in Equation (7.1), the log-likelihood of the GERGM cannot be directly calculated and must be approximated for parameter estimation. In this section, we describe maximum likelihood inference of the parameters θ and γ via MCMC-MLE. We present the Gibbs sampling procedure proposed by Desmarais and Cranmer (2012b), which relies on an important restriction of model specification. We then present the sampling via Metropolis–Hastings, developed by Wilson et al. (2017), which is more generally applicable but requires more manual supervision.

7.4.1 Approximate Maximum Likelihood Inference

Given a specification of statistics $\mathbf{h}(\cdot)$, transformation function T^{-1}, and observations $Y = y$ on the support of the distribution 7.2, our goal is to find the maximum likelihood estimates (MLEs) of the unknown parameters θ and γ, namely, to find values $\widehat{\theta}$ and $\widehat{\gamma}$ that maximize the log-likelihood:

$$\ell(\theta, \gamma \mid y) = \theta' \mathbf{h}(T(y, \gamma)) - \log C(\theta) + \sum_{ij} \log t_{ij}(y, \gamma), \qquad (7.3)$$

TABLE 7.1 *Summary of network statistics used in the specification of a GERGM in this work.*

Network statistic	Parameter	Value
Reciprocity	θ_R	$\left(\sum_{i<j} x_{ij} x_{ji} \right)^{\alpha_R}$
Cyclic Triads	θ_{CT}	$\left(\sum_{i<j<k} (x_{ij} x_{jk} x_{ki} + x_{ik} x_{kj} x_{ji}) \right)^{\alpha_{CT}}$
In-Two-Stars	θ_{ITS}	$\left(\sum_{i} \sum_{j<k\neq i} x_{ji} x_{ki} \right)^{\alpha_{ITS}}$
Out-Two-Stars	θ_{OTS}	$\left(\sum_{i} \sum_{j<k\neq i} x_{ij} x_{ik} \right)^{\alpha_{OTS}}$
Edge Density	θ_E	$\left(\sum_{i\neq j} x_{ij} \right)^{\alpha_E}$
Transitive Triads	θ_{TT}	$\left(\sum_{i<j<k} (x_{ij} x_{jk} x_{ik} + x_{ij} x_{kj} x_{ki} + x_{ij} x_{kj} x_{ik}) + \sum_{i<j<k} (x_{ji} x_{jk} x_{ki} + x_{ji} x_{jk} x_{ik} + x_{ji} x_{kj} x_{ki}) \right)^{\alpha_{TT}}$

Note. These are the α-outside specification of five commonly used network statistics.

where

$$C(\theta) = \int_{[0,1]^m} \exp(\theta' \mathbf{h}(z)) dz.$$

The maximization of (7.3) can be achieved through iteratively maximizing with respect to $\gamma \mid \theta$ and $\theta \mid \gamma$. Specifically, the MLEs $\widehat{\theta}$ and $\widehat{\gamma}$ can be calculated by following two iterative optimization steps given below. For $r \geq 1$, iterate until convergence:

1. Given $\theta^{(r)}$, estimate $\gamma^{(r)} \mid \theta^{(r)}$:

$$\beta^{(r)} = \arg\max_{\gamma} \left(\theta^{(r)} \mathbf{h}(T(y, \gamma)) + \sum_{ij} \log t_{ij}(y, \gamma) \right). \quad (7.4)$$

2. Set $\hat{x} = T(y, \gamma^{(r)})$. Then estimate $\theta^{(r+1)} \mid \gamma^{(r)}$:

$$\theta^{(r+1)} = \arg\max_{\theta} \left(\theta' \mathbf{h}(\hat{x}) - \log C(\theta) \right). \quad (7.5)$$

For fixed θ, the likelihood maximization in (7.4) is straightforward and can be accomplished numerically using gradient descent (Snyman 2005). In the case that $t_{i,j}$ is log-concave and $\mathbf{h} \circ T$ is concave in γ, optimization with a hill-climbing algorithm will be effective.

The maximization in (7.5) is much more challenging due to the intractability of the normalizing constant, $C(\theta)$. A substantial literature has developed to address estimation of ERG-style models with intractable normalizing constants. For example, Strauss and Ikeda (1990) consider the use of the maximum pseudo-likelihood estimate (MPLE) for θ, in which the maximization of the log-likelihood is replaced with the maximization of the product of conditional probabilities of each component of the adjacency matrix given the other adjacency matrices. van Duijn et al. (2009) show, however, that the MPLE often exhibits bias, and is less efficient than the MCMLE, especially in the presence of strong network dependencies. The methodology that is generally preferred to MPLE is MC-MLE, which is based on stochastic approximation of the normalizing constant. As we reviewed in Chapter 5, MC-MLE has proven to be an effective solution for estimation in ERGM (Geyer & Thompson 1992; Hunter & Handcock 2006). We describe the MCMC framework for estimating θ, which includes both Gibbs and Metropolis-Hasting approaches to constructing Markov chains of networks.

7.4.2   Monte Carlo Maximum Likelihood for the GERGM

Let θ and $\widetilde{\theta}$ be two parameter vectors in $\mathbb{R}^p$ and $lC(\cdot)$ is defined as in (7.3). The approach to optimization of (7.5) using Monte Carlo simulation is based on an important property of exponential family distributions (Geyer & Thompson 1992):

$$\frac{C(\theta)}{C(\widetilde{\theta})} = \mathbb{E}_{\widetilde{\theta}}\left[\exp\left((\theta - \widetilde{\theta})'\mathbf{h}(X)\right)\right]. \tag{7.6}$$

The expected value in (7.6) cannot be computed directly; however, a first-order approximation of the expectation can be calculated using a first moment estimate:

$$\mathbb{E}_{\widetilde{\theta}}\left[\exp\left((\theta - \widetilde{\theta})'\mathbf{h}(X)\right)\right] \approx \frac{1}{M}\sum_{j=1}^{M}\exp\left((\theta - \widetilde{\theta})'\mathbf{h}(x^{(j)})\right), \tag{7.7}$$

where $x^{(1)}, \ldots, x^{(M)}$ is a random sample from pdf $f_X(\cdot, \widetilde{\theta})$.

Let $\ell(\boldsymbol{\theta} \mid \hat{x}) := \boldsymbol{\theta} \mathbf{h}(\hat{x}) - \log C(\boldsymbol{\theta})$. Then maximizing $\ell(\boldsymbol{\theta} \mid \hat{x})$ with respect to $\boldsymbol{\theta} \in \mathbb{R}^p$ boils down to maximizing $\ell(\boldsymbol{\theta} \mid \hat{x}) - \ell(\widetilde{\boldsymbol{\theta}} \mid \hat{x})$ for $\widetilde{\boldsymbol{\theta}} \in \mathbb{R}^p$. Equations (7.6) and (7.7) imply that

$$\ell(\boldsymbol{\theta} \mid \hat{x}) - \ell(\widetilde{\boldsymbol{\theta}} \mid \hat{x}) \approx (\boldsymbol{\theta} - \widetilde{\boldsymbol{\theta}})'\mathbf{h}(\hat{x}) - \log\left(\frac{1}{M}\sum_{j=1}^{M} \exp\left((\boldsymbol{\theta} - \widetilde{\boldsymbol{\theta}})'\mathbf{h}(x^{(j)})\right)\right).$$

(7.8)

Estimation of $\boldsymbol{\theta}$ is done by maximizing (7.8). The estimate in the $r + 1$st iteration $\boldsymbol{\theta}^{(r+1)}$ in (7.5) is calculated by using Monte Carlo methods to iterate between the two following steps: given $\boldsymbol{\gamma}^{(r)}, \boldsymbol{\theta}^{(r)}$, and $\hat{x} = T(y, \boldsymbol{\gamma}^{(r)})$,

1. simulate networks $x^{(1)}, \ldots, x^{(M)}$ from density $f_X(x, \boldsymbol{\theta}^{(r)})$;
2. update:

$$\boldsymbol{\theta}^{(r+1)} = \arg\max_{\theta}\left(\boldsymbol{\theta}'\mathbf{h}(\hat{x}) - \log\left(\frac{1}{M}\sum_{j=1}^{M}\exp\left((\boldsymbol{\theta} - \boldsymbol{\theta}^{(r)})'\mathbf{h}(x^{(j)})\right)\right)\right).$$

(7.9)

The first step of MC-MLE involves simulation from the density $f_X(x, \boldsymbol{\theta}^{(r)})$. As it is not possible to directly calculate a function from which to draw independent samples from $f_X(x)$, MCMC methods are used for the approximation involved in estimation.

7.5 APPLICATIONS IN THE LITERATURE

Since the GERGM is a much newer method than the other methods we cover in this book, there have not been many published applications, but we review a few of them in detail in the current section. Desmarais and Cranmer (2012b) used the GERGM to study a network of the fifty US states, in which the value of the edge from state i to state j is the change from the previous year to the next in the number of people who migrated from state i to state j. The edge value was negative if there was a decrease in the migration rate, and positive if there was an increase. Since the edge values had a lot of outliers, they used the Cauchy distribution for the edge distribution – a bell-shaped distribution with heavy tails to model outliers (Cane 1974). They included parameters in the model to account for the effects of common covariates on the median change in migration (e.g., the unemployment rate in a state, the population in a state) and also included dependence parameters to account for transitivity, reciprocity, cycling, popularity, and activity effects. They found a strong tendency toward transitivity (i.e., if there is a big increase in people moving from state i to state j, and from state j to state k, there is likely to be a large increase in people moving directly from state i to state k). They also found a large negative cycling effect, which indicates that if there is a big increase in people moving from state i to state j, and from state j to state k, there is likely to be a decrease in people moving from state k to state i. This was the first published application of the GERGM, as it was included in the article in which the methodology was introduced.

Abramski (2018) uses the GERGM to study refugee networks defined on countries as vertices. In this network, the value of the edge from i to j was given by the number of refugees living in country j that are from country i (in the year 2015). To specify the GERGM, the edge distribution was set as the log-Cauchy distribution, such that the natural logarithm of the edge value has a Cauchy distribution. There were some zero-valued edges in the network, to which the value 0.01 was added to avoid taking the natural log of zero. The model included the effects of many exogenous covariates on the median of the log edge values. Covariates included the geographic distance between countries, the unemployment rate in the sending and receiving countries, and measures of ethnic and political unrest in both the sender and receiving countries. The dependence terms included measures of reciprocity, activity, and popularity effects. Abramski (2018) fit this model to four separate networks of countries, each centered around a different country (Syria, DRC, Myanmar, and Ukraine). Reciprocity was statistically significantly positive in two of the four networks. The activity effect (out-two-stars) was statistically significantly positive in three of the four networks, and significantly negative in one (the network centered around Myanmar). The popularity effect was significantly negative in two of the networks, and significantly positive in one (again, the network centered around Myanmar). The covariate effects were strong, and many in their expected directions. For example, more populous countries both sent more refugees and received more refugees in all four networks. This is another example of the GERGM being used to study networks based on migration patterns, but with countries as vertices.

In the final GERGM example we discuss, Stillman et al. (2019) use a special case of the GERGM, the correlation GERGM (cGERGM), that can be used to model a correlation matrix as a network. They study networks of activity in the human brain. The network in this application is defined with vertices as regions of the brain, and undirected edges defined as the correlation between the functional activation levels in the brain regions. The vertices were subdivided into twelve networks, each corresponding to a different task type (e.g., auditory, default function). The objective in their analysis was to evaluate the degree to which these networks exhibited a consistent generative structure. They found consistent patterns across subnetworks based on cGERGM results. Specifically, each subnetwork exhibited a positive triads term, and a negative two-stars term, indicating, respectively, that there is significant clustering in the co-activation network, and that the degree distributions in interregion correlations do not have heavy tails – that ties are evenly spread across the vertices. This last application, in neuroscience, departs from most of the social network examples presented in this book, but highlights the versatile applicability of generative models for networks.

Running Example: ACC Basketball Scoring Network

The GERGM is implemented in the R package by the same name. Its functionality is similar to that of the binary ERGM implemented in the ERGM package. Here we illustrate the application of the GERGM using the ACC basketball network presented above. The formula is used to specify the effects we wish to include in the model. The functions "sender" and "receiver" model the relationship between the vertex-level covariate "enrollment," and the points scored by and against a team, respectively. The function "netcov" is used to account for the number of games played between two teams. The function "mutual" adds the Reciprocity statistic from Table 7.1 to the model, with α specified below 1 to avoid degeneracy. The term "edges" adds an intercept term to the regression component of the model, to account for the median edge value on the observed scale. In this example, we follow Desmarais and Cranmer (2012b) and specify $g()$ to be a Cauchy density. The results of GERGM estimation are presented in the table following the code snippet.

```
1  ## Specify the formula to include the desired effects
2  formula <- adjacencyMatrix ~ sender("enrollment") +
       receiver("enrollment") +
3     netcov(nGames) + mutual(alpha=.9) + edges
4
5  ## Set the random number seed to assure replicability
6  set.seed(5)
7
8  ## Run the gergm
9  gergmResults <- gergm(formula,                 # use the formula we
       defined
10     covariate_data=covariateData,              # point to the covariate
          data
11     number_of_networks_to_simulate=100000,  # large value = accuracy
12     MCMC_burnin=10000,                         # large value speeds
          convergence
13     thin=1/10,                  # don't keep all of the simulated
          networks
14     transformation_type="Cauchy") # specify a distribution for g()
15
16 Estimate_Plot(gergmResults)
17 Trace_Plot(gergmResults)
18
19 ## Extract matrix of estimates and standard errors
20 EstSE <- rbind(t(attributes(gergmResults)$theta.coef),
21                t(attributes(gergmResults)$lambda.coef))
22
23 ## Create a LaTeX table
24 library(xtable)
25 xtable(EstSE, dig=4)
```

	est	se
intercept	3.2387*	0.0920
mutual	0.8298*	0.3874
enrollment_sender	0.0034*	0.0011
enrollment_receiver	0.0045*	0.0113
nGames_netcov	0.4826*	0.0153
dispersion	−2.6733*	0.1016

We see that all of the effects we included in the model are statistically significant. Median points scored, as indicated by the nGames
effect, increase by around 50 points per game played. The median
points scored and given up both increase by between 3 and 5 points per

each 10,000 students. Lastly, we find reciprocity in the points-scored network. This may result from the fact that a team's top scorers are more likely to remain in the game when playing against a team that is performing well.

The fit assessment produced at the end of the example code is plotted below. The fit is generally good, with most of the observed statistics lying within the boxes in the box plots. However, further development of this model could improve upon the fit to the in-degree distribution.

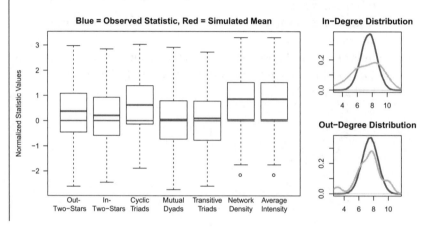

7.6 WRAPPING UP

The same types of dependencies that characterize binary networks can be found in weighted networks. ERG-style analysis of weighted networks can be used to test theory regarding – and for the existence of – these dependencies. Whether using the count ERGM or the GERGM, researchers do not need to settle for thresholding weighted networks.

7.7 SELF-STUDY PROBLEMS

Select a weighted network dataset to study using GERGM, but avoid using the data from ina that was used in this chapter. Be sure that the dataset includes at least one vertex attribute. If you do not have a dataset that you would like to use for this exercise, we recommend that you use the cosponsorship dataset from ina, which is introduced in Section 10.1. Using this dataset, complete a report that includes the following information:

1. **Description of the dataset:** What does the dataset cover? Where did it come from? Has it been used in any prior studies?

2. **Hypotheses:** Describe and test at least one hypothesis regarding a vertex attribute and at least one hypothesis regarding interdependence among the ties. Describe these hypotheses

3. **Model specification:** Identify a model specification that you believe is capable of testing your hypotheses.

4. **Estimates:** Present the estimates of the GERGM in either graphical or tabular form.

5. **Diagnostics:** Evaluate whether this GERGM fits your network adequately.

6. **Interpretation:** Substantively interpret your results. Do you find support for your hypotheses? Do you think the effects that you find are large?

PART III

LATENT SPACE NETWORK MODELS

8

The Basic Latent Space Model

8.1 INTRODUCTION

In the previous sections of this book, we focused on modeling networks with the exponential random graph model (ERGM), as well as the closely related temporal exponential random graph model (TERGM) and stochastic actor-oriented model (SAOM). As we saw, by allowing the explicit modeling of endogenous network features, those models offer flexible means of modeling network formation in a more or less holistic fashion. In this section, we change directions with the introduction of an alternative modeling approach, the latent space family of models. These models differ from the ERGM approach in that they place greater priority on modeling the local contexts of individual ties and vertices at the expense of emphasizing broader network processes. This approach to modeling dependencies in networks was introduced by Hoff, Raftery, and Handcock (2002), while they have been extended to include methods for clustering (Handcock, Raftery & Tantrum 2007), random effects (Krivitsky et al. 2009), more flexible functional forms (Hoff et al. 2014), and dynamic networks (Sewell and Chen 2015). But despite this important work, latent space models have traditionally received less attention from network scholars than has the ERGM approach. However, as we will see in the following three chapters, the latent space approach does offer a great deal of flexibility for modeling networks, and has been extended to cover several types of network data.

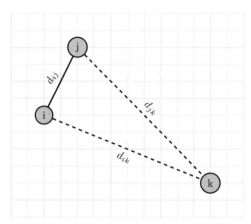

FIGURE 8.1 A simple network of three vertices (i, j, and k). Here the smaller distance between i and j, d_{ij}, in the latent space means the probability of observing a tie is higher than it is between i and k and j and k.

8.2 MOTIVATION: THEORETICAL AND MATHEMATICAL PERSPECTIVE

The latent space model (LSM) formulated by Hoff et al. (2002) is based on a simple premise: that dependencies in network data can be viewed as being the result of the distances between individuals in some social, physical, or other latent space.[1] Simply put, the LSM postulates that the closer individuals (i.e., vertices) are in this latent social space, the more likely there will be a tie between these individuals (vertices). For instance, in an adolescent friendship network, the observed ties between individuals could be representative of unobserved positions in a social space; for example, perhaps social class or other unobserved traits of children's parents make it more likely that certain individuals in a school have formed friendships.

To make this idea more concrete, observe the simple network in Figure 8.1. Here we see three vertices – i, j, and k – embedded in a two-dimensional latent space, represented by the grid in the background. Notice that, as depicted, vertices i and j are close together and that k is located further away. In the LSM, this suggests that the probability of a tie between i and j is greater than the probability of a tie between i and k or between j and k. In the figure, this greater probability of a tie is represented by the thick solid line connecting the vertices. The distance

---

[1] Recent research has moved on to treating the LSM to be specific subtype in a broader class of the latent *variable* models for networks; e.g., see Rastelli, Friel, and Raftery (2016).

between k and the other two vertices, on the other hand, is greater; thus, the probability of a tie is lower, so a dashed line connects these dyads.

The LSM is a conditional independence model, where the probability of a tie (or the strength of a tie in a weighted network) is considered conditional on the locations of the vertices in the latent space. With greater distances between vertices, the less likely we expect to see a tie. Considering the model for binary ties developed by Hoff et al. (2002), the log-odds of a tie between two vertices i and j is

$$\log\left(\frac{\Pr(N_{ij} = 1)}{1 - \Pr(N_{ij} = 1)}\right) = \eta_{ij} = \beta_0 - d(\mathbf{z}_i, \mathbf{z}_j). \tag{8.1}$$

Here, $\Pr(N_{ij} = 1)$ is the probability of the tie between i and j (or the tie from i to j in a directed network), $\mathbf{z}_i$ and $\mathbf{z}_j$ represent the locations of vertices i and j in some s-dimensional latent space, d is a distance function that satisfies the triangle inequality,[2] and β_0 is some baseline for the likelihood of a tie (i.e., an intercept term). Importantly, notice that the distance between vertices i and j is subtracted from the baseline rate – distances are always positive, and an increase in the distance between two vertices is associated with a decrease in the log-odds of a tie between those vertices.

In a network of binary ties, the log probability of the observed graph, conditional on $\eta = \{\eta_{ij}\}$, is

$$\log \Pr(N \mid \eta) = \sum_{i \neq j} \left[\eta_{ij} N_{ij} - \log(1 + \exp(\eta_{ij})) \right], \tag{8.2}$$

where N_{ij} is a tie between vertices i and j. It should be clear from Equation (8.2) that this version of the LSM has the same functional form as a logistic regression model for binary ties. This model works for both undirected and directed networks though, as we will see, interpretation of the latter models can be tricky.

Running Example: Strike Communication Network

In this chapter, we will be using data from Michael (1997) to demonstrate the workings of the latent space model. Data are from a study of communication between twenty-four striking workers at a sawmill, for thirty-eight undirected ties (density of 0.14). Ties in this network were

[2] Recall that if a, b, and c represent the lengths of three sides in a triangle, the triangle inequality says that the sum of the lengths of two of these sides should be greater than or equal to the length of the third side; i.e., $a + b \geq c$.

determined by a survey of the strikers. Each striker was asked to rank on a 5-point Likert scale how often they communicated with each of the other strikers. If at least one person in each dyad said they communicated at a level of 3 or greater, then this was characterized as an undirected tie between those workers.

The data for this network are available in the ina package via the dataset named Strike. The data are stored as a network object, which includes vertex attributes. The network can be loaded and visualized using the latentnet package (Krivitsky & Handcock 2008) as follows.

```
1   ## Load the latentnet package for estimating latent space models.
2   ## This will also load the network and ergm packages.
3   library(latentnet)
4
5   ## Load Michael's (1997) sawmill strike data, contained in ina
6   ## package.
7   data("Strike", package="ina")
8
9   ## Look at the network object, and the help file for the data.
10  Strike
11  help("Strike")
12
13  ## Plot the network, labeling vertices with strikers' names
14
15  set.seed(10)
16  lab <- network.vertex.names(Strike)
17  plot(Strike, vertex.cex=1.5, label=lab, edge.col="gray",
```

Figure 8.2 presents the resultant communication network. In this plot, vertex colors denote specific groups of strikers. Group 1 (in triangles) are four Spanish-speaking workers under thirty years old, group 2 (squares) comprises nine English-speaking workers under thirty, and group 3 (circles) consists of eleven English-speaking workers over thirty. In the plot, the connections between Alejandro and Bob can be explained by the fact that Alejandro speaks English, while Bob speaks some Spanish. Ozzie is the father of Karl, explaining their connection, while Norm helped get Bob the job at the mill. As we will see, this communication network is an excellent introductory example for demonstrating the capabilities of the latent space model.

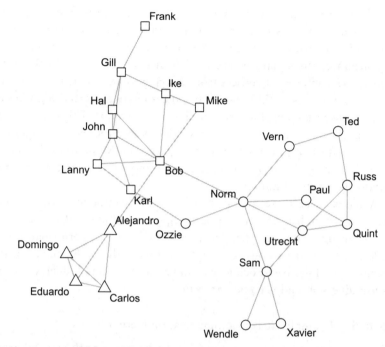

FIGURE 8.2 Michael's Michael: 1997 communication network among striking sawmill workers. Young Spanish-speaking workers are shown as triangles, young English-speaking workers are squares, and older English-speaking workers are shown as circles.

8.3   THE EUCLIDEAN LATENT SPACE MODEL

The previous section said nothing about how the distance metric, $d(\cdot)$, is defined, except to say that it must satisfy the triangle inequality. The most common, and default, distance metric used by practitioners is the standard Euclidean distance. In two dimensions, this is defined as

$$d_{ij} = d(\mathbf{z}_i, \mathbf{z}_j) = \sqrt{(z_i^1 - z_j^1)^2 + (z_i^2 - z_j^2)^2}\,, \qquad (8.3)$$

where the notation z_i^1 indicates the location of vertex i in dimension $s = 1$ of the latent social space. Of course, this generalizes easily to many dimensions:

$$d_{ij} = d(\mathbf{z}_i, \mathbf{z}_j) = \sqrt{\sum_s [(z_i^s - z_j^s)^2]}\,. \qquad (8.4)$$

The Euclidean distance is often used due to practitioners' familiarity with the metric as well as its interpretability and ease of calculation. However, other metrics can often perform better in practical applications. For instance, the square of the Euclidean distance, $(d_{ij})^2$ in the notation above, can prevent vertices from straying too far apart by penalizing larger distances more than shorter distances (analogous to using squared errors rather than absolute error in linear regression). This can be especially useful in relatively sparse networks, where the lack of edges can have the effect of "pushing" vertices apart. The Manhattan distance – $d_{ij}^M = \sum_s | z_i^s - z_j^s |$ – would have a similar, though less extreme effect of penalizing greater distances.

While each of these metrics can be useful in practical applications, the Manhattan distance has not been implemented in the R packages we will be using in this chapter. Thus, exploration of its performance will be left to the reader; however, we will compare the performance of the Euclidean and squared-Euclidean distances in the examples below, where its usefulness should become apparent.

Running Example: Strike Communication Network

Returning to our running example of the strike network, we will begin by estimating a two-dimensional ($s = 2$) latent space model for this network. This will estimate $1 + (2 \times 24) = 49$ parameters – two latent positions for each of the vertices and one parameter for the intercept. This doesn't include a number of additional parameters that are estimated for the priors in the Bayesian formulation of the model. This will be discussed further in Section 9.5. The choice of the dimension of the latent space will be discussed in Section 8.6.2.

The latent space model can be estimated with the `ergmm` function, available in the `latentnet` package in R (Krivitsky & Handcock 2008). In its minimal invocation, one needs only specify the network to model and the desired distance model. For instance, a two-dimensional model using the Euclidean distance can be specified as follows (here we set the seed for replicability):

```
1    ## Estimate a 2-dimensional latent space model using a Euclidean
2    ## distance metrics for the sawmill strike communication network.
3    strike.2d <- ergmm(Strike ~ euclidean(d=2), verbose=TRUE,
         seed=125)
4    summary(strike.2d)
```

The summary method for the model fit object presents the information one would expect, including details about the model type (Bernoulli in this case, because of the binary ties between striking workings), the sample size and burn-in for the MCMC algorithm, point estimates for the intercept term in the model, and the BIC measure of model fit. One should note that two point estimates for the intercept are provided, one being the posterior mean of the MCMC samples, including 95 percent credible intervals, and the other being the value where the Kullback-Leibler divergence (Corcuera & Giummolè 1999) is minimized. Our discussion of the results will largely focus on the posterior means.

```
 1   ============================
 2   Summary of model fit
 3   ============================
 4
 5   Formula:    Strike ~ euclidean(d = 2)
 6   Attribute: edges
 7   Model:      Bernoulli
 8   MCMC sample of size 4000, draws are 10 iterations apart, after
        burnin
 9       of 10000 iterations.
10   Covariate coefficients posterior means:
11              Estimate    2.5%  97.5% 2*min(Pr(>0),Pr(<0))
12   (Intercept) 2.00293 0.56519 3.7855                 0.002 **
13   ---
14   Signif. codes:  0 '***' 0.001 '**' 0.01 '*' 0.05 '.' 0.1 ' ' 1
15
16   Overall BIC:           308.1124
17   Likelihood BIC:        127.3764
18   Latent space/clustering BIC:      180.736
19
20   Covariate coefficients MKL:
21              Estimate
22   (Intercept) 0.1717308
```

Since the only parameters included in our initial specification of this latent space model included only the intercept, and the latent space parameters, there is only a limited amount we can learn from the output of the model summary. For this reason, we will first turn to a plot of the estimated vertex locations. Figure 8.3 provides a plot for this model, which is obtained with the plot method for the estimated model fit object. By default, latentnet plots the Minimum Kullback-Leiber (MKL) estimates for the positions. This can be overridden by specifying what="pmean" for the posterior mean in the call to plot.ergmm.

Other options are also available, including plotting the maximum likelihood estimates (what="mle", the posterior mode (what="pmode"), and a cloud of posterior draws (what="cloud").

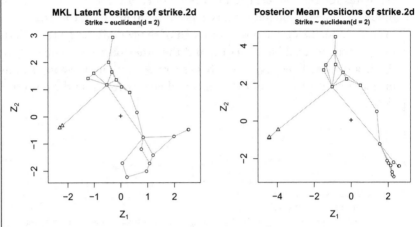

FIGURE 8.3 Estimated two-dimensional latent locations for Michael's (1997) communication network among striking sawmill workers. Vertex shape indicate their language/age groupings, as in Figure 8.2.

To make interpretation easier, vertex shapes are the same as in Figure 8.2 and remove a circle indicating the intracluster variance (plot.vars=FALSE), which is of limited use for this model.

```
## Plot estimated latent locations.
par(mfrow=c(1,2))
plot(strike.2d,
    plot.vars=FALSE, pad=0)
plot(strike.2d, what="pmean",
    plot.vars=FALSE, pad=0)
```

There are a few things to notice about the estimated vertex locations in Figure 8.3. First, the relative configuration of the vertices in the estimated two-dimensional latent space model is quite similar to that of the original descriptive plot of Figure 8.2. In other words, the vertices colored light triangles, squares, and circles (representing the three language/age groupings, as in the previous figure) are located more closely together in the latent social space. This natural grouping is a direct consequence of the greater density of ties between these vertices than between vertices of different groups. In the latent space model, the greater density of ties between groups of vertices is indicative of those vertices being closer in the latent social space. But it should be emphasized that, unlike in this example, positions estimated with the LSM will not necessarily closely resemble those derived from a network graphing routine in all networks one may be interested in modeling. The exploratory graph of Figure 8.2 was generated using a heuristic, force-directed algorithm that was developed for the purpose of generating graphical representations of the networks that are visually appealing and useful for exploratory analysis. One typical feature of such algorithms is to prevent vertices from overlapping. For exploratory purposes, this is a nice attribute to have; however, for inference, preventing vertex overlap is inappropriate.

This leads us to the second observation about the latent positions estimated from the LSM. As Figure 8.3 shows, multiple vertices can occupy the same estimated locations in the latent social space. This occurs when two (or more) vertices have the same, or nearly the same, set of connections, while also being connected to each other (i.e., they are structurally equivalent; Faust 1988). Assuming an absence of anything else to distinguish the vertices, such as exogenous covariate information, the probability of the graph will be maximized when the distance between vertices is zero (i.e., the positions are the same). For the strike communication network, we can see this happening with the Spanish speakers (triangles vertices) as well as the older English speakers (circles vertices). In this network, Domingo, Eduardo, and Carlos have the same set of connections. Consequently, they have essentially the same estimated locations and appear as a single point on the network plot. Alejandro, on the other hand, has the same set of ties but, in addition, is also connected to Bob. This pulls Alejandro's estimated location slightly away from the other three Spanish speakers and toward the group of squares vertices, to which Bob belongs. Likewise, in the group of older English speakers, Xavier and Wendle have connections to each other, while each also has a tie to Sam (this may be easiest to see if the original plot of Figure 8.2). The estimated LSM reflects this by producing the same latent positions for each of these vertices.

While in this small network, overlap of vertices in the latent space is relatively easy to see from the plot of estimated locations, such relationships can often be difficult to discern in larger and denser networks. When dealing with larger networks, it's sometimes easier to inspect the estimated latent locations directly. The `loc` function in the `ina` package makes this straightforward. For instance, we can extract the posterior mean locations for the Spanish-speaking group as follows:

```
## Extract posterior mean locations for the Spanish speakers
spanish <- c("Alejandro", "Domingo", "Eduardo", "Carlos")
spanish_locations <- loc(strike.2d)[spanish,]
```

For this model, this produces a 4 × 2 matrix of locations, where each row represents the posterior mean location for a selected vertex in the network:

```
print(spanish_locations)
                 Z1         Z2
Alejandro  3.952046  -0.6411787
Domingo    4.377462  -1.0934701
Eduardo    4.376854  -1.0938438
Carlos     4.360271  -1.0727964
```

As was evident from the network plot, we can see that according to the model Domingo, Eduardo, and Carlos have nearly the same estimated locations, while Alejandro is shown to be a bit further away. Using the `dist` function, we can see precisely how close these vertices are in the latent social space.

```
> dist(loc(strike.2d)[spanish,])
              Alejandro        Domingo       Eduardo
Domingo 0.6209235534
Eduardo 0.6207799423  0.0007133156
Carlos  0.5940891199  0.0268869245  0.0267951752
```

By inspecting estimated vertex distances as well as the latent locations produced by the LSM, practitioners can glean useful insight into a network. While interpreting the latent *dimensions* can be tricky – as will be discussed in the following chapter – one can use the estimated locations along with familiar tools of data analysis to better understand the relationships between vertices. As one simple example, k-means or other methods of clustering could be used on the latent positions to discover whether actors in the network can be usefully partitioned into distinct groups or to identify those actors in the network that are outliers with respect to their relationships to others. The short snippet below provides the steps one would take to estimate a k-means model with three clusters and then produce a plot of the results.

```
1    ## Use k-means to find clusters based on the estimated posterior
2    ## means of the 2-dimensional latent space model
3    set.seed(15)
4    strike.km <- kmeans(loc(strike.2d), centers=3)
5
6    ## Plot the model results with k-means cluster centers
7    plot(strike.2d, what="pmean", plot.vars=FALSE, pad=0,
8         main="Posterior Mean Positions of strike.2d with k-means
              Cluster Centers")
9    points(strike.km$centers[,1], strike.km$centers[,2], pch="+",
           cex=3.
```

The cluster centers estimated from the k-means routine are shown in Figure 8.4 as large crosses. These results offer no surprises, with the cluster centers located amongst the three groups already discussed. Given prior information – that is, the known age and language barriers separating groups – as well as the network structure that clearly emerged in the earliest plot of Figure 8.2 and the subsequent plots of the two-dimensional LSM, we would have expected the cluster centers to be located near the three age/language groups discussed previously. Chapter 10 will present a more advanced method of model-based clustering within the latent space modeling framework. In that model, proper inference about group membership may be performed based on draws from the posterior estimates of the model.

8.4 MODEL CONVERGENCE

In the last two sections, we introduced the basic theory underlying the latent space model for network data, and discussed the distance metrics typically used in applying these models to real world problems. We also explored a basic application of the model to a small communication network between striking workers at a sawmill. In this section, we focus on model checking, and demonstrating the methods used to verify that a fitted LSM has converged to stable parameter estimates. Models for network data can be difficult to estimate. For this reason, it's important that

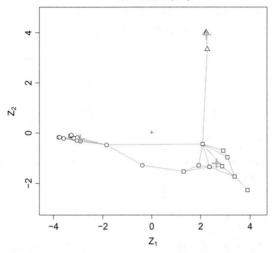

FIGURE 8.4 Estimated two-dimensional latent locations for Michael's (1997) communication network among striking sawmill workers, including the identified centers from a k-means clustering model with three clusters, which are denoted with large crosses.

one carefully checks model estimates to verify model convergence before moving on to refining model specification and assessing model fit (each of which be discussed in the following two sections).[3]

The standard method of estimation/inference with latent space models is Bayesian inference via Markov chain Monte Carlo (to be discussed in detail in Section 9.5) (Donovan & Mickey 2019). We can apply standard diagnostic tools to check for model convergence. At a minimum, this would include checking for proper stable random noise in the chains through visual inspection of chains using trace plots. A more rigorous approach could also be taken, such as that shown for ERG models in Chapter 5, by using various statistical tests for convergence in MCMC, such as that proposed by Geweke (1992a) or Gelman and Rubin (1992) in the case of multiple chains.

---

[3] To some, the order of topics in this section may seem backward. In other words, it could be argued that checking model diagnostics should follow specification, which itself should be derived from the theoretical question at hand; however, it's our experience that there is often little theoretical guidance on how to specify the latent space itself, and that final model specification will be the result of an iterative process of estimation, model checking, and appropriate model refinement.

However, in the latent space approach to modeling network dependencies, simply checking that individual parameters have converged is not always sufficient for verifying overall model convergence. Recall that the likelihood of the graph, under the LSM, is a function of the *distances between vertices* in the latent space and not simply on individual locations of vertices in the latent space. For this reason, one should verify that the estimated distances between vertices have also converged. In other words, just because z_i and z_j appear to have converged, that does not necessarily mean that $d(z_i, z_j)$ has converged; accordingly, $d(z_i, z_j) \, \forall \, i \neq j$ should also be checked for convergence alongside individual parameters.

Running Example: Strike Communication Network

Here we perform basic model checking as suggested in the previous text for our two-dimensional latent space model of the strike communication network. We begin by demonstrating the built-in capabilities for model diagnostics provided by the `latentnet` package. We then show, using tools from the `ina` package, how to inspect trace plots for the estimated distances between vertices.

The `mcmc.diagnostics` function from the `latentnet` package provides autocorrelation and trace plots as well as correlation and Raftery-Lewis statistics for latent space models estimated with `ergmm`. By default, the function provides results for the first four parameters in the model. In case of this model, that includes `lpY`, the log-probability of the graph; `beta.1`, the intercept term; and `Z.1.1` and `Z.1.2`, the first vertex's (Frank's) positions in the two-dimensional latent space. Here we will focus on inspecting the trace and autocorrelation plots and leave an inspection of correlation and Raftery-Lewis statistics to the reader.

Autocorrelation plots can be produced by specifying `which.diags="acf"` in the call to `mcmc.diagnostics`, while trace plots are analogously produced by specifying `which.diags= "trace"`:

```
## ACF plot
mcmc.diagnostics(strike.2d, which.diags="acf")

## Trace plot
mcmc.diagnostics(strike.2d, which.diags="trace")
```

The results of running the above code block are provided in Figures 8.5 and 8.6.

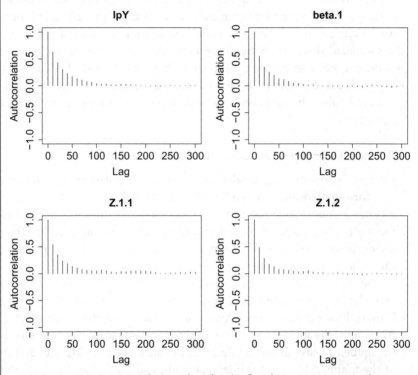

FIGURE 8.5 Autocorrelation plots for the first four parameters in the two-dimensional latent space model for the sawmill strikers' communication network.

The ACF plot in Figure 8.5 shows some autocorrelation between posterior samples from the model. This is indicated by the high positive values for the lower-lag terms; however, at around a lag of 50, the autocorrelation is fairly small. This pattern is expected with a Markov chain, as the current sample is typically very similar to the previous one in value. The chain can be "thinned" to reduce autocorrelation (King et al. 2009), which amounts to discarding steps in the Markov chain between subsequent samples. By default, the chains in ergmm are thinned by sampling every tenth step in the Markov chain. Moving to the trace plots shown in Figure 8.6 we also see that there is fairly good mixing in the MCMC chains for these same four parameters. The only possible exception is apparent in the density plot for Z.1.1 – the first latent position for the first vertex in the network – which appears to be slightly bimodal, though this is far from extreme. This

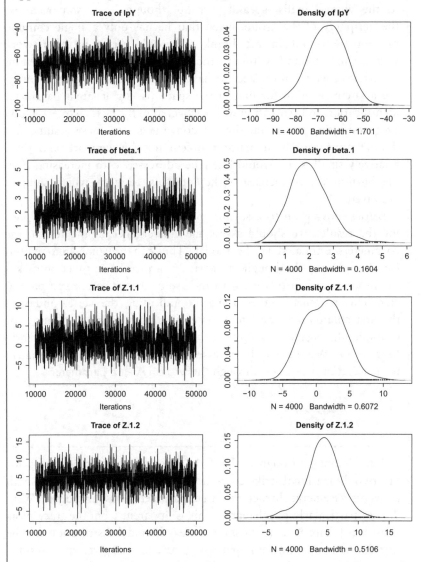

FIGURE 8.6 Trace plots for the first four parameters in the two-dimensional latent space model for the sawmill strikers' communication network.

latent location parameter belongs to Frank which, given his positioning in the network, makes an excellent choice for assessing the convergence of the model. Referring back to Figure 8.2, notice that Frank belongs to the young English-speaking group, though he is somewhat on the periphery of the group, given that he has only a single communication tie to Gill. In fact, Frank is the only person in the network with a single tie and, without other information (such as exogenous covariates), we would expect to have some difficulty clearly identifying a latent position for him in the space (issues of latent parameter identification and estimation will be covered in the next chapter). However, restricting our evaluation of convergence to these results, this doesn't appear to be a major problem for this network and these relatively small issues would likely be addressed with increasing sample burn-in or by increasing the intervals between which samples are saved.

Before moving on to assessing model fit and, ultimately, interpreting the results, we should assess the convergence of the rest of the parameters estimated in the model. This can be somewhat tedious for a large network, though the mcmc.diagnostics function makes the process straightforward with the use of the which.vars parameter. This parameter takes a matrix indicating the vertex index in the first column and the latent dimension in the second column. For example, the posterior samples for the latent positions for the twenty-four vertex (Wendle) can be accessed by passing the following matrix to mcmc.diagnostics through the which.vars parameter:

```
> (z.24 <- cbind(24, 1:2))
     [,1] [,2]
[1,]   24    1
[2,]   24    2
```

After looking through each of the latent parameter estimates for our two-dimensional strike communication network, some issues with convergence emerge. In fact, the latent parameters associated with Wendle are particularly problematic. This is apparent from the trace plots shown in Figure 8.7, which show a clear bimodal distribution for the first dimension parameter in particular. As expected given these results, the ACF plot (not shown here) also reports high levels of autocorrelation for these parameters. These diagnostics suggest the need for greater care in model estimation for the network.

However, we will leave these issues with estimation aside for the moment and move on to assessing the mixing of the distances between vertices. As we mentioned above, the likelihood of the model is based on the distance between vertices, not the locations themselves. Thus, it's wise to look at the posterior samples of these distances.

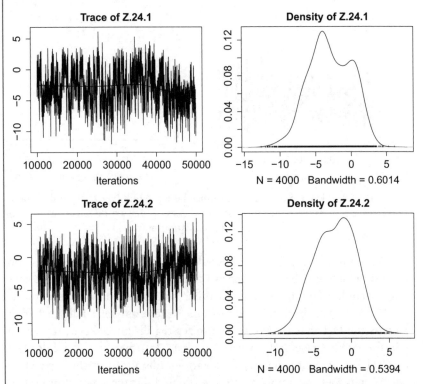

FIGURE 8.7 Trace plots for the first four parameters in the two-dimensional latent space model for the sawmill strikers' communication network.

For our purposes, we choose to look just at the sample distances between Gill (vertex 2) and Wendle (vertex 24). We can do so using the `mcmc_distance` function from the `ina` package. This function extracts the pairwise samples from the `ergmm` object for the specified vertices and returns a `coda` object, which makes performing diagnostics easy. For example, the following block of code creates a trace plot of these distances, which is shown in Figure 8.8.

```
1   ## Plot posterior distances of between vertex 2 (Gill) and
2   ## vertex 24 (Wendle).
3   plot(mcmc_distance(strike.2d, 2, 24))
```

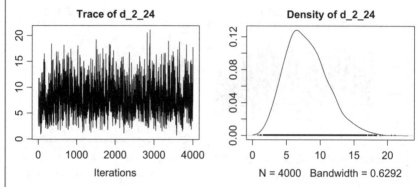

FIGURE 8.8 Trace plots for the distance between Gill (vertex 2) and Wendle (vertex 24) as taken from the posterior draws of the two-dimensional LSM in the strike communication network.

At initial glance, the trace plot doesn't appear to raise serious concerns, which may be a bit surprising given the issues with the estimates for Wendle's latent position. In other words, we may have expected a bimodal distribution of the distances here as well. This just highlights the fact that the model optimizes the distances between vertices in the latent space and not the locations. In other words, while there may be issues with identifying locations (discussed in the next chapter), that does not imply that the estimated distances between vertices have not converged to stable estimates. However, this is not a general rule; that is, we will not always see bimodal locations and stable distances. In a more serious application, all of the pairwise distances should be inspected. But this can be a daunting task in a large network. In this small example, there are $(24 \times 23)/2 = 276$ pairwise distances to be estimated and reviewed. Thus, in larger networks, it would be useful to use other tools (such as `geweke.diag` and `autocorr.diag` from `coda`) to identify potentially problematic parameters in a more automated way.

8.5 MODEL FIT

The previous section discussed some ways to assess model convergence for latent space models. Once there is confidence that the model has converged to stable parameter estimates, one should move to determining whether the model returns results that appear to be reasonable with respect to the original network. In other words, does the model fit the network that is being analyzed? For binary ties and a model that excludes covariates, this would suggest comparing predicted network densities to the original network. The expectation is that the model predicts network densities that are in line with the network being modeled. Going further, one should check that the model does a reasonable job of predicting individual edges between vertices. This can be done with standard tools, such as by calculating the area under the receiver operator curve, F1 statistic, evaluating precision, recall or, in the case of weighted edges, RMSE or another appropriate metric.

Running Example: Strike Communication Network

Here we begin by checking to see whether the two-dimensional model for the strike communication network we estimated above reasonably

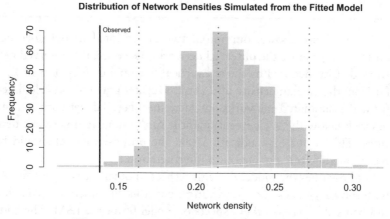

Distribution of Network Densities Simulated from the Fitted Model

FIGURE 8.9 Histogram comparing simulated densities of networks generated by the proposed two-dimensional LSM to the observed strike communication network. The solid vertical line shows the density of ties in the observed network, while the vertical gray lines mark the 2.5 percent, 50 percent, and 97.5 percent quantiles of the densities for 500 networks simulated from the proposed model.

reflects the observed network. We will first compare the density of ties in the original network to the density expected under the estimated model. As was the case with the ERGM, the easiest way to do this is to simulate many networks from the model and then calculate the density for each. The following code block shows how this can be done for the estimated model. It simulates 500 networks from the model, calculates the network density for each, and then produces a histogram of the results along with a comparison to the observed network. The results are shown in Figure 8.9.

```
1    ## Simulate from the fitted model, calculate the network density
2    ## for each of those networks.
3    set.seed(123)
4    densities <- sapply(simulate(strike.2d, 500)[[2]],
                network.density)
5
6    ## Create a histogram comparing the densities of the simulated
                networks
7    hist(densities, breaks="FD",
8            main="Distribution of Network Densities Simulated from
9                    the Fitted Model",
10           xlab="Network Density")
11   abline(v=network.density(Strike), col="black", lty=1, lwd=3)
12   abline(v=quantile(densities, probs=c(0.025, 0.5, 0.975)),
13                    lty=2, lwd=3)
```

As the figure shows, our initial two-dimensional model does not faithfully reproduce the observed network. As we see, the observed network density, denoted by the red vertical line (at a density of 0.138), is far from the median density of 0.210 (the center gray line) as calculated from the simulated networks. In fact, the observed network density lies well below the 2.5 percent quantile of the simulated network densities. This is our first indication that the proposed model should be reevaluated before moving on to interpretation.

But how does the model do with respect to other measures of fit? As with the ergm package, latentnet has a useful function, gof, that can be used to assess other aspects of model fit for the LSM. The code below, for example, performs a similar process as above to evaluate model fit. Here, we use the function to simulate 500 networks from the estimated model, calculate the degree distribution and minimum geodesic distance distribution for each of the simulated networks, and then plot these distributions along with those of the original network.

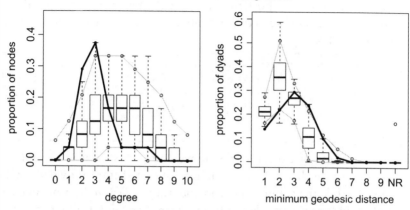

FIGURE 8.10 GOF plots for the proposed two-dimensional LSM for the strike communication network, suggesting a poor fit to the network.

```
par(mfrow=c(1, 2))
plot(gof(strike.2d, GOF= ~ degree + dist, nsim=500))
```

Figure 8.10 again shows that the two-dimensional model we have estimated for the strike communication network does not fit the observed network well. In the plot on the left, we see that the degree distribution for the observed network (represented as the black line) shows many more 2° and 3° vertices than the simulated networks, which tend to have many more high-degree vertices. In the plot on the right, we also see that the minimum geodesic distances in the observed network are typically greater than the simulated networks. Each of these is a symptom of the estimated model producing networks that are too dense, which suggests that, on average, the distances between vertices in the latent space is too small.

The preceding analysis makes it clear that more work should put into fitting a model to the strike communication network. However, for pedagogical purposes, it may be interesting to explore the performance of the model despite its shortcomings. To that end, we will now look at the model's performance with respect to how well it predicts individual ties observed in the network. In a network with binary ties, one of the easiest ways to do that is to calculate the confusion matrix, which compares the predicted outcomes for the model to those of the network itself. The snippet below provides the R code to produce a confusion matrix based on the posterior mean of the parameters for prediction from the model (a predictive probability of 0.5 is used as the cutoff in this example).

```
1   ## Create confusion matrix for the estimated model using
2   ## posterior mean estimates for prediction
3   y_star <- predict(strike.2d, type="pmean")
4   y <- as.matrix(summary(strike.2d)$model$Yg)
5   cm <- table(prediction=y_star[lower.tri(y_star)] > 0.5,
6                truth=y[lower.tri(y)] == 1)
```

The results of executing the above code are shown in the following output. In the table, rows indicate the prediction provided by the model, while the columns indicate the truth (TRUE indicating an edge, FALSE indicating no edge). Overall, using the counts along the diagonals – which correspond to the true negatives and true positives – we see that 82.6 percent $((192 + 36)/276)$ of the ties in the network were correctly predicted by the model. More interesting, perhaps, is that the confusion matrix makes the breakdown between false positives and false negatives readily apparent. As shown, the vast majority of the errors produced by the model are false positives (46 vs. 2 false negatives). Given the results presented above in the goodness-of-fit plots, this is unsurprising, the predicted model has a tendency to overpredict ties.

```
1   print(cm)
2              truth
3   prediction FALSE TRUE
4        FALSE   192    2
5         TRUE    46   36
```

The confusion matrix offers one last opportunity to look more closely at the performance of the proposed model. Since there are just two false negatives – observed ties that the model did not predict would exist – we may want to look more closely at which vertices were involved with these ties. Inspecting the prediction and adjacency matrices, we find that the false negatives produced by the model involve the ties between Bob and Alejandro and between Bob and Norm. Recalling the description of the network, we shouldn't be surprised at these predictions. As was mentioned in that discussion, Bob and Alejandro are likely connected because Alejandro is the only Spanish speaker with a knowledge of English, while Bob was the only English speaker with Spanish experience. At the same time, Norm helped get Bob his job, which helps explain their connections. These are relationships that the model should have a hard time uncovering given the pattern of ties these actors have in the network overall. However, even in this ill-fitted model, it shows the usefulness of the LSM approach. By inspecting where the model fails, we may be able to uncover exogenous factors that drive tie formation. And by incorporating such exogenous factors into the model-building process, ideally we can improve our understanding of the overall network formation process.

8.6 MODEL SPECIFICATION

The previous sections showed how one fits a basic LSM to a network, verifies that the estimation converged, and inspects model fit and predictive performance. Here we look more closely at model specification. Specifically, in Section 8.6.1, we look at how exogenous covariates – predictors that are generated outside of the network but are expected to affect edge formation – can be incorporated into a latent space model. In this discussion there will be many parallels to that found in the ERGM chapters. Then in Section 8.6.2, we tackle the issue of choosing the dimensions of the latent space. This appears to be something that is not approached in a systematic or consistent manner in the literature, primarily because standard tools for model selection (e.g., Bayesian information criterion) have not been shown to be valid for this purpose. We will consider some alternative approaches to choosing the latent dimension, once again leveraging posterior predictive checks and predictive performance.

8.6.1 Exogenous Covariates and Vertex-Specific Effects

Up to this point, we have looked at estimating minimalist latent space models in which only the latent locations for vertices in the latent space and an intercept term were included. But such barebones models are not always of use to practitioners, who may be interested in exogenous characteristics of actors beyond their structural location in networks. For example, scholars of international trade may be interested in assessing the importance of countries' GDP or geographic proximity in understanding trade imbalances (Ward, Ahlquist & Rozenas 2013); sociologists may wish to assess the role of sex or race in adolescent friendships formation (Shrum, Cheek & MacD. Hunter 1988); and political scientists may study the influence of budget and industry group on development of interest group networks in US politics (Box-Steffensmeier & Christenson 2014). Luckily, as with the ERGM, the latent space model can readily accommodate the inclusion of vertex- or dyad-level covariates, making it possible to explore questions such as these. As in the ERGM chapters, we discuss two types of exogenous covariates in the section below: vertex-level covariates and edge-level covariates.

As the reader may recall, vertex-level covariates are included in the model when it's suspected that some attribute of an individual actor affects the number of ties sent to and/or from the actor. Vertex-level covariates come in four general flavors: measures of sociality, popularity, degree prediction, and homophily. In the first case, you may believe, for instance, that a directed tie from i to j is more likely if some covariate value of the sender, X_i, is larger. In other words, you hypothesize:

$$\Pr(N_{ij} = 1 \mid X_i \text{ is large}) > \Pr(N_{ij} = 1 \mid X_i \text{ is small}). \qquad (8.5)$$

One would expect the coefficient on X_i to be positive and statistically significant when included in an LSM. This is an example of a *sociality* term – an exogenous characteristic that is associated with greater sending of ties. Terms could also be added to capture the reverse tendency – a *popularity* term – where a change in some exogenous factor is expected to change the number of connections an actor receives. For example, in a model of communication networks, an analyst may expect cities with higher population to receive a greater number of inbound telephone calls, and in an online social network, one may expect Hollywood actors who make more movies to gain more followers.

These substantive features of sociality and popularity do not apply to undirected networks, of course, where there is no directionality to ties. To capture similar effects in undirected networks we can instead include what are a referred to as *degree prediction* terms in our latent space models. These statistics are calculated from one or more exogenous covariates of *both* vertices in a dyad and, as the name suggests, are covariates that are expected to increase (decrease) the number of connections a vertex has. For example, for numeric covariates, it's common for this statistic to be the sum of each actors' value on the covariate. So, in a model explaining international trade, the sum of each country's GDP would be included in an LSM to account for the expectation that trade would be more common when total economic output of the countries was larger.

The final major category of vertex-level terms we will discuss is *homophily*. Recall that homophily is an inclination for actors of the same type to be more likely to interact. For example, in adolescent friendship networks, friendship ties may be stronger or more common between people of the same sex or race. When a vertex-level covariate, call it X_i, is categorical, homophily terms are defined simply as

$$X_{ij} = \begin{cases} 0, & \text{if } X_i \neq X_j \\ 1, & \text{if } X_i = X_j. \end{cases} \tag{8.6}$$

Here, a positive coefficient on X_{ij} would indicate that homophily is an important component in tie formation in a network, whereas a negative and significant coefficient would be indicative of heterophily – the tendency for opposites to attract. Continuous or numeric exogenous covariates can also be used to capture homophily effects in latent space models. In this case, one would use some function of X_i and X_j, such as the absolute difference, as the term in the model.[4]

As in the ERGM, edge effects can also be included in latent space models. These are characteristics that are measured at the level of the dyad (either directed or undirected) in a network, which makes it possible to incorporate information from other types of relations into a model. For instance, in analyzing international trade, one may want to include geographic distance between two countries as a factor affecting the amount of trade, and in a model explaining friendships in a high school, the number of shared classes could be included to account for shared interests. One strength of the LSM over the ERGM with respect to edge effects is that edge-weights are often not necessary in the LSM as they can be directly accounted for in the left-hand-side (i.e., as a weighted edge, N_{ij}) of the modeling equation, though incorporating them as part of the edge itself does change the nature of the questions being asked. See Chapter 10 for a discussion of latent space models with weighted edges.

As should be clear, the terms discussed above are directly comparable to those discussed in the ERGM chapters. Vertex- or edge-level covariates can be treated pretty much the same in both models. And with respect to the interpretation of the estimated coefficients for those models, the similarities remain and should be familiar to practitioners used to working with more standard applied regression models; that is,

---

[4] It's important to note the difference between homophily terms and degree prediction terms in undirected networks. In the homophily terms, there is an explicit comparison made between the covariate values, such as the difference between ages of two people. In degree prediction, an aggregate of the two values is used. This is an important distinction to make when interpreting these effects.

the statistical significance of exogenous covariates can be assessed with an inspection of coefficient standard errors or, better, the credible intervals calculated from the posterior (since most implementations take a Bayesian approach due to the complexity of the models). Beyond statistical significance, however, the interpretation of the *practical* significance of a particular covariate is more complex and requires its own detailed discussion, which can be found in Section 8.7.

The similarities between the LSM and ERGM mentioned in foregoing discussion of exogenous covariates should not, however, be viewed as extending to endogenous network characteristics. In other words, it is not possible to use just any modeling terms from the ERGM framework in an LSM. Broadly speaking, one can freely incorporate modeling terms that are "dyad-independent." But this is somewhat confusing terminology. As we saw above, one can include terms in the LSM that incorporate effects based on the value of a covariate (or set of covariates) from one or both actors making up a dyad; that is, it's quite okay to include dyad-level variables in the model (e.g., homophily), and this is often a desire of practitioners to include such terms. The dyad-independence of modeling terms, in the terminology of network analysis, refers to the independence *between different dyads*; that is, they are terms that do not depend on the existence or absence of ties between *other* dyads. On the other hand, dyad-dependent terms are those that render the likelihood of a tie between two vertices dependent on the states of one or more of the other ties in the network. These are the terms that make the ERGM approach to modeling networks so powerful, such as k-star, triangle, and mutuality terms. Why can't we (or shouldn't we) include dyad-dependent terms in an LSM? Recall that the LSM is a model that assumes independence of edges conditional on the latent locations of vertices in the latent space (and exogenous covariates). Including such terms induces dependence between dyads.

Running Example: Strike Communication Network

In this section, we extend our strike communication network example to include exogenous covariates. The network object itself contains just a single covariate, group, as described in the first example section of this chapter. However, as noted, the group variable is itself a composite of the actors' ages and language usage. For example, Alejandro belongs to the young Spanish-speaker group, making it possible to define two covariates for him: young=TRUE and spanish=TRUE. Alejandro also speaks English, meaning we can set english=TRUE. In the code below, we define these three vertex-level covariates for each of the actors in the network. Clearly, spanish and english are indicators of whether the individual speaks that language, while young is an indicator of whether the individual is in the younger or older group of workers. In an ideal situation, we would have had a greater amount of information about the ages of the actors in this network; however, the only other detail we get with respect to ages from the original analysis is that in the older group, none of the workers were younger than thirty-eight years of age (Michael 1997).

We also construct a single dyad-level covariate, relations, which reflects additional information gleaned from the original paper, where Michael (1997) attributes a few of the observed ties to exogenous relationships among the. These include the facts that Frank and Gill are cousins, Ozzie is Karl's father, and Norm was instrumental in getting Bob his job at the sawmill. We use these relations to create a matrix (the same size as the network), where a 1 indicates whether there is an exogenous relationship between two individuals, and 0 otherwise. Obviously, this is a very sparse matrix, but it will help demonstrate the usage of dyadic covariates in the model.

```
1   ## Create two covariates indicating whether the actors speak
2   ## Spanish and English
3   grp <- Strike %v% "group"
4   spanish <- ifelse(grp == 1, 1, 0)
5   english <- ifelse(grp != 1, 1, 0)
6   young <- ifelse(grp != 3, 1, 0)
7
8   ## Bob speaks some Spanish and Alejandro speaks English
9   spanish[Strike %v% "vertex.names" == "Bob"] <- 1
10  english[Strike %v% "vertex.names" == "Alejandro"] <- 1
11
12  ## Add to the network object
13  Strike %v% "spanish" <- spanish
14  Strike %v% "english" <- english
15  Strike %v% "young" <- young
16
17  ## Construct the relations matrix (24 x 24)
18  relations <- matrix(0, nrow=length(grp), ncol=length(grp))
19  colnames(relations) <- rownames(relations) <- Strike %v%
        "vertex.names"
20  relations["Frank", "Gill"] <- relations["Gill", "Frank"]<- 1
21  relations["Ozzie", "Karl"] <- relations["Karl", "Ozzie"]<- 1
```

```
22   relations["Norm", "Bob"]  <- relations["Bob", "Norm"]<- 1
23   Strike %e% "relations"  <- relations
```

The first vertex-level covariate we will include in our model for the strike communication network is the indicator for Spanish-speaking ability. Since the variable has been coded as a zero or one, we can use the nodecov term from latentnet (if it were a factor with more than two levels, we would use nodefactor, which adds $l - 1$ variables to the model, where l is the number of levels in the factor). By default, this will add a variable to the model equal to the sum of the two values. For example, the value of the covariate for Alejandro and Bob will be 2, since both of these actors speak Spanish. On the other hand, for Norm and Gill the value will be 0, since neither of them speaks Spanish. This variable is what we referred to above as a "degree prediction" variable – it's a vertex-level covariate that captured the association between that covariate and the likelihood a tie will form within that dyad.

So, the question remains: what would we hypothesize about the relationship between the number of people in the dyad speaking Spanish and whether they often communicate with each other? This is something of a strange question. On the one hand, we know from the original plot that when *both* speakers speak Spanish, there is a high likelihood of an edge between them. In fact, if we look just at the Spanish speakers, including Bob, and constrain the network to just those five vertices, the density is 0.7, compared to the English-speaker network, which has a density of 0.15. Furthermore, the degree centrality of these vertices is also higher, on average, than the rest of the network. On average, Spanish speakers have a degree centrality of 4 in the complete network, while English speakers have a degree centrality of 3.19 (note that Bob and Alejandro are included in both of these groups). Knowing all of this, we would expect a positive effect on the nodecov term for Spanish. However, one may still wonder what we should expect when just a single person in a dyad speaks Spanish. Would we still expect a positive coefficient? We know that there are only two actors in the network that can speak a second language, which suggests that a nodecov term value of 1 would be associated with *less* communication (it's difficult to communicate if you don't speak the same language). All of this is to say that there very well could be a heterogeneous effect for the three unique values of the nodecov term: a positive effect for zero Spanish speakers, a negative effect for one Spanish speaker, and a positive effect for two Spanish speakers. In other words, `nodecov` may not be the most appropriate method of accounting for Spanish-speaking ability and the likelihood of edge formation in dyads. In subsequent sections, we model iterations, we will reevaluate this issue but, for now, what does the model say?

The code for estimating a two-dimensional LSM that includes a `nodecov` term for Spanish is show in the code block below. Note that we increase the burn-in to assure convergence.

```
## Estimate model with nodecov for spanish vertex covariate.
## Increase burn-in to help with convergence.
> strike.2d.cov1 <- ergmm(Strike ~ nodecov("spanish") +
+                         euclidean(d=2),
+                         control=control.ergmm(burnin=250000),
+                         seed=10,
+                         verbose=TRUE)
> summary(strike.2d.cov1)


===========================
Summary of model fit
===========================

Formula:   Strike ~ nodecov("spanish") + euclidean(d = 2)
Attribute: edges
Model:     Bernoulli
MCMC sample of size 4000, draws are 10 iterations apart, after
          burnin
       of 250000 iterations.
Covariate coefficients posterior means:
               Estimate    2.5%  97.5% 2*min(Pr(>0),Pr(<0))
(Intercept)    1.82703 0.43675 3.6104                0.007 **
nodecov.spanish 1.45573 0.27459 2.8882               0.011 *
---
Signif. codes: 0 '***' 0.001 '**' 0.01 '*' 0.05 '.' 0.1 ' ' 1

Overall BIC:          314.4861
Likelihood BIC:       119.5065
Latent space/clustering BIC:      194.9795


Covariate coefficients MKL:
               Estimate
(Intercept)    -0.0158795
nodecov.spanish 1.0778107
```

According to the model, the `nodecov.spanish` term is statistically significant at the standard 0.05 level. This indicates that when more Spanish speakers are present in a dyad, the more likely there will be an edge (in this case, an established pattern of communication).

However, for the reasons we discussed above, this modeling term probably doesn't address the question we want to answer. What we want know is whether shared language understanding is associated with a greater probability of an edge forming. In other words, we want to check for the importance of language homophily in edge formation. We turn to that next.

Homophily can be included in the model using the `nodematch` terms from `latentnet`. By default, a single *uniform* homophily term is included, which just means the effect for different levels of a covariate (i.e., both members of a dyad being Spanish speakers, and both members of a dyad being non-Spanish speakers) are assumed to be the same. Specifying `diff=TRUE` in the call to `nodematch` incorporates *differential* homophily into the model, where it is assumed that common values of different levels of the input covariate could have different effects on edge formation. In the example below, we include the second formulation since we expect that two members of a dyad speaking Spanish will have a different effect than neither speaking Spanish.

```
## Estimate model with nodematch for spanish, a homophily term.
> strike.2d.cov2 <- ergmm(Strike ~ nodematch("spanish",
    diff=TRUE) +
+                              euclidean(d=2),
+                              control=control.ergmm(burnin=250000),
+                              seed=10,
+                              verbose=TRUE)
> summary(strike.2d.cov2)


==========================
Summary of model fit
==========================

Formula:   Strike ~ nodematch("spanish", diff = TRUE) +
    euclidean(d = 2)
Attribute: edges
Model:     Bernoulli
MCMC sample of size 4000, draws are 10 iterations apart, after
    burnin
    of 250000 iterations.
Covariate coefficients posterior means:
                        Estimate     2.5%   97.5% 2*min(Pr(>0),Pr(<0))
(Intercept)             1.26563 -0.83212 3.8349                 0.2860
nodematch.spanish.0     0.32000 -1.28739 1.8851                 0.6775
nodematch.spanish.1     5.50932  2.28391 9.8797                 0.0005
                        ***
---
Signif. codes:  0 '***' 0.001 '**' 0.01 '*' 0.05 '.' 0.1 ' ' 1
```

```
25
26   Overall BIC:          300.407
27   Likelihood BIC:       134.4763
28   Latent space/clustering BIC:        165.9307
29
30   Covariate coefficients MKL:
31                         Estimate
32   (Intercept)           -0.3787111
33   nodematch.spanish.0   0.1384549
34   nodematch.spanish.1   3.2003674
```

We see from the results above that there is a strong positive effect for the Spanish homophily term (estimated coefficient of 5.5 and statistically significant at the 0.05 level). On the other hand, there is not a statistically significant effect for *neither* vertex in a dyad speaking Spanish. Since spanish is a binary variable, we can reinterpret this as meaning there is no difference in the rate of tie formation between dyads in which both vertices do not speak Spanish, and dyads in which just one vertex speaks Spanish. From what we know about the network, this is unsurprising. The density of connections between English speakers is close to the overall density of the network (since the majority of the network are English-only speakers), so we wouldn't expect there to be an effect for this covariate.

Now we will turn to looking at the importance of age in the formation of the strike communication network. Given the observed network, it's reasonable to believe that having shared membership in an age cohort is positively associated with increased communication ties. Homophily with respect to age is a common finding in social network analysis (e.g., Mazur & Richards 2011, Utz & Jankowski 2016). This effect may also be highly correlated with language (all Spanish speakers are young, after all). To test the importance of age cohort membership, we include a differential homophily term for the young in the next model version.

```
1   ## Include differential homophily for age
2   > strike.2d.cov3 <- ergmm(Strike ~ nodematch("spanish",
        diff=TRUE) +
3   +                         nodematch("young", diff=TRUE) +
4   +                         euclidean(d=2),
5   +                 control=control.ergmm(burnin=250000),
6   +                 seed=10,
7   +                 verbose=TRUE)
8   > summary(strike.2d.cov3)
9
```

```
10   =============================
11   Summary of model fit
12   =============================
13
14   Formula:    Strike ~ nodematch("spanish", diff = TRUE) +
             nodematch("young",
15       diff = TRUE) + euclidean(d = 2)
16   Attribute: edges
17   Model:     Bernoulli
18   MCMC sample of size 4000, draws are 10 iterations apart, after
             burnin
19       of 250000 iterations.
20   Covariate coefficients posterior means:
21                       Estimate     2.5%   97.5%
                               2*min(Pr(>0),Pr(<0))
22   (Intercept)         -1.556556 -3.933093 0.8279        0.187
23   nodematch.spanish.0  0.058742 -1.738096 1.7471        0.939
24   nodematch.spanish.1  3.742177  0.876206 7.1817        0.010 **
25   nodematch.young.0    4.082358  2.242321 6.6392        <2e-16 ***
26   nodematch.young.1    3.666500  1.895247 5.8823        <2e-16 ***
27   ---
28   Signif. codes:  0 '***' 0.001 '**' 0.01 '*' 0.05 '.' 0.1 ' ' 1
29
30   Overall BIC:           274.138
31   Likelihood BIC:        128.0477
32   Latent space/clustering BIC:       146.0903
33
34   Covariate coefficients MKL:
35                         Estimate
36   (Intercept)         -2.5210468
37   nodematch.spanish.0 -0.1162707
38   nodematch.spanish.1  2.3515437
39   nodematch.young.0    3.1795619
40   nodematch.young.1    2.7869530
```

There are a few things to note from the above model estimate. First, both terms for homophily are statistically significant, suggesting (as we suspected) that shared age cohort membership is an important factor in determining whether actors in the network communicate. Second, the inclusion of these effects did decrease the magnitude of the coefficient on the Spanish-speaking homophily, though the effect is still strong and statistically significant. Finally, the effect sizes for age cohort homophily

– nodematch.young.0 and nodematch.young.1 – are quite
similar. This suggests using a *uniform* homophily term for young may
be warranted. In other words, the effect of shared age cohort membership appears to be the same across cohorts. We test this with the
following model.

```
> strike.2d.cov4 <- ergmm(Strike ~ nodematch("spanish",
      diff=TRUE) +
+                               nodematch("young", diff=FALSE) +
+                               euclidean(d=2),
+                           control=control.ergmm(burnin=250000),
+                           seed=10,
+                           verbose=TRUE)
> summary(strike.2d.cov4)


==========================
Summary of model fit
==========================

Formula:   Strike ~ nodematch("spanish", diff = TRUE) +
      nodematch("young",
      diff = FALSE) + euclidean(d = 2)
Attribute: edges
Model:     Bernoulli
MCMC sample of size 4000, draws are 10 iterations apart, after
      burnin
      of 250000 iterations.
Covariate coefficients posterior means:
                    Estimate    2.5%  97.5% 2*min(Pr(>0),Pr(<0))
(Intercept)         -1.79720 -4.02524 0.4140          0.1060
nodematch.spanish.0  0.18404 -1.40034 1.6854          0.7860
nodematch.spanish.1  3.60021  0.82602 6.9351          0.0095 **
nodematch.young      3.85421  2.34784 5              <2e-16 ***
---
Signif. codes:  0 '***' 0.001 '**' 0.01 '*' 0.05 '.' 0.1 ' ' 1

Overall BIC:            267.8256
Likelihood BIC:         126.3129
Latent space/clustering BIC:      141.5127

Covariate coefficients MKL:
                       Estimate
(Intercept)          -2.773310077
nodematch.spanish.0  -0.002957289
nodematch.spanish.1   2.263955442
nodematch.young       3.059124134
```

As suspected, the uniform homophily term for age cohort membership retains its statistical significance in the above model, while the coefficient is in line with the terms for differential age cohort homophily in the previous model. The principle of parsimony suggests the latter model is a better fit for the strike communication network.

The final exogenous covariate we will look at for this network is the `relations` edge-level covariate we defined above. As discussed, this variable captures the various relationships identified by Michael (1997). Since these were mentioned as explaining particular connections in the network, we expect them to have a strong, positive association with edge formation in the network. The code below shows the results of including this variable in the model.

```
> strike.2d.cov5 <- ergmm(Strike ~ nodematch("spanish",
  diff=TRUE) +
+                               nodematch("young", diff=FALSE) +
+                               edgecov(relations) +
+                               euclidean(d=2),
+                      control=control.ergmm(burnin=250000),
+                      seed=10,
+                      verbose=TRUE)
> summary(strike.2d.cov5)


===========================
Summary of model fit
===========================

Formula:   Strike ~ nodematch("spanish", diff = TRUE) +
       nodematch("young",
       diff = FALSE) + edgecov(relations) + euclidean(d = 2)
Attribute: edges
Model:     Bernoulli
MCMC sample of size 4000, draws are 10 iterations apart, after
       burnin
       of 250000 iterations.
Covariate coefficients posterior means:
                      Estimate    2.5%   97.5% 2*min(Pr(>0),Pr(<0))
(Intercept)           -3.34657 -6.38819 -0.5404         0.0220 *
nodematch.spanish.0    0.21255 -1.59221  1.8555         0.7975
nodematch.spanish.1    3.83665  0.97807  7.3548         0.0105 *
nodematch.young        5.35213  3.05593  8.3650         <2e-16 ***
edgecov.relations     28.92336  8.13349 69.3756         <2e-16 ***
---
Signif. codes:  0 '***' 0.001 '**' 0.01 '*' 0.05 '.' 0.1 ' ' 1
```

```
30
31    Overall BIC:          252.8761
32    Likelihood BIC:       109.1342
33    Latent space/clustering BIC:      143.742
34
35    Covariate coefficients MKL:
36                              Estimate
37    (Intercept)             -3.8801715
38    nodematch.spanish.0      0.0479944
39    nodematch.spanish.1      2.3600172
40    nodematch.young          4.1248230
41    edgecov.relations        8.6238276
```

As we surmised, the coefficient for edgecov.relations is large and statistically significant. The inclusion of this variable didn't affect the conclusions regarding the effects of other terms included in the model, but it seems to have improved the fit of the model. How can we tell that fit has improved? In comparing different LSM specifications – and where the only change we make is in the exogenous covariate terms – we can leverage the Bayesian information criterion (BIC) (Wang 2009) to help select the best performing model. The code below calculates the BIC for each of the last five model variants and presents the results as a table.

```
1    > strike.bic <- sapply(list(strike.2d.cov1, strike.2d.cov2,
         strike.2d.cov3,
2    +                             strike.2d.cov4, strike.2d.cov5),
         bic.ergmm)
3    > colnames(strike.bic) <- paste("Model",1:5)
4    > strike.bic
5               Model 1   Model 2   Model 3   Model 4   Model 5
6    Y          119.5065  134.4763  128.0477  126.3129  109.1342
7    Z          194.9795  165.9307  146.0903  141.5127  143.742
8    sender     0         0         0         0         0
9    receiver   0         0         0         0         0
10   sociality  0         0         0         0         0
11   overall    314.4861  300.407   274.138   267.8256  252.8761
```

The output of the bic.ergmm function is the BIC associated with each component of the model, including the likelihood of the graph

(Y); the latent locations (Z); sender, receiver, and sociality effects; and the overall BIC, which is what we are concerned with.

According to the results, the last model – model 5, which includes the Spanish differential homophily terms, the uniform homophily term for age cohort, and the relations edge covariate – results in the best fit, with a BIC of approximately 252.9. Accordingly, without any other information, this is the model one should select. However, it's also interesting to look at the predictive performance of these models. And this is an area where the LSM approach to modeling network data often shines. While they are far less parsimonious than, for instance, ERGM, the flexibility of the high-dimensional parameter space of the LSM, along with its explicit focus on modeling individual dyadic outcomes, makes the LSM excel at prediction.

In   Figure   8.11,   which   can   be   created   using   the `model_performance` function from the `ina` package, we provide

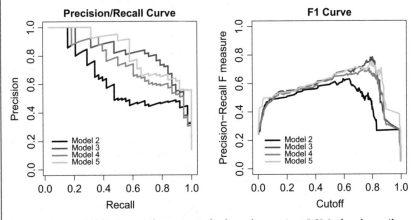

FIGURE 8.11 Predictive performance of selected covariate LSMs for the strike communication network. The plot on the left shows the precision-recall curves for the last four covariate model estimates. The plot on the right shows the associated F1 score for those models.

within-sample precision-recall and F1 curves detailing the predictive performance of the selected models (we excluded the model 1 with the misspecified covariate term from the charts, just as we did when comparing BICs). Neither of these plots provide unambiguous guidance on which model performs the best. In the precision-recall curve on the left, model 5 – the one also selected according to the BIC above – seems to be "higher" for lower ranges of recall, though for a good portion of the plot, model 3 appears to be the best performer. Similarly, in the plot on the right, which includes the F1 statistics, where every point is calculated as geometric mean of precision and recall – the formula for the F1 score is 2 × ((precision × recall)/(precision + recall)) – there is very little difference in the apparent performance of the last three models. Digging in further, one can calculate the area under the ROC curve (AUC), which indicates model 5 is the best performer, with an AUC of 0.968 versus 0.962 for model 3. Overall, given the results of comparing the BIC and the model performance, we would select model 5.

The question remains though whether we picked the right number of dimensions for the model. We will turn to answering this question after addressing the important problem of selecting the appropriate dimensions for the latent space.

8.6.2 Considering the Dimension of the Latent Space

This section addresses something we have ignored until now: the issue of specifying the dimensions of the latent space. This is an important theoretical and modeling decision that needs to be made when taking the LSM approach to applied network analysis. Unfortunately, this is a topic largely ignored in the statistical literature, where practitioners seem to default – as we have done in the foregoing examples – to using two dimensions due to the ease with which one can visualize the space. But in practical applications, where the objective is to uncover the generative process behind the network, this is an unsatisfying approach to modeling, which can inhibit our understanding of the network being studied.

How should applied work approach the issue of dimension selection? There are two approaches typically used in the literature. First, one should always lean on theory, when possible. Occasionally, there are good theoretical reasons to choose a particular number of dimensions. For instance, when estimating a latent space model for party switching in the Polish parliament in his dissertation, one of the authors chose a two-dimensional latent space that was consistent with the literature on political competition in the country (Morgan 2015, Chapter 2).

But how many dimensions should we choose when there is little theoretical guidance? Practitioners often lean on a second approach of applying standard model fitting criteria to determining the number of dimensions that should be used in a model. For example, posterior predictive checks, as we used in Section 8.5, can provide a clear indication of how well models with different numbers of dimensions fit the observed network. And when there is little apparent difference between models with respect to these checks, practitioners can often glean more insight with a comparison of predictive performance of the models. Precision and recall measures (and the derivative F1 score) are often particularly useful in networks with binary ties, since simple accuracy metrics can be distorted by the overall sparcity of network connections. One important thing to note is that other commonly applied tools, such as the Bayesian information criterion (BIC), are not known to be valid for model selection with respect to the dimension of the model.[5]

But from a practical perspective, the question remains whether choosing the wrong dimension for the latent space is such a bad thing. For example, in large and complex networks, it is certainly possible to specify models with a high number of dimensions – say, five or even ten. However, at a minimum, specifying such a large model violates the principle of parsimony. More worrisome though are issues of overfitting, since each added dimension requires that the model estimate one new parameter for each vertex in the network. Luckily, in our experience, networks can often be fit well with far fewer dimensions. This is in line with an argument by Hoff et al. (2002) in their original formulation of the LSM. They argue that, for undirected binary networks at least, and absent covariate data, even complex network dependencies are "representable" by relatively low-dimensional latent spaces (Hoff et al. 2002, pp. 1091–1092). They show, for example, that the Florentine Family data are representable by a two-dimensional model.

However, there may sometimes be good reasons to increase the number of dimensions beyond the range of one to three most often found in the literature,[6] but when doing so, one needs to contend with something analogous to the curse of dimensionality in the nearest neighbor or clustering models. This is because increasing the number of dimensions in the model increases the average distance between vertices, even if the data in any single dimension follow a "reasonable" distribution.

---

[5] In fact, in the `latentnet` R package, a warning is shown whenever a model summary is printed stating this fact.
[6] One situation may be in the case of affiliation networks, where one wants to model several different affiliations simultaneously, giving each their own dimension.

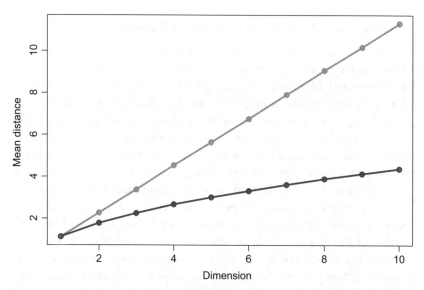

FIGURE 8.12 Mean Euclidean and Manhattan distance between points in latent spaces of various dimensions.

Figure 8.12 demonstrates this relationship between distance and dimensionality for one-through ten-dimension distances. For each latent space, the chart shows the mean Manhattan (L_1) and Euclidean (L_2) distance for points in these spaces when each point is generated by a multivariate normal distribution.[7] As is clearly the case, the mean distance for each metric increases as the dimension increases despite the centroid of the data being fixed at the origin. From a theoretical perspective, the mean distances increasing with increased dimensionality shouldn't matter too much because the model should adapt by pulling the vertices closer together to compensate. But from a practical perspective, computation and model convergence often becomes a concern in higher dimensions.

As a general rule – one that may seem somewhat dissatisfying – we suggest keeping the number of dimensions in the latent space small. If there are issues with fit, look for exogenous covariates that may help improve things before aggressively increasing the dimensions.

---

[7] This chart was produced by simulating 10,000 points from an s-dimensional multivariate normal for each $s \in 1, 2 \ldots, 10$ and then calculating the mean distance between the simulated points.

Running Example: Strike Communication Network

In the previous example sections, we estimated a basic two-dimensional latent space model for the strike communications network. We then supplemented this model with the addition of three exogenous covariate terms: a differential homophily term for Spanish speaking, a uniform homophily term for age cohort, and an edge covariate indicating whether two actors in a dyad had an established relationship outside of work, which may have contributed to their communications at work.

One important aspect of LSM fitting that was ignored in these discussions was how we decided on a two-dimensional latent space. In fact, the choice was made for pedagogical convenience, as it facilitated a comparison with heuristic plotting methods and simplified interpretation of the model. However, this was a strong assumption that, in a serious modeling exercise, should be validated by comparing results to models estimated with different dimensions for the latent space. Here we revisit this decision with a comparison of model performance and goodness of fit for different numbers of dimensions.

We will specifically focus on comparing the performance and goodness of fit for models of 1- through four-dimensions. As we mentioned in the theoretical discussion of dimension choice, even complex networks can often be fit with relatively few dimensions. Furthermore, the principle of parsimony and modeling concerns leads us to begin with specifying models with fewer dimensions.

The code block below estimates four models for one through four dimensions. For this set of models, we make two changes to our estimation process. First, we have switched to using the squared-Euclidean distance instead of the standard Euclidean distance that we used in previous models. This was done by specifying `euclidean2` in the model formula. We made this change because it helped speed convergence somewhat, while it also showed marginally better performance on the goodness-of-fit tests. Second, we have increased the number of iterations for the MCMC burn-in as well as the sampling interval. This was necessary to achieve reasonable mixing of the three- and four-dimensional models. While likely unnecessary, to assure comparable results, these settings were used for all models.

```
1   ctrl <- control.ergmm(burnin=750000, interval=100)
2   strike.1d2 <- ergmm(Strike ~ nodematch("spanish", diff=TRUE) +
3                       nodematch("young", diff=FALSE) +
4                       edgecov(relations) +
```

```
 5                               euclidean2(d=1),
 6                   control=ctrl, seed=10, verbose=TRUE)
 7
 8      strike.2d2 <- ergmm(Strike ~ nodematch("spanish", diff=TRUE) +
 9                          nodematch("young", diff=FALSE) +
10                          edgecov(relations) +
11                          euclidean2(d=2),
12                   control=ctrl, seed=10, verbose=TRUE)
13
14      strike.3d2 <- ergmm(Strike ~ nodematch("spanish", diff=TRUE) +
15                          nodematch("young", diff=FALSE) +
16                          edgecov(relations) +
17                          euclidean2(d=3),
18                   control=ctrl, seed=10, verbose=TRUE)
19
20      strike.4d2 <- ergmm(Strike ~ nodematch("spanish", diff=TRUE) +
21                          nodematch("young", diff=FALSE) +
22                          edgecov(relations) +
23                          euclidean2(d=4),
24                   control=ctrl, seed=10, verbose=TRUE)
```

We begin by checking to verify that our decision to use the squared-Euclidean distance didn't change the results significantly. Below we provide a summary of the two-dimensional model, which we can compare back to the best-performing model discussed in the last section. Notice from the summary output that while some of the coefficients changed in magnitude, substantively, the results did not change.

```
 1      > summary(strike.2d2)
 2
 3      ==========================
 4      Summary of model fit
 5      ==========================
 6
 7      Formula:   Strike ~ nodematch("spanish", diff = TRUE) +
                   nodematch("young",
 8          diff = FALSE) + edgecov(relations) + euclidean2(d = 2)
 9      Attribute: edges
10      Model:        Bernoulli
11      MCMC sample of size 4000, draws are 100 iterations apart, after
                   burnin
12          of 750000 iterations.
13      Covariate coefficients posterior means:
14                      Estimate    2.5%   97.5% 2*min(Pr(>0),Pr(<0))
15      (Intercept)     -3.39890 -6.38197 -0.7675            0.0100 **
16      nodematch.spanish.0 -0.47804 -2.87848  1.4972        0.6975
17      nodematch.spanish.1  8.52252  1.82188 19.8170        0.0065 **
```

```
18    nodematch.young        5.74889  3.32841  9.1216              <2e-16 ***
19    edgecov.relations     32.41736  9.81798 69.7834              <2e-16 ***
20    ---
21    Signif. codes:  0 '***' 0.001 '**' 0.01 '*' 0.05 '.' 0.1 ' ' 1
22
23    Overall BIC:              210.132
24    Likelihood BIC:           95.0792
25    Latent space/clustering BIC:        115.0528
26
27    Covariate coefficients MKL:
28                            Estimate
29    (Intercept)           -3.7571757
30    nodematch.spanish.0   -0.3765211
31    nodematch.spanish.1    2.9980509
32    nodematch.young        4.2992159
33    edgecov.relations      8.3489846
```

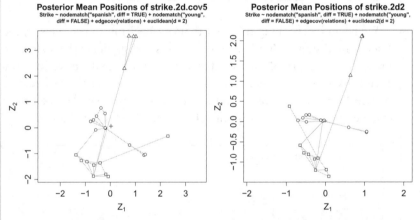

FIGURE 8.13 Comparing the posterior means for the latent locations estimated for models' Euclidean distance (left plot) and the squared-Euclidean distance (right plot).

It's also useful to compare the latent locations estimated for each of these models. Figure 8.13 below provides this comparison. The plot on the left shows the posterior estimated for the latent locations in the model using the standard Euclidean distance, while the plot on the right shows the locations for the model using the squared-Euclidean distance. (Note that the locations for the plot on the left were rotated to facilitate comparison with the other plot.) Overall, the relative locations of the points are quite similar in both models. The biggest difference between the models is the range of the latent space: the range of latent locations on each of the axes is approximately half the size in the second model. This is not surprising. The squared-Euclidean distance penalizes large distances to a much greater degree, forcing the distances to be closer together. For comparison, the average distance between vertices in the Euclidean distance model is approximately 2.42, while it is 1.40 for the squared-Euclidean model.

One difference between these models is the predicted location of Frank in these two spaces. Frank is represented by the outlier squares vertex in the plots. In the first model, he is estimated as having a positive value, somewhat "above" the other young English speakers, but nearer to a small group of older English speakers. In the second model, his estimated latent location is "below" the group of young English speakers, but he remains relatively close to the older English speakers. Recall that Frank only communicates with Gill, so it's not surprising that his location tends to shift between models. What is surprising is that he is located so close to the older English speakers, with whom he doesn't have any connections (the minimum geodesic distance between him and the nearest older English speaker is 4, while he's within 3 from all other young English speakers). In fact, in the second model, Frank is actually closer, on average, to the other group.

Another interesting characteristic to note is the relative positions of the Spanish-speaking group (triangles) and the young English speakers (squares). Somewhat unexpectedly, they are on the opposite sides of the space from each other, when they are connected by the edge between Bob and Alejandro. We would have expected these groups to be closer to each other given what we know about the network. Broadly speaking, these are patterns that can result when choosing the wrong dimension for the model and is something we will look at further below.

We now return to comparing the models with different numbers of specified dimensions. As was mentioned in the theoretical section, BIC is not known to be an appropriate metric for selecting the number of latent dimensions. For this reason, we begin by comparing the goodness-of-fit statistics for these four models. The code to do so can be found in the following snippet. The results can be found in Figure 8.14.

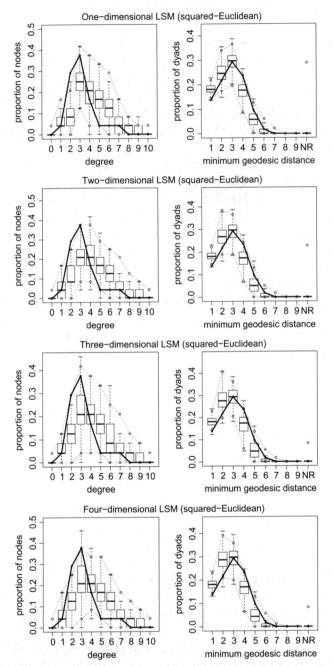

FIGURE 8.14 Goodness of fit plots for one- to four-dimensional latent space models for the strike communication network. Squared-Euclidean distance was used for these models.

```
 1    par(mfrow=c(1, 2))
 2    plot(gof(strike.1d2, GOF= ~ degree + dist, nsim=500, seed=10),
 3        main="1-dimensional LSM (squared-Euclidean)")
 4
 5    par(mfrow=c(1, 2))
 6    plot(gof(strike.2d2, GOF= ~ degree + dist, nsim=500, seed=10),
 7        main="2-dimensional LSM (squared-Euclidean)")
 8
 9    par(mfrow=c(1, 2))
10    plot(gof(strike.3d2, GOF= ~ degree + dist, nsim=500, seed=10),
11        main="3-dimensional LSM (squared-Euclidean)")
12
13    par(mfrow=c(1, 2))
14    plot(gof(strike.4d2, GOF= ~ degree + dist, nsim=500, seed=10),
15        main="4-dimensional LSM (squared-Euclidean)")
```

Inspecting these plots, we don't see a lot of major differences in fit between them. All models still have trouble capturing the lower-degree distribution found in the original network. The posterior predictive checks for the minimum geodesic distances look better, but they also don't differ great across models, nor are they much different than the first two-dimensional model we predicted at the beginning of the chapter. If we were restricted to these results, we would likely want to move forward with the simplest, one-dimensional model.

Before making our final decision about which model to retain, we should inspect the precision-recall curves and other performance metrics for these four models. The precision-recall curves are shown in Figure 8.15. As is clear, the four-dimensional model does the best job at predicting ties in this network. In fact, the AUC score for this model is over 0.99, while the previous two-dimensional model that used the standard Euclidean distance had an AUC of 0.96 (the model with squared-Euclidean distance had an AUC of 0.98).

These results are somewhat disappointing. From a scientist's perspective, it's not very satisfying to add forty-eight new parameters (twenty-four for each of the added dimensions) to gain just a few points in predictive performance. Furthermore, looking at the confusion matrices for the two- and four-dimensional models (not shown), we see that adding these parameters only improves the model by decreasing the false positives by five, while no false negatives are reported by either model. Overall, unless the objective was to produce the best in-sample

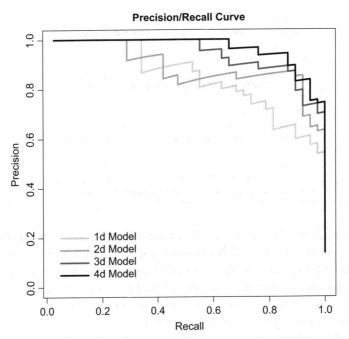

FIGURE 8.15 Precision-recall curves for estimated one- to four-dimensional LSMs for Michael's (1997) communication network among striking sawmill workers. Squared-Euclidean distance used.

predictive model possible without regard to interpretability or parsimony, we'd say that adding the complexity of estimating an additional forty-eight parameters for the four-dimensional model would not be worth the trouble in this case, and in doing so, we have likely overfit the data.

8.7 INTERPRETATION OF LATENT SPACE MODELS

While the mathematical formulation of the LSM is fairly straightforward and familiar for someone used to working with generalized linear models, the interpretation of these models can be complicated. Here we list several aspects of LSMs that practitioners should keep in mind when reviewing the results from these models.

First, as we have done numerous times in this chapter, it's common to present latent space model results in graphical form as network plots showing the locations of the vertices in the estimated latent space. However, these are not as informative as one would expect. Recall that the probability of an edge existing between two vertices is conditional on the *distances* between those vertices. In other words, the locations of those vertices don't matter except in as much as they affect the distances between vertices. In fact, unless there is care taken to define latent space, the locations themselves are not interpretable. This complication, and possible remedies, will be discussed in more detail in the next chapter.

Second, the interpretation of exogenous covariate effects is complicated by their association with the distances between vertices in the latent space. In other words, one cannot interpret a coefficient estimate on an exogenous covariate without simultaneously considering the distances between vertices in the space. This means that it's difficult to isolate the effect of the covariate from the latent space. Furthermore, this close association between important exogenous covariates and the latent distances between vertices can sometimes have surprising effects: sometimes, coefficient estimates can take on signs opposite of what one would expect (Cranmer et al. 2017). For this reason, it's important for practitioners to assess the importance of exogenous covariates of interest with an analysis of the posterior samples – which should reflect the covariance of latent distances and the covariates – from the model and not to rely on the point estimates of individual parameters.

Running Example: Strike Communication Network

In this brief example, we demonstrate how the latent space can change with the addition of exogenous covariates.

In our example application of the strike communication network, we saw a close association between language ability and communication patterns between striking workers. Unsurprisingly, according to the model, people who speak the same language are more likely to communicate with each other. Because of the higher density of ties within language group, the model (`strike.2d`) also placed members of the same language group more closely together in the latent space (see Figure 8.3). In a subsequent model, we included a `nodematch` term for Spanish-speaking homophily to test for this hypothesized relationship between communication and language knowledge. This model, `strike.2d.cov2`, found a positive effect for Spanish-speaking homophily, but no significant effect for non-Spanish (English) speaking.

But what happens to the estimated distances between vertices with the addition of the homophily term? Figure 8.16 shows the posterior distribution of distances between Alejandro and Carlos, two of the Spanish speakers, for each of these models. The first histogram shows

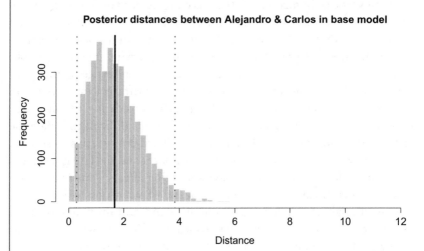

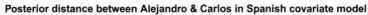

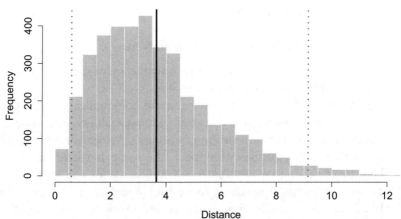

FIGURE 8.16 Posterior distances between Alejandro and Carlos in two two-dimensional latent space models. The top panel shows the posterior of the distances between these vertices in the baseline model. The bottom panel shows the posterior of the distances in the model, including differential homophily on Spanish.

the posterior distances between these two actors under the first baseline two-dimensional model that did not include the homophily terms. In the second histogram, the posterior distances are plotted for the model with the Spanish homophily term. In both histograms, the solid vertical line represents the posterior mean, while the dotted lines show the 95 percent credible interval.

We note two features of these plots. First, under the baseline model, the posterior distance is much smaller at $\bar{d}_{ij}^{\text{base}} = 1.65$, while in the second plot it has increased more than two-fold to $\bar{d}_{ij}^{\text{spanish}} = 3.73$. Second, the distribution of the posterior is also narrower under the first model. The differences between these posterior distances reflects the explanatory effect of the Spanish homophily term. Adding the Spanish term takes away the need for the latent distances to "soak up" the increased probability these vertices will form an edge. In other words, because the Spanish homophily effect is so important to edge formation, once it is added to the model, the estimation algorithm has a more difficult time identifying latent locations that further increase the probability of the graph.

Practitioners are not often interested in the distances between two vertices, nor are they particularly interested in individual covariate values. Instead, they want to know whether a certain exogenous covariate has a positive or negative effect on an outcome. To that end, in the next two histograms, we show the posterior predicted probabilities for ties between Alejandro and Carlos under the same two models. Once again, the solid line is the posterior mean and the dotted lines are the 95 percent credible intervals.

A comparison between the histograms in Figure 8.17 clearly shows the importance of the Spanish language homophily in edge formation between these vertices. Overall, the mean predicted probability of a tie increased by approximately 0.29 with the inclusion of the term. That is despite the fact that the posterior distances between the vertices in the latent space increased (which, all else equal, would lead to a *decrease* in the probability of a tie). This demonstrates the necessity of conditioning the assessment of covariate effects on the latent distances and not, as is usually the case with generalized linear models, relying on parameter point and uncertainty estimates for inference.

Here we have considered the importance of an exogenous covariate for just one dyad. In a more in-depth analysis of this network,

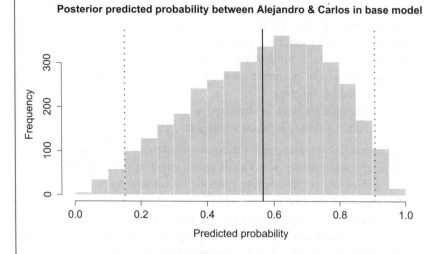

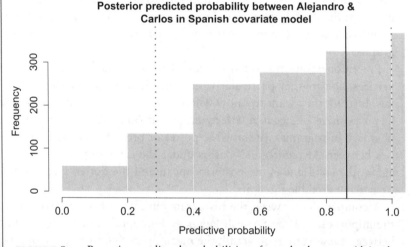

FIGURE 8.17 Posterior predicted probabilities of an edge between Alejandro and Carlos in two two-dimensional latent space models. The top panel shows the posterior of the predicted probability between these vertices in the baseline model. The bottom panel shows the posterior of predicted probability in the model, including differential homophily on Spanish.

one would want to investigate the change in predicted probabilities across groups of vertices in the network in order to gauge its overall importance. By doing so, interesting patterns may emerge, which can offer greater insight into the process generating the network.

8.8 STRENGTHS, ASSUMPTIONS, AND LIMITATIONS OF THE LATENT SPACE MODEL

In this chapter we have presented the basic theory underpinning the latent space network model. This framework for dealing with relational data has some clear strengths. For one thing, the model is fairly easy to understand for anyone familiar with standard generalized linear modeling. Furthermore, implementation of the model in software is relatively straightforward. The LSM framework also has the strength of being quite flexible. As we will show in Chapter 10, the LSM can be extended to accommodate weighted edges, clustering and random vertex-level intercepts. There has also been some interesting research done in recent years on extendeding the model to temporal networks (Sarkar and Moore 2005, Sewell and Chen 2015, 2016. Finally, if the objective is prediction and not inference about the generative process behind edge formation, then the LSM provides a set of powerful, flexible methods to meet that objective.

However, as with all models, there are some clear assumptions underpinning the LSM. First, as was mentioned in Section 8.2, there is a strong conditional independence assumption in the model. That is, the model assumes the ties are generated independently conditional on the location of the vertices in the latent space and the attribute covariates included in the model. This may be a strong assumption, particularly when taken with the second assumption that we correctly identify the true dimension of the latent social space. There is often little theory about the number of dimensions that should be chosen, making it difficult to judge when a model is capturing the structure underlying network formation or simply overfitting.

That leads us to some possibly more concerning and fundamental limitations of the LSM. The most glaring limitation, as alluded to above, is that the latent space model is not designed to concisely model higher-order dependencies in the data. This is the strength of the ERGM, discussed in detail in previous chapters. In that model, higher-order dependencies can be explicitly modeled, and inferences can be made about the importance of those dependencies in the formation of the network. In contrast, in the LSM the locations in the latent space reflect these dependencies, but those are not made explicit (i.e., dependencies are not summarized by individual parameters in the LSM). This lack of precise dependence modeling can, however, be seen as a strength if the researcher is not sure which dependence terms should be included in an ERGM. Second, when compared to the alternatives, the LSM is far from parsimonious. In the standard LSM, each dimension requires an additional n parameters to be estimated. This is particularly a problem in large network, which makes estimation for large networks difficult, though there has been some recent research in this area (Raftery et al. 2012). Third, the interpretation of the latent space model, particularly with regard to exogenous covariates, can be tricky. As discussed in Section 8.7, when covariates are highly correlated with the latent space, which they often are, the magnitude of parameters on the covariates can sometimes be highly attenuated or of the opposite sign, even when the covariate is known to be instrumental to the underlying network generating process (as an example, see Cranmer et al. 2017). Limitations aside, the LSM represents a powerful tool in the network analysts tool kit, and is particularly useful when the researcher is not sure what to specify in formulating an ERGM for modeling the network, and/or the primary interest is in the development of a predictive model.

8.9 WRAPPING UP

The latent space approach to modeling network data assumes that each vertex in a network is embedded in a latent social space. The fundamental assumption of the model is that the likelihood (or strength) of relations between vertices is a function of their distance from each other in that space. Coupled with the use of a distance metric that satisfies the triangle inequality, these assumptions help account for often-seen features of networks, including transitivity and reciprocity. As long as the researcher is not focused on testing specific structural hypotheses, such as those specified in ERGM, the LSM offers a powerful approach to capturing network structure and covariate effects. As a modeling tool, the latent space approach is deceptively easy to use, though proper care must be taken to account for the fundamental connection between the estimated position of vertices in the latent space and any observed exogenous covariates when making inferences.

8.10 SELF-STUDY PROBLEMS

Select a network dataset to study using LSM, but avoid using the data from ina that were used in this chapter. Be sure that the dataset includes at least one vertex attribute. If you do not have a dataset that you would like to use for this exercise, we recommend that you use the Hookups dataset from `ina`, which is introduced in Section 4.2. Using this dataset, complete a report that includes the following information:

1. **Description of the dataset:** What does the dataset cover? Where did it come from? Has it been used in any prior studies?

2. **Hypotheses:** Describe and test at least one hypothesis regarding a vertex attribute.

3. **Model specification:** Identify a model specification that you believe is capable of testing your hypotheses. Add a two-dimensional Euclidean latent space to the model. Estimate the model and assure that the MCMC has converged.

4. **Estimates:** Present the coefficient estimates of the LSM in either graphical or tabular form.

5. **Exploration:** Plot the latent positions. Comment on whether you learn anything about the structure of the network from visualizing the latent positions.

6. **Interpretation:** Substantively interpret your results. Do you find support for your hypotheses? Do you think the effects that you find are large?

9

Identification, Estimation, and Interpretation of the Latent Space Model

In the last chapter, we introduced the latent space model for networks. That chapter touched on the motivating theory behind the model, basic model specification, model checking and fit, and discussed model interpretation. In this chapter we focus on the computationally intensive issue of the statistical inference with the LSM.

While parameter identification tends to be treated as an estimation detail in much of the statistical literature, we believe that for practitioners wanting to apply the LSM to substantive questions, a greater understanding of the problem will help them build better models tailored to their substantive concerns. Due to the computationally expensive, and at times unstable, algorithms used to estimate the models, users of inferential network analysis benefit from understanding the implementation and diagnostics associated with estimation. Furthermore, a basic understanding of parameter identification and the strategies different software implementations could use to deal with it should help users to employ the statistical software more effectively and help them identify different problems in estimation when they arise.

We believe the same benefits apply with respect to understanding the algorithms used to estimate the standard latent space model. By providing readers with an overview of how the software works, we hope practitioners can better understand the problems that can occur during the estimation process. We also hope that our review of the algorithms can help the reader better understand how some of the extensions described in the next chapter are implemented. Finally, for those wanting to explore the latent space class of models further – possibly with an eye to extending the model to new problem domains – the content in this chapter should provide a good initial introduction to doing so.

9.1 PARAMETER IDENTIFICATION

This section discusses the issue of parameter identification in the latent space model. Stated succinctly, the primary challenge in parameter identification is this: without placing suitable constraints on the positions of vertices in the latent space, those positions cannot be uniquely identified.

Recall that the LSM models the existence (or strength) of a tie between two vertices as a function of the distance between the vertices in the latent space (as well as exogenous covariates). For the case of binary ties, we can model this as a logit model: $\Pr(N_{ij} = 1 \mid \beta, z_i, z_j) = \text{logit}^{-1}\{\beta^T X_{ij} - d(z_i, z_j)\}$. Clearly, the greater the distance between the two vertices, the less likely we are to observe a tie between i and j. As Hoff et al. (2002) point out, the likelihood for this model is concave in distances, so maximization is possible through standard hill-climbing methods. However, there will be $n(n-1)/2$ distances to estimate, while there is also a need to enforce dependence in the distances. In other words, if you change the distance between one pair of vertices, the model should necessarily change the distances between those vertices and others. The solution to these problems is to develop a model to estimate locations for each vertex in an s-dimensional latent space and use those as inputs for calculating the distance between vertices. This approach carries with it a few important advantages. First, it means there are many fewer parameters to estimate. Instead of there being $n(n-1)/2$ distances to estimate, by estimating latent locations, there will be $n \times s$ parameters. Second, estimating locations enforces the desired dependence between vertices. If an estimation algorithm moves a vertex to increase the probability of a tie between two vertices, it has to contend with the fact that this may decrease the probability of a tie with another. Coupled with a distance metric that satisfies the triangle inequality, estimating locations creates the requisite dependencies between distances among dyads. However, estimating latent locations instead of distances does introduce at least one significant issue: the issue of parameter identification.

There are four aspects of latent spaces that we need to contend with when we talk about parameter identification in the LSM. But to summarize the problem, the likelihood is not invariant to issues of translation, scale, reflection, and rotation. This challenge is rooted in the fact that any given distance matrix can be derived from infinitely many vertex embeddings. To put it another way, for any particular set of the latent locations, there is some transformation that can be done to these locations that, due to an unchanged distance matrix, does not change the likelihood of the model, yet does change the locations of the vertices in the latent space. Consequently, there is not a set of unique latent locations that maximize the likelihood, and without some principled set of restrictions on the latent space, estimated locations of vertices will not be unique. This complicates model estimation and interpretation. We will cover each of these aspects of invariance in the next four sections.

9.1.1 Translation

The first form of invariance we will discuss is translational invariance, or invariance to a constant shift to all points in any direction. The invariance of the likelihood with respect to vertex translation is easy to see. Consider a network of three vertices with the following set of latent locations in a two-dimensional space:

$$
Z = \begin{bmatrix} -1.5 & 0.0 \\ 0.0 & 2.0 \\ 1.5 & -2.0 \end{bmatrix}.
$$

In Z, each row represents the location of the vertex in the space, with the first column being the first dimension and the second column being the second. For the purposes of this section, we'll call these the x (horizontal) and y (vertical) dimensions, respectively.

These vertices are represented graphically in Figure 9.1. On the left – the vertices i, j, and k – we have the initial positions (Z) of three vertices with distances between them of d_{ij}, d_{ik}, and d_{jk}. If we translate the vertices to the right (shown by the arrows), each by the same amount, Δ_x,

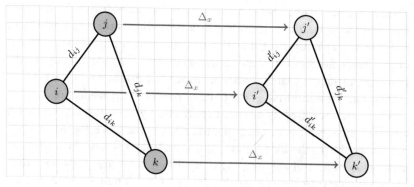

FIGURE 9.1 Translation invariance in the latent space model.

we get the new translated locations, i', j', and k'. These new points have dyadic distances of d'_{ij}, d'_{ik}, and d'_{jk}. It should be clear, visually, that the distances between the vertices are the same in each configuration.

We can also show this invariance of the distances to translation algebraically. Suppose that each vertex location (row in Z) will be translated by $\Delta = [\Delta_x, \Delta_y]$. Then the distance between these vertices is $d'_{ij} = d'(z_i + \Delta, z_j + \Delta)$. Equation (9.1) shows this equivalence for the Euclidean distance:

$$
\begin{aligned}
d(z_i + \Delta, z_j + \Delta) & \\
&= \sqrt{([z_{ix} + \Delta_x] - [z_{jx} + \Delta_x])^2 + ([z_{iy} + \Delta_y] - [z_{jy} + \Delta_y])^2} \\
&= \sqrt{([z_{ix} - z_{jx}] + [\Delta_x - \Delta_x])^2 + ([z_{iy} - z_{jy}] + [\Delta_y - \Delta_y])^2} \\
&= \sqrt{(z_{ix} - z_{jx})^2 + (z_{iy} - z_{jy})^2} \\
&= d(z_i, z_j).
\end{aligned}
\tag{9.1}
$$

But what does this mean for model estimation and interpretation? Recall Equation (8.1), which defined the log-odds of a tie between two vertices in a network as $\text{logit}\{\Pr(N_{ij} = 1 \mid \cdot)\} = \eta_{ij} = \beta_0 - d(z_i, z_j) = \beta_0 - d_{ij}$. Because the probability of the graph is dependent on the locations of the vertices only through their pairwise distances and, as we have shown, $d_{ij} = d'_{ij}$, this means the overall probability of the graph does not change with translation. Because of this invariance, any optimization algorithm maximizing the likelihood of the graph will need some way to fix the location in order to identify the model. Otherwise, the likelihood surface will be multimodal, preventing convergence to a single best set of parameter estimates.

Running Example: Identification of the Latent Locations

We will treat the examples in this section of the book a bit differently than in the previous ones. Here, rather than providing detailed examples using real-world data, we instead replicate in code what was discussed in the previous section.

It's easy to show the equivalence of the distances under translation in R. We begin by defining our location matrix, Z, as we did above (we also name the rows to remain consistent with the example).

```
1  > Z <- matrix(c(-1.5,  0.0,
2  +                0.0,  2.0,
3  +                1.5, -2.0), ncol=2, byrow=TRUE)
4  > rownames(Z) <- c("i", "j", "k")
5  > Z
6    [,1] [,2]
7  i -1.5   0
8  j  0.0   2
9  k  1.5  -2
```

The distances between each pair of vertices can be calculated with the dist function. By default, the Euclidean distance is the metric used by dist, though several other metrics are available using the function's method argument.

```
1  > dist(Z)
2           i         j
3  j 2.500000
4  k 3.605551 4.272002
```

Now we will translate the matrix of latent locations, Z, by 3 units to the right along the *x*-axis and recalculate the distances between the vertices.

```
1   > Z.trans <- Z
2   > Z.trans[,1] <- Z.trans[,1] + 3
3   > Z.trans
4     [,1] [,2]
5   i  1.5   0
6   j  3.0   2
7   k  4.5  -2
8   >
9   > dist(Z.trans)
10          i         j
11  j 2.500000
12  k 3.605551 4.272002
```

As was shown in test, the distances between vertices didn't change with the translation. Consequently, any likelihood calculated based on these locations wouldn't change, either.

9.1.2   Scale

The scale of the latent space raises a second problem for the estimation and interpretation of the LSM. Unlike issues of translation, though, the scale of the latent space only becomes a problem when the complete model is taken into account. This is because the probability of a graph is not invariant to scale; in fact, changing the scale of the latent space – for instance, by multiplying each vertex's latent location by a constant – has a clear impact on the likelihood, holding all else equal.

To see this, take the three-vertex network used in the last section along with their latent locations, Z. Vertices i and j had locations of $(-1.5, 0.0)$ and $(0.0, 2.0)$, respectively. The Euclidean distance between these vertices is 2.5, as we saw before. If we observe a (binary) tie between these vertices, and assume a zero intercept, the log probability of the graph is $-2.5 - \log(1 + \exp(-2.5)) = -2.58$, per Equation (8.2). If we were to scale each of the vectors by $\alpha = 2$, the distance between the vertices increases to 5, while the log probability changes to $-5.0 - \log(1 + \exp(-5.0)) = -5.01$. Clearly the likelihood varies with the scaling of the latent space.

There remains a complication: the invariance of the likelihood to scale only holds if we do not include an intercept in the model. But we almost always want to include an intercept because it represents (roughly) the average probability of a tie in the network. If we exclude an intercept, in a network with binary ties the highest probability of a tie would be 0.5 (at a distance of zero). We could never have a model that has predictions for a tie with more than 50 percent. However, including an intercept in the model and trying to estimate it along with the latent locations will result in a nonunique maxima and, without applying proper constraints, prevent convergence of the model.

Running Example: Identification of the Latent Locations

We can show this by implementing the above example in R.

First, we will define a function that calculates the log-likelihood of a network with binary ties (to simplify things, this assumes there is a tie between every pair of vertices in the network, as is the case in our running example), and calculates the log-likelihood of the graph given Z and an intercept of 0.

```
## Log-likelihood of a network given vector of etas, the intercept
## minus the distance between vertices.
loglik <- function(etas)
{
    sum(etas - log(1 + exp(etas)))
}
```

```
 8   > etas0 <- 0 - dist(Z)
 9   > loglik(etas0)
10   [1] -10.49711
```

Now we define another function that calculates the difference in the log-likelihood when we vary the intercept and assume αZ, where $\alpha = 2$. Using the `uniroot` function, we then find the point at which the log-likelihoods are equal.

```
1   diff <- function(intercept)
2   {
3       loglik(intercept - dist(Z * 2)) - loglik(etas0)
4   }
5
6   > uniroot(diff, interval=c(0,5))[["root"]]
7   [1] 3.496429
```

What this shows is that for an intercept of approximately 3.50, the log-likelihoods are the same. In other words, there is not a unique set of β_0 and α in $\eta_{ij} = \beta_0 - \alpha d(\mathbf{z}_i, \mathbf{z}_j)$ that maximize the log-likelihood. Model parameters are not uniquely identified without imposing some restrictions on the estimation method.

9.1.3   Reflection

The third source of invariance in the LSM is due to reflection – the multiplication of one or more dimension by -1. Figure 9.2 demonstrates this. In the left panel, we see one configuration of the network. The dashed vertical line is a line of reflection. If we reflect the points to the other

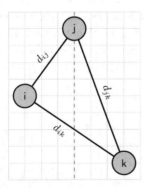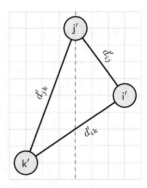

FIGURE 9.2 Reflection in the latent space model.

side of this line, we get the panel on the right. In this case, none of the distances change, thus the probability of the graph does not change, even though the latent locations do.

Running Example: Identification of the Latent Locations

Again, we can show the invariance to reflection with a little snippet of R. To reflect points in two-dimensions across the y-axis, we can simply postmultiply Z by a 2×2 matrix of the form

$$R = \begin{bmatrix} -1.0 & 0.0 \\ 0.0 & 1.0 \end{bmatrix}.$$

In R, we can now define this reflection matrix, postmultiply Z, and calculate the distances between the points.

```
1   > R <- matrix(c(-1, 0,
2   +                   0, 1), ncol=2, byrow=TRUE)
3   >
4   > Z %*% R
5      [,1] [,2]
6   i  1.5    0
7   j  0.0    2
8   k -1.5   -2
```

Notice that in the first column of the reflected matrix of positions – representing the locations of the vertex in the first dimension – each value has the opposite sign compared to the original Z, while y positions remain the same. These reflected locations correspond to the locations of the vertices in the right panel of Figure 9.2.

As suspected, the distances between the reflected vertices has not changed with this reflection:

```
1   > dist(Z %*% R)
2          i        j
3   j 2.500000
4   k 3.605551 4.272002
```

We can go further and reflect along both axes simultaneously by setting $R_{1,1} = R_{2,2} = -1.0$. This results in the same set of distances between vertices, as shown in the following snippet of R code.

```
1  > R2 <- matrix(c(-1,   0,
2  +                   0,  -1), ncol=2, byrow=TRUE)
3  >
4  > dist(Z %*% R2)
5             i            j
6  j 2.500000
7  k 3.605551  4.272002
```

9.1.4 Rotation

Rotation – the motion of an embedding relative to a fixed point (e.g., the origin, a vertex's position) – of the latent space is the final source of invariance in the LSM. This is demonstrated graphically in Figure 9.3. In this figure, the unlabeled vertices represent the original locations of the vertices of Z, while the labeled vertices are the locations rotated by 45°.

Is should be clear from the figure that rotating a set of points has no effect on the distances between those points. And because the distances don't change with rotation, the likelihood is invariant to this rotation. We can easily demonstrate that the distances are invariant to rotations in R. First, we need to define a function in R to construct a matrix to rotate the Z. Clockwise rotation of a set of locations in two-dimensional space can be performed by postmultiplying the coordinates by

$$\text{ROT}(\theta) = \begin{bmatrix} \cos(\theta) & -\sin(\theta) \\ \sin(\theta) & \cos(\theta) \end{bmatrix},$$

where θ is the degrees of rotation.

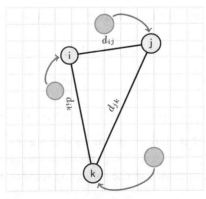

FIGURE 9.3 Rotation in the latent space model.

Running Example: Identification of the Latent Locations

In R, the trigonometric functions take radians, not degrees. So the following function first converts the desired rotation in degrees to radians before constructing the 2×2 rotations matrix, ROT(θ).

```
1   rotation_matrix <- function(degree)
2   {
3       rad <- (degree * pi) / 180
4       matrix(c( cos(rad), -sin(rad),
5                 sin(rad),  cos(rad)), ncol=2, byrow=TRUE)
6   }
```

Using this function, we can then postmultiply any $n \times 2$ matrix of locations to get a rotated set of points:

```
1   > Z %*% rotation_matrix(45)
2           [,1]       [,2]
3   i -1.0606602  1.060660
4   j  1.4142136  1.414214
5   k -0.3535534 -2.474874
```

As expected, this rotation has no effect on the distances between vertices in the network and, consequently, does not change the likelihood.

```
1   > dist(Z)
2           A         B
3   B 2.500000
4   C 3.605551  4.272002
5   > dist(Z %*% rotation_matrix(45))
6           A         B
7   B 2.500000
8   C 3.605551  4.272002
```

9.2 IDENTIFICATION: SOME SOLUTIONS

The previous sections detailed how distances between vertices embedded in a latent social space are not uniquely defined when one estimates the distances via estimating vertex locations. As we showed, the distances between vertices are invariant to scale (when also estimating an intercept), translation, reflection, and rotation. This complicates estimation, while also raising issues with model interpretation. Consequently, we need some principled way to deal with these problems. There are generally two ways to go about dealing with the identification problem.

The first way to deal with parameter identification in the LSM is to fix the positions of a set of vertices in the latent space. In a two-dimensional model, for example, you can fix one point to eliminate translational invariance, fixing a second point will eliminate rotational and scale invariance, and fixing a third point will eliminate the invariance to reflection. More generally, all four of these types of invariance can be eliminated by fixing $s + 1$ vertices in an s-dimensional latent space. Initially, this may seem to be an attractive way to deal with this issue, and it's a method that is quite commonly used in similar situations (Poole & Rosenthal 1985, Bafumi et al. 2005). However, the method does raise some significant problems.

One problem with fixing vertices is deciding how to choose which vertices to fix. Clearly, fixing the positions of isolates in the network won't do any good in helping identify the locations of the other vertices. It may also be tempting to identify vertices with relatively high degree centrality, but this only works well when there are several such vertices in the network *and* the network is not too sparse. In sparse matrices there are often isolated groups of vertices (i.e., components; Hawe, Webster & Shiell 2004) that are disconnected from each other. When this is the case, it doesn't matter if there is a set of well-connected vertices in the main component, the latent positions for the isolated groups will resist identification without further fixing of vertices in those individual groups.

The second problem that arises when fixing vertex locations is that doing so imposes a great deal of structure on the latent space, affecting (by design) the latent locations of the other vertices, but also imposing potentially detrimental constraints on the parameters for exogenous covariates. For instance, imagine setting the latent positions for i and j in a one-dimensional space, where there exists an edge between them. Not only does this impose a scale restriction on the network (usually adjusted for through the intercept term), if there are any covariates that are important in defining that tie, the parameter capturing the importance of that covariate will also be affected.

An alternative to fixing a set of vertices in the latent space is to apply informative Bayesian priors to their positions (Morgan 2015, Chapter 2). However, while being somewhat more flexible and less likely to harm inferences for any exogenous covariates in the model, this approach doesn't obviate the need to select which vertices to which to apply the priors, nor is it effective in sparse networks.

The second method of dealing with parameter identification in the LSM is to use post-processing of the latent positions to transform them into something consistent. In other words, during the estimation phase, the algorithm is allowed to sample latent positions from an unconstrained space.[1] Once this process is complete, a transformation is made to the sampled latent positions, which translates, rotates, and scales them to resemble some set of reference locations. This is the method of identification most often used in the literature, including in Hoff et al. (2002). Specifically, a Procrustes transform is used (Borg & Groenen 1997, Chapter 19). A Procrustes transformation is a method according to which one set of points is transformed to be as similar as possible to a reference set of points without affecting the distance matrix produced by the transformed set of points. In classic Procrustes transformation, "similarity" is measured according to the squared difference between the the locations of the units in each space (Castillo & Colosimo 2011). The formula for this transformation is shown in Equation (9.2):

$$Z^* = Z_{\text{ref}} Z^T (Z_{\text{ref}}^T Z_{\text{ref}} Z^T)^{-1/2} Z \tag{9.2}$$

Here, Z_{ref} refers to a set of reference positions, while Z is the matrix of sampled points with the same dimensions as Z_{ref}.

Using the Procrustes transformation to get a set of stable posterior samples for the latent positions seems preferable to fixing vertices in the latent space or applying tight priors; however, it also requires an important decision to be made: choosing Z_{ref}. Luckily, it's often straightforward to estimate the latent positions through maximum likelihood using a nonlinear optimization routine. And when there are issues with estimating these reference positions, it can often help to obtain starting positions through multidimensional scaling of geodesic distances between vertices (Hoff et al. 2002, p. 1093), though one needs to place constraints on any isolates in the network.

9.3   INTERPRETING THE LATENT SPACE

In light of the discussion in the last section, it should be clear that interpreting the latent space model by comparing the locations of vertices in that space can be problematic. In the LSM, the likelihood is invariant to translation, scale, reflection, and rotation – only the distances between vertices matter for the model. Because of this, latent locations that

---

[1] The space is not completely unconstrained, as there are often a set of priors placed on the location and scale of the space, but these are often fairly weak.

maximize the likelihood could take on infinite specific configurations. How could interpretablity be achieved? Two methods seem tempting.

First, constraints could be placed on the space in such a way to make the locations interpretable. For example, in ideal point models for US politicians, a set of reference legislators are often given fixed positions in some political space (e.g., a one-dimensional space ranging from liberal to conservative). The rest of the legislators are then compared against the resulting space to determine their place on the political spectrum. The same could be done in, for example, an LSM for cosponsorship networks. Two legislators could be fixed at some points in the space and then the rest of the legislators positions could be compared to them. However, as was mentioned in Section 9.2, fixing positions in an LSM can cause estimation issues by distorting the latent space.

Second, interpretability could be achieved through postprocessing to a particular set of reference positions. This has the advantage of not distorting the latent space to follow some structure not supported by the data. But even after postprocessing, practitioners need to be careful in how they interpret the distances between vertices in the space. For one thing, the distance metric used in the fitting process needs to be accounted for in making inferences. For instance, suppose we have a model where the estimated intercept was $\beta_0 = 3$, the estimated location for i was $z_i = 2$, and the location for j was $z_j = 4$. In a model for binary edges using the standard Euclidean distance, the predicted probability of a tie would be $\text{logit}^{-1}\{3 - (4 - 2)\} = 0.73$; however, if a squared-Euclidean distance was used to estimate the model, the predicted probability under the model would be $\text{logit}^{-1}\{3 - (4 - 2)^2\} = 0.27$. Likewise, the nonlinearity of the relationship between the distance and the outcome need to be kept in mind. Just as in a logistic regression model, a one unit increase is not always the same; for example, in a binary LSM, moving from a distance of 0 to 1 is much more significant than moving from a distance of 1 to 2. For these reasons, practitioners need to be very careful about how they compare locations and distances in the estimated latent space. Certain comparisons that seem natural – for instance, making statements such as "vertex i is 50 percent further away from j than is k" – are fraught with inferential peril.

9.4 THE PROBLEM WITH ISOLATES

Thus far we haven't discussed isolates and the issues they raise for the latent space model. Simply put, isolates are something of a problem. This is because without any edges connecting them to the rest of the network, there is no way for the model to locate them in the latent space. As a result, it's typically the case that the latent positions for isolates will not converge to a stable distribution, and multimodal posteriors are often the result. Consequently, practitioners should be wary of making any formal inferences about isolates and their relation to other vertices. That said, isolates don't usually cause too much of an issue with estimation as long as there aren't too many in the network. Researchers need not worry about the applicability or appropriateness of the LSM for networks with isolates. But when there is a large number, convergence of parameter estimates for the nonisolates can be slow. Just like with `ergm`, the convergence of estimates can be checked using the `mcmc.diagnostics` function in the `latentnet` package.

9.5 ESTIMATION

In this final section, we review a straightforward algorithm for estimating the standard latent space model. This Bayesian approach resembles the one used by Hoff et al. (2002) and is attributed to Shortreed, Handcock, and Hoff (2006), who present some improvements to the original. In that paper, the authors were primarily concerned with evaluating different point estimates for the latent positions, which is where the point estimates obtained from minimizing the Kullback-Leibler divergence (MKL estimates) were originally formulated. However, this section will not cover that derivation (though, it isn't complicated, and we direct interested readers to their original paper).

There are three primary steps to estimating the LSM. First, starting values – including the reference latent locations, Z_{ref}, for the final Procrustes transformation step – are estimated. Second, these starting values are used to kick off a sampling routine, which should be run to convergence. Third, the raw posterior samples of the latent locations obtained from the second step are transformed with the Procrustes procedure, the output of which are the final posterior distributions of the vertices' positions in the latent space.

More specifically, the steps are as follows:

Step 1: Obtain starting values and reference positions.
Obtain maximum likelihood estimates for β°, a vector of covariate parameters as well as the intercept, and Z°, a set of latent locations in an s-dimensional latent space, using the standard optimization techniques. When such techniques fail (e.g., it's not uncommon for

parameter values to explode given the scale invariance discussed in Section 9.1.2), place reasonable box or other constraints on problematic parameters, where "reasonable" is defined relative to the outcome (i.e., the distribution of the edge weights). If there aren't too many isolates in the network, the minimum geodesic distances between vertices can be used as an input to a multidimensional scaling routine to get starting values for the latent locations.

Step 2: Run Markov chain sampling.

Set S to be the number of desired samples from the posterior and ζ be the interval between samples. Set initial state of the starting positions and intercept found in previous step; that is, $Z^m = Z^\circ$, $\beta^m = \beta^\circ$.

Run a Markov chain for $S \times \zeta = M$ iterations. For each of these iterations, $m \in \{0, 1, 2, \ldots, M\}$:

1. Sample a set of proposal embedding, $\hat{Z}$, from a multivariate Gaussian distribution, each embedding centered at Z_n^m, where n indexes vertices in the network.

2. Perform a Metropolis-Hastings step, setting

$$
Z^{m+1} = \begin{cases} \hat{Z} & \text{with probability } \min\left\{1, \dfrac{\Pr(N \mid \hat{Z}, \beta^m) \Pr(\hat{Z})}{\Pr(N \mid Z^m, \beta^m) \Pr(Z^m)}\right\} \\ Z^m & \text{otherwise,} \end{cases}
$$

where $\Pr(Z)$ is a prior (typically Gaussian, centered at zero), on the latent positions.

3. Sample a proposal for $\hat{\beta}$ from a multivariate (possibly correlated) Gaussian centered at zero.

4. Perform a Metropolis step, setting

$$
\beta^{m+1} = \begin{cases} \hat{\beta} & \text{with probability } \min\left\{1, \dfrac{\Pr(N \mid Z^m, \hat{\beta}) \Pr(\hat{\beta})}{\Pr(N \mid Z^m, \beta^m) \Pr(\beta^m)}\right\} \\ \beta^m & \text{otherwise,} \end{cases}
$$

where $\Pr(\beta)$ is a prior on β.

5. Save sample after every ζ iterations.

Step 3: Postprocess latent locations.

For each of the saved samples in the posterior of the latent locations, perform the Procrustes transformation using Z_{mle} as the set of reference positions.

9.6 WRAPPING UP

In the LSM an edge between two vertices is dependent only on the distances between vertices in the latent space (and exogenous covariates). Consequently, the likelihood of the model is invariant to transformations that are distance preserving. This can cause complications with estimation and interpretation. Two potential remedies to this issue are easy to implement. Reference vertices can be fixed in the latent social space or posterior estimates of the latent positions can be post-processed to help make them comparable. The latter option of postprocessing is preferable given the distorting effects of fixing vertices. But, postprocessing does not obviate the need to be careful when analysts interpret the latent locations of vertices.

10

Extending the Latent Space Model

10.1 INTRODUCTION

In Chapter 8, we introduced the basic latent space model for undirected networks with binary ties. In the last chapter, we provided a detailed review of the particular issues one may encounter when fitting and interpreting these models.

In this chapter we present some extensions of the LSM, including models for weighted networks, a variant of the model that includes clustering the vertices in the latent space, as well as a model for incorporating random sender, receiver, and sociality effects into the LSM. We also provide a brief introduction to a new latent variable model for networks – the latent factor model. At the end of the chapter, we also briefly discuss the extensions to the LSM, including the projection modeling and approaches to modeling temporal networks. Luckily, because of the flexibility of the original formulation of the LSM, the bulk of the theory needed to understand these models has already been covered. Consequently, this chapter will be heavy on application and somewhat lighter on theory.

Running Example: Scottish Schoolgirl Friendship Network

Our example network for this chapter comes from the *Teenage Friends and Lifestyle Study* (Michell & Amos 1997; Pearson & Michell 2000; West & Sweeting 1996). This is a friendship network comprising girls from a Scottish school. The girls were surveyed over three years starting when they were about thirteen years old in 1995. During each survey period, the girls were asked to name up to twelve girls as friends. This is a directed network; that is, while girl i may identify j as being one of her close friends, that doesn't mean j said the same about i. For other research in which this network data are used, see Pearson and West (2003), Pearson, Steglich, and Snijders (2006), and Steglich, Snijders, and West (2006). This is stored as the ScottishSchool dataset in the ina package. The dataset consists of four network objects, each with vertex attributes. One network corresponds to each survey wave, and there is also an aggregated network object – combining the information across all three waves.

The network also contains some interesting vertex-level covariates. During each of the survey years, the girls were asked whether they smoked, drank alcohol, used drugs (cannabis), were active in sports, or if there had been a family event in the past year leading to the change in the number of people living in the household.

The three friendship networks summarizing these data are presented in Figure 10.1. Note that the plot locations of each vertex has been fixed for each of the three periods — using the second period as a reference — to help make the plots more comparable.

1995   **1996**   **1997**

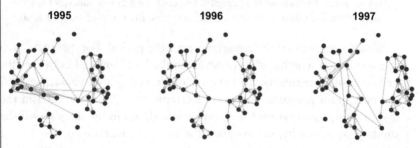

FIGURE 10.1 Friendship networks in a Scottish school, 1995–97. Three directed networks are shown, one for each period. Vertex positions were fixed at those calculated for the 1996 period.

For the purposes of this chapter, we have combined the three periods into a single directed, weighted network. Edge weights were created by the taking the sum of the mentions over the three periods. In other words, if i mentioned j in two of the three periods, the directed edge weight was set to $N_{ij} = 2$. This aggregated network is shown in Figure 10.2. In this plot, the edge colors and widths correspond to the strength of the connection. A light arrow indicates that in just one of the periods the sending vertex indicated that the receiver was amongst her friends, while grey indicates the sender mentioned the receiver twice, and black indicates the sender mentioned the receiver in all three periods.

1995 – 1997

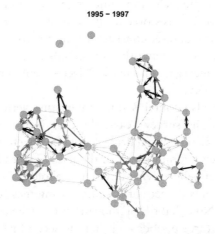

FIGURE 10.2 Friendship network for fifty girls in a Scottish school, 1995–97 (aggregated). Periods were aggregated to create weighted edges, where the edges sum the number of times a girl specified the receiver as her friend.

We also aggregated the covariates over the period. For instance, each girl was asked whether she (1) never smoked, (2) smoked occasionally, or (3) smoked regularly. To create a single aggregated value, we took the maximum response value; for example, if a girl responded in the first and third surveys that she never smoked, but in the second said she smoked occasionally, we assigned the smoke covariate for her as a 2 (the maximum of the three responses).

These covariates provide some useful insight into the relationship between friendship ties and behavior, which shapes our subsequent analysis. For instance, in Figure 10.3 we have recreated the previous plot, but this time coloring the vertices according to the aggregated smoke covariate. In the plot, vertices colored white are those that indicated they never smoked, grey vertices said they occasionally smoked, and the black vertices represent girls that said they smoked regularly. A strong pattern between friendships and smoking is clearly apparent in this plot. The smokers (black) are grouped together on the right side of the plot, while the nonsmokers (white) populate the left, with very few connections between them. Drug and alcohol use followed similar patterns, but the clustering was not a strong.

Tobacco use: 1995 – 1997

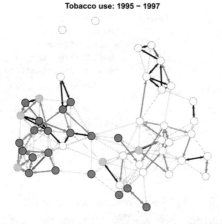

FIGURE 10.3 Friendship network for fifty girls in a Scottish school, 1995–96 (aggregated). Vertices are colored to correspond to each girl's stated tobacco use, where white indicates no use, grey occasional use, and dark grey regular use.

We begin modeling the friendship network with a simple binary LSM, excluding any covariates. While we know that smoking is related to friendship ties, and we know the ties are weighted, we begin with a simple baseline model for comparing subsequent models. For pedagogical purposes, we also stick to estimating a two-dimensional latent space. As we will see in the examples below, the two-dimensional model does provide a reasonable fit.

One modeling note: in each of the models estimated below, we set rather aggressive MCMC control parameters to assure convergence. While this isn't a requirement for convergence of the simpler model specification, the more complex models do benefit from the longer burn-in and sampling interval. For comparability, we have used the same control parameters for all models.

```
1    library(ina)
2    data(ScottishSchool)
3    CONTROL  <- control.ergmm(burnin=150000, interval=100)
```

```
 4    girls.2d.base <- ergmm(Girls ~ euclidean(d=2), control=CONTROL,
          seed=12)
 5    girls.2d.x1   <- ergmm(Girls ~ absdiff("smoke") +
 6                           euclidean(d=2), control=CONTROL,
                               seed=12)
 7    girls.2d.x2   <- ergmm(Girls ~ absdiff("smoke") +
 8                           absdiff("alcohol") +
 9                           absdiff("drugs") +
10                           absdiff("sports") +
11                           nodeofactor("family") +
12                           euclidean(d=2), control=CONTROL,
                               seed=12)
13    girls.2d.x3   <- ergmm(Girls ~ absdiff("smoke") +
14                           absdiff("drugs") +
15                           euclidean(d=2), control=CONTROL,
                               seed=12)
```

The results for the baseline model without any covariates are shown in R output below. We also include the network plot in Figure 10.4 showing the posterior mean positions for each vertex in the two-dimensional space. Once again, we have colored the vertices according to their smoking values. We have not included goodness-of-fit plots or MCMC diagnostic plots; however, a review proved that the baseline specification was quite good for an initial model.

```
 1    ============================
 2    Summary of model fit
 3    ============================
 4
 5    Formula:   Girls ~ euclidean(d = 2)
 6    Attribute: edges
 7    Model:     Bernoulli
 8    MCMC sample of size 4000, draws are 100 iterations apart, after
          burnin
 9       of 150000 iterations.
10    Covariate coefficients posterior means:
11              Estimate   2.5% 97.5% 2*min(Pr(>0),Pr(<0))
12    (Intercept)  3.2890 2.6234  3.98              < 2.2e-16 ***
13    ---
14    Signif. codes:  0 '***' 0.001 '**' 0.01 '*' 0.05 '.' 0.1 ' ' 1
15
16    Overall BIC:         1176.092
17    Likelihood BIC:      574.5201
18    Latent space/clustering BIC:     601.5718
```

```
19
20      Covariate coefficients MKL:
21                  Estimate
22      (Intercept) 2.229005
```

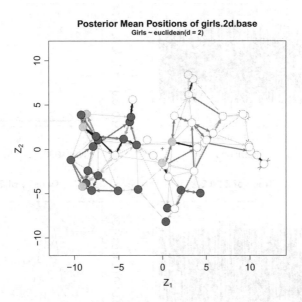

Posterior Mean Positions of girls.2d.base
Girls ~ euclidean(d = 2)

FIGURE 10.4 Estimated two-dimensional latent locations for the girls' friendship network model. This baseline model used unweighted edges and excluded covariates. Vertices are shaded according to their stated tobacco use.

One curious thing should be noted, however, about the results of this model: the isolates (the vertices colored black) are not located at the periphery of the plot, as they were in Figure 10.3. Instead, the model has estimated positions for them in the *center* of the latent space, very near the origin. For this reason, and given the discussion of isolates from the previous chapters, it is instructive to look at the trace plots for the latent positions of these vertices. In Figure 10.5, we show these for vertex number 20. Notice how the distribution of the posterior samples for the first dimension is clearly bimodal with the greatest densities at approximately ± 12. The reason for this is, of course, that because of their lack of edges to other vertices in the network, the model has little information on where to locate these isolates in the latent space. Consequently, the positions it produces are driven by the priors placed on Z and on the Procrustes transformation used in the postprocessing step. We will return to analyzing the position of the isolates in future versions of the model.

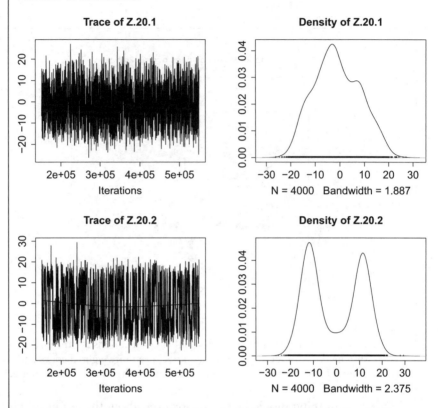

FIGURE 10.5 [Trace plots for the posterior latent positions of an isolate (vertex 20) derived from the baseline two-dimensional LSM for the girls' friendship network.

Our next step was to incorporate the covariate data. To that end, we estimated three models with different covariate specifications. In the first model, we include an `absdiff` term for the smoking vertex-level covariate. As the reader may recall, the `absdiff` term is a homophily term for numeric covariates. For this term, as two nodes grow one unit apart in the attribute value, the log-odds of a tie changes by the respective coefficient value, with a negative coefficient indicating homophily. While our measure is technically ordinal, for our purposes, the term provides a straightforward way of incorporating this important covariate into the data. From the network plot of Figure 10.3, we would expect the coefficient on this term to be negative as it relates to ties: the greater the difference in the smoking covariate, the less likely a friendship edge would be sent.

The second model we estimate is a saturated model, where we include terms for each of the covariates available in the data. This includes an absdiff terms for alcohol consumption, drug use, and participation in sports, as well as the term for smoking. We hypothesize that each of these would have a negative effect on friendship ties. We also include a nodeofactor term indicating whether the sender in each directed dyad had recently experienced a family event, resulting in a change in the number of people living in a household. Finally, the third model we estimate is slightly more parsimonious, where the only covariates that were included were the absdiff terms for smoking and drug use. The results of these three models are presented in the code blocks below.

```
> summary(girls.2d.x1)


============================
Summary of model fit
============================

Formula:   Girls ~ absdiff("smoke") + euclidean(d = 2)
Attribute: edges
Model:     Bernoulli
MCMC sample of size 4000, draws are 100 iterations apart, after
     burnin
     of 150000 iterations.
Covariate coefficients posterior means:
              Estimate     2.5%    97.5% 2*min(Pr(>0),Pr(<0))
(Intercept)    3.53160  2.81798   4.2908              <2e-16 ***
absdiff.smoke -0.50477 -0.85483  -0.1539               0.004 **
---
Signif. codes:  0 '***' 0.001 '**' 0.01 '*' 0.05 '.' 0.1 ' ' 1

Overall BIC:             1169.957
Likelihood BIC:          576.7817
Latent space/clustering BIC:      593.1757

Covariate coefficients MKL:
               Estimate
(Intercept)    2.4824687
absdiff.smoke -0.4439364

> summary(girls.2d.x2)
```

```
29
30    ============================
31    Summary of model fit
32    ============================
33
34    Formula:   Girls ~ absdiff("smoke") + absdiff("alcohol") +
             absdiff("drugs") +
35             absdiff("sports") + nodeofactor("family") + euclidean(d = 2)
36    Attribute: edges
37    Model:     Bernoulli
38    MCMC sample of size 4000, draws are 100 iterations apart, after
             burnin
39         of 150000 iterations.
40    Covariate coefficients posterior means:
41                          Estimate    2.5%   97.5%
                              2*min(Pr(>0),Pr(<0))
42    (Intercept)           4.051999 3.263189  4.9120
             <2e-16 ***
43    absdiff.smoke        -0.456011 -0.800137 -0.1075
             0.0105 *
44    absdiff.alcohol      -0.127627 -0.533060  0.3187
             0.5440
45    absdiff.drugs        -0.920655 -1.248011 -0.5998
             <2e-16 ***
46    absdiff.sports        0.090879 -0.553943  0.7564
             0.7890
47    nodeofactor.family.2  0.081646 -0.416718  0.5693
             0.7440
48    ---
49    Signif. codes:  0 '***' 0.001 '**' 0.01 '*' 0.05 '.' 0.1 ' ' 1
50
51    Overall BIC:          1168.572
52    Likelihood BIC:        597.117
53    Latent space/clustering BIC:     571.4555
54
55    Covariate coefficients MKL:
56                         Estimate
57    (Intercept)          2.88090309
58    absdiff.smoke       -0.39410284
59    absdiff.alcohol     -0.15275492
60    absdiff.drugs       -0.73615887
61    absdiff.sports       0.10077055
62    nodeofactor.family.2 -0.01900235
63
64    > summary(girls.2d.x3)
65
66    ============================
67    Summary of model fit
68    ============================
69
```

```
70    Formula:    Girls ~ absdiff("smoke") + absdiff("drugs") +
          euclidean(d = 2)
71    Attribute: edges
72    Model:      Bernoulli
73    MCMC sample of size 4000, draws are 100 iterations apart, after
          burnin
74        of 150000 iterations.
75    Covariate coefficients posterior means:
76                    Estimate    2.5%    97.5% 2*min(Pr(>0),Pr(<0))
77    (Intercept)      3.97285 3.21976  4.7686                <2e-16 ***
78    absdiff.smoke   -0.45471 -0.80309 -0.0979                0.011 *
79    absdiff.drugs   -0.89374 -1.22870 -0.5597               <2e-16 ***
80    ---
81    Signif. codes:  0 '***' 0.001 '**' 0.01 '*' 0.05 '.' 0.1 ' ' 1
82
83    Overall BIC:          1154.829
84    Likelihood BIC:        591.8083
85    Latent space/clustering BIC:     563.0211
86
87    Covariate coefficients MKL:
88                    Estimate
89    (Intercept)     2.5519122
90    absdiff.smoke  -0.3996937
91    absdiff.drugs  -0.6987539
```

A few things are noteworthy in these results. First, as we suspected, smoking is closely associated with edge formation in this friendship network. The effect is negative and statistically significant, also as we hypothesized; that is, smokers are more likely to be friends with other smokers, and nonsmokers are likewise more likely to be friends with nonsmokers. Second, the only other covariate that is closely related to friendships according to these models is drug (cannabis) use, which actually has a stronger effect than smoking tobacco. Once these two covariate terms are included in the model, the homophily terms for alcohol consumption and sports participation are not significant, while neither is the family event sociality effect.

Given all of that, which model appears to provide the best fit to the friendships network? Comparing the overall BIC scores for the four models, the third model that restricts the model to the homophily terms for smoking and drug use has a lower BIC than the saturated model. While a more thorough/complete analysis would try alternative covariate specifications, we will continue with this model version for the ongoing examples in the rest of this chapter.

For completeness, a plot of the estimated latent positions is shown in Figure 10.6. We include two plots. On the left, the vertices are labeled according to the smoking covariate, on the right we have done the same with the drug use covariate. In the latter, white indicates "no use," light grey "used once," grey "use occasionally," and black "use regularly." The black vertices indicate the isolates in both plots.

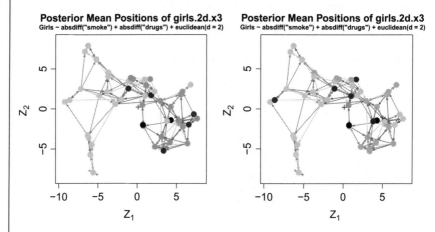

FIGURE 10.6 Estimated two-dimensional latent locations for the girls' friendship network model. This baseline model used unweighted edges and included homophily terms for tobacco and drug use. In the left panel, vertices are shaded according to their stated tobacco use, while on the right, they are shaded for drug use.

Before moving on, we'll look again at the posterior samples for the latent location for vertex 20, the same isolate we looked at before. Figure 10.7 shows the trace plot for the model with the smoking and drug use covariates. The posterior samples for the first dimension is once again bimodal. This demonstrates the problems with modeling isolates in the LSM framework. Isolates are not "anchored" in any way by their connections to other vertices in the network, so the model cannot easily locate them in the latent space. And this isn't simply a symptom of not running the MCMC algorithm for enough iterations; that is, the instability of the estimates doesn't go away with increasing the number of burn-in iterations (to test this, the reader should try increasing the burnin parameter to 2 million iterations — the same pattern emerges). From a practical standpoint, it turns out not to matter much for the estimation of this particular network, since just two of the fifty vertices are isolates – if these vertices are removed from the network, the substantive and statistical results for the covariates included in the previous or following models do not change appreciably. However, in smaller networks, or networks with a proportionally larger number of isolates, overall performance of the estimation algorthm can suffer. And even in the best case scenarios, one needs to be careful about making inferences about the location of isolates in the latent space or about their relation to other vertices in the network.

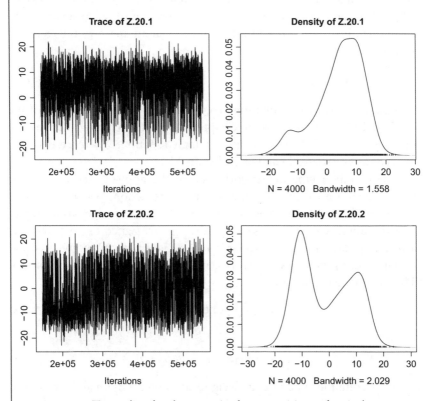

FIGURE 10.7 Trace plots for the posterior latent positions of an isolate (vertex 20) derived from the two-dimensional LSM, including tobacco and drug use homophily terms for the girls friendship network.

10.2 VALUED-EDGE NETWORKS

To this point, we have focused on applying the LSM to binary networks. In this section we start to explore some of the flexibility of the latent space modeling framework with the first application to weighted, or valued-edge, networks. Conceptually, weighted networks are quite straightforward, though as we saw in Chapter 7, a rigorous analyis of such networks presents some significant challenges. Despite these challenges, there is a significant need for models that deal with valued-edge networks. Weighted networks are quite common in empirical applications (e.g., networks of countries are often measured in weighted terms, such as trade in dollars and tariffs in rates; Chen 2011). Luckily, the standard binary LSM can be readily extended to accommodate valued edges. The general form for the model follows that of the generalized linear model, just with a term that relates the latent space to the expected values of the elements of the adjacency matrix:

$$E(N_{ij} \mid \beta, X_{ij}, \mathbf{z}_i, \mathbf{z}_j) = g^{-1}\left\{\beta^T X_{ij} - d(\mathbf{z}_i, \mathbf{z}_j)\right\}. \tag{10.1}$$

It should be clear that Equation (10.1) is just a generalized form of the original LSM we specified in Chapter 8. In that chapter, the inverse link function, $g^{-1}(\cdot)$, was the inverse logit function. X_{ij} represents any exogenous covariates included in the model.

One common type of network seen in the applied literature is one where edges are weighted by the count of interactions between vertices. For example, in a Senate cosponsorship network, the edges could represent the number of times a senator (the sender) signed on to cosponsor a piece legislation with the sponsor (the receiver) during a given period (Fowler 2006). For these networks, it's natural to use a Poisson model. This is specified as follows:

$$N_{ij} \mid \eta_{ij} \sim \text{Poisson}(\eta_{ij}), \tag{10.2}$$

where

$$\eta_{ij} = \exp\{\beta^T x_{ij} - d(\mathbf{z}_i, \mathbf{z}_j)\}. \tag{10.3}$$

Another common type of edge weight takes on a binomial distribution, where there are a certain number successes in a number of trials. For instance, instead of modeling the cosponsorship network as a count model, where the maximum value is not constrained by a fixed number of possible cosponsorships, we may want to control for the fact that senators sponsor a limited number of bills each period, thus limiting the maximum value of the edge. (We'll see another example of this in our application.) The binomial model is defined as shown in Equation (10.4):

$$\Pr(N_{ij} = p_{ij} \mid \eta_{ij}) \sim \text{Binomial}(P_{ij}, \eta_{ij}), \qquad (10.4)$$

where P_{ij} is the number of trials (e.g., the number of sponsorships by senator j in a specific time period) for edge ij, $p_{ij} \in 1, \ldots P_{ij}$ is the observed number of successful trials, η_{ij} is defined as in Equation (10.3). Of course, possibly the most common edge weights are continuous. We see these, for example, in trade networks where the edges represent the value of imports and exports between countries (Ward et al. 2013). It's natural to model such edges as following a Gaussian process; that is,

$$N_{ij} \mid \eta_{ij}, \sigma \sim \text{Normal}(\eta_{ij}, \sigma). \qquad (10.5)$$

In terms of estimation, there isn't anything particularly different about the LSM for valued-edge networks when compared to the binary LSM. With the appropriate changes to the likelihood calculation, the algorithm outlined in Section 9.5 still applies. This is quite unlike the complexity of estimating the GERGM, which we saw in Chapter 7. The one significant difference with models for valued-edge networks, as we will see, is that the interpretation of the estimated models must change (just as it would for different generalized linear models).

Running Example: Scottish Schoolgirl Friendship Network

We begin our examples of estimating a valued-edge LSM with a Poisson model for the girls friendship network. Recall that in the aggregated network, edge weights represent the number of times vertex i mentioned vertex j as being her friend. Strictly speaking, a Poisson model is not the most appropriate for this network. Since the there are just three periods, the count represented by the `mentions` edge weights has a maximum value of 3; thus, a binomial model may me more sensible. However, since count data are so common in network data, we think it's useful to see an application and to compare the results to a binomial model in a subsequent example.

To specify a Poisson LSM, one needs to specify a response variable to use as well as a response family in the call to `ergmm`. For our network this is done by specifying `response="mentions"` and `family="Poisson"`. We show how to do this in the following code block, where we also show the summary results for the model. Note that we also retain the rest of the model specification from the previous model.

```
> girls.2d.pois <- ergmm(Girls ~ absdiff("smoke") +
    absdiff("drugs") +
                        euclidean(d=2),
                    response="mentions", family="Poisson",
                    control=CONTROL, seed=12)
> summary(girls.2d.pois)


==========================
Summary of model fit
==========================

Formula:   Girls ~ absdiff("smoke") + absdiff("drugs") +
    euclidean(d = 2)
Attribute: mentions
Model:     Poisson
MCMC sample of size 4000, draws are 100 iterations apart, after
    burnin
    of 150000 iterations.
Covariate coefficients posterior means:
                Estimate    2.5%    97.5% 2*min(Pr(>0),Pr(<0))
(Intercept)      2.05605  1.76306  2.3708               <2e-16 ***
absdiff.smoke   -0.21313 -0.42943  0.0268               0.0805 .
absdiff.drugs   -0.60812 -0.81221 -0.4043               <2e-16 ***
---
Signif. codes:  0 '***' 0.001 '**' 0.01 '*' 0.05 '.' 0.1 ' ' 1

Overall BIC:              1490.398
Likelihood BIC:            965.7598
Latent space/clustering BIC:       524.6385

Covariate coefficients MKL:
                Estimate
(Intercept)    1.6445602
absdiff.smoke -0.2239747
absdiff.drugs -0.5817440
```

From the results we see that drug use is still a strong correlate with friendship in this model, though the smoking covariate doesn't seem to have as strong of an association under the Poisson model (no longer statistically significant at the conventional 95 percent level). Both of these homophily covariates retain the expected negative sign, however, indicating that fewer friendship mentions are "sent" from i to j when there are different levels of smoking and drug habits between i and j.

The estimated latent locations for this model are shown in the right panel of Figure 10.8, where it is compared to the binary model on the left. We have rotated the results from the Poisson model to match the previous model using the Z.ref argument to plot.ergmm. There are very few significant differences between the relative latent locations estimated in these two models. The biggest difference that should be noted is the scale of the latent space, which is somewhat smaller in the Poisson model and is simply the result of changing the dependent variable in the model.

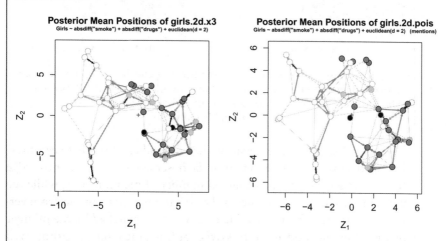

FIGURE 10.8 Estimated two-dimensional latent locations for the girls' friendship network models. The panel on the left shows results for the unweighted model shown in Figure 10.6. The panel on the right shows the Poisson model. Both models include homophily terms for tobacco and drug use. Vertices are shaded according to their stated tobacco use.

But how does the Poisson model perform? Figure 10.9 uses the predict_response_hist function from the ina package to simulate 1,000 networks (the default) from the estimated Poisson model, extract the predicted edge value between two vertices in the network, then plot the results as a histogram. We have chosen to look at the edge values between vertex 30 and 19, who are two relatively connected vertices. In the chart, the solid vertical line indicates the observed number of mentions, while the dotted line is the mean value seen in the simulations.

Predicted edge values from 19 to 30

Predicted edge values from 30 to 19

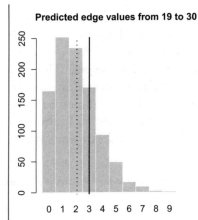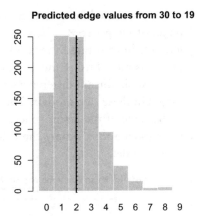

FIGURE 10.9 Posterior predicted number of friendship mentions between vertices 19 and 30 in the girls' friendship network based on the Poisson model. The vertical solid line represents the truth, while the vertical dotted line is the mean predicted value.

As the plots show, the mean predicted number of ties between these two vertices is fairly close to that of the observed networks. For the edge from vertex 19 to 30, the observed number of mentions is 3, while the mean predicted value is around 2. For the number of mentions from vertex 30 to 19, we observe a value of 2, which is matched by the number predicted by the model. For this dyad, at least, the model performs well as far as mean predictive accuracy is concerned. However, there is one way in which the model doesn't perform well: some of the predictions are nonsensical in that they exceed the number of mentions possible in the network. To remedy this, we will next estimate a binomial model for this network.

The code block below shows how to specify a binomial model in the call to `ergmm`. This is analogous to the Poisson call – simply specify `response="mentions"` and `family="binomial"` — but there is one further complication. In addition to specifying the response and family, for binomial models, one also has to specify the number of trials, P_{ij} in our notation above, for each of the edge weights. This can be done by adding a `fam.par` argument, that takes a list with a `trials` element. In this example, we specify `fam.par=list(trials=3)`, because each girl could have only mentioned another girl a maximum of three times. However, it should be noted that there is a significant limitation in the LSM for binomial models as implemented in `latentnet`: the number of trials must be fixed across dyads; in other words $P_{ij} = P \ \forall i \neq j$. This doesn't affect our analysis, but it does limit the application of `ergmm` to those in which the number of trials varies by dyad. For example, Bonsón, Royo, and Ratkai (2015) measure a citizen's engagement with a local government's Facebook page, in part, by the number of posts liked by the citizen out of the number of total posts. A network formed through relations such as this would, ideally, adjust for the number of posts by a user as a trials variable that varies by user.

```
> girls.2d.binom <- ergmm(Girls ~ absdiff("smoke") +
    absdiff("drugs") +
                            euclidean(d=2),
                            response="mentions", family="binomial",
                            fam.par=list(trials=3),
                            control=CONTROL, seed=12)
> summary(girls.2d.binom)


==========================
Summary of model fit
==========================


Formula:   Girls ~ absdiff("smoke") + absdiff("drugs") +
    euclidean(d = 2)
Attribute: mentions
Model:       binomial
MCMC sample of size 4000, draws are 100 iterations apart, after
    burnin
    of 150000 iterations.
Covariate coefficients posterior means:
                Estimate    2.5%   97.5% 2*min(Pr(>0),Pr(<0))
(Intercept)    2.68132  2.24675  3.1469          <2e-16 ***
absdiff.smoke -0.27050 -0.54493  0.0158          0.0655 .
absdiff.drugs -0.89738 -1.14954 -0.6401          <2e-16 ***
---
Signif. codes:  0 '***' 0.001 '**' 0.01 '*' 0.05 '.' 0.1 ' ' 1

Overall BIC:         1463.477
Likelihood BIC:       869.3855
Latent space/clustering BIC:     594.091

Covariate coefficients MKL:
                Estimate
(Intercept)    1.9829093
absdiff.smoke -0.2649620
absdiff.drugs -0.8061366
```

There are no surprises in the binomial version of the model. Substantively, the drug homophily covariate still appears to have a close association with friendship mentions and, as in the Poisson model, the smoking homophily is no longer statistically significant at conventional levels. Figure 10.10 provides a side-by-side comparison of the estimated latent locations for the Poisson and binomial models (locations have been rotated for comparability).

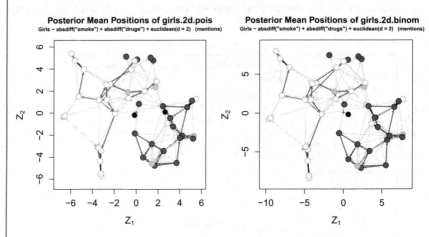

FIGURE 10.10 Estimated two-dimensional latent locations for the girls' friendship network models. The panel on the left shows results for the Poisson model shown in Figure 10.8. The panel on the right shows the binomial model. Both models include homophily terms for tobacco and drug use. Vertices are shaded according to their stated tobacco use.

A comparison of the plots shows no surprises in the locations of the vertices in the estimated latent space. But what about the predictive performance of the binomial model? In Figure 10.11 we again the show histograms of predicted outcomes for edges connecting vertex 19 and 30. While histograms may not be the best way to visualize binomial distributions, once again, we can see that the model performs relatively well, though not significantly different than the Poisson model in terms of mean predictive error. However, where it does excel is in not producing nonsensical predictions that go beyond the range of possible outcomes.

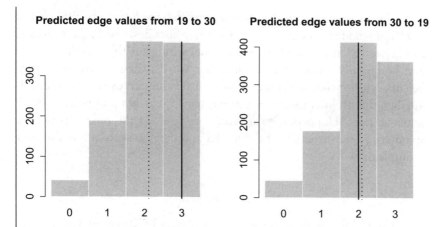

FIGURE 10.11 Posterior predicted number of friendship mentions between vertex 19 and 30 in the girls friendship network based on the binomial model. The vertical solid line represents the truth, while the vertical dotted line is the mean predicted value.

10.3 CLUSTER MODELS

It is often the case that we know, or suspect, the vertices in a network are grouped together by some characteristic or set of characteristics. For instance, we may think that in an adolescent friendship network, girls and boys would cluster into distinct groups, where close friendships would be more common within gender groups than between them.

We may want to take this clustering into account in our modeling of the latent space. Of course, in the models we have discussed previously, we could just include a homophily effect if the vertex characteristic is known. However, it is often the case that datasets of interest may exclude important vertex attribute data (e.g., we may be studying political communication on social media, and not know the political party affiliations of users). Furthermore, we often don't know if or why a group of vertices group together. We may have a theory about why they should group together. If this is an exploratory analysis, we may want to see if the network itself can uncover some structure in the data.

In this section we introduce another model, the latent position cluster model of Handcock et al. (2007). As the authors describe it, their "model can be viewed as a stochastic blockmodel with transitivity within blocks and homophily on attributes." In other words, each vertex is a member of a cluster that is denser within-cluster than across clusters, and is attributed with latent positions along which it is homophilous with all other vertices (Handcock et al. 2007, p. 303). In the next section, we summarized the structure of the model and then go on to apply it to our example network.

10.3.1 The Model

In the notation we used before, the clustered LSM (or, as the authors called it, the latent position cluster model; LPCM) for binary networks is defined as follows:[1]

$$\Pr(N_{ij} = 1 \mid \beta_0, \beta_1, \mathbf{z}_i, \mathbf{z}_j) = \text{logit}^{-1}\left\{\beta_0 - \beta_1 d(\mathbf{z}_i, \mathbf{z}_j)\right\}. \quad (10.6)$$

By now, this should be mostly familiar. The only difference between this portion of the model and the basic LSM is the β_1 term. This term acts to scale the latent space, which is needed because of a further constraint the model places on the latent positions. Specifically, the latent positions are restricted to have a unit root mean square:

$$\sqrt{\frac{1}{n}\sum_i |z_i|^2} = 1. \quad (10.7)$$

Placing this constraint help identifies the scale of the other coefficients in the model. The difference with this model when compared to the others we have reviewed is how the latent positions for each vertex are modeled. Instead of being drawn from a single distribution, the LPCM assumes each vertex is generated from a mixture of Gaussian distributions:

$$\mathbf{z}_i \sim \sum_{g \in G} \lambda_g N(\mu_g, \sigma_g^2 I_s). \quad (10.8)$$

In Equation (10.8), g indicates one of G groups (clusters) to which each vertex can belong, where $\lambda_g \geq 0$ is the probability of membership in group g. $N(\mu_g, \sigma_g^2 I_s)$ is the Gaussian distribution centered at μ_g with variance of $\sigma_g^2 I_s$. The parameter $\sigma_g^2 I_s$ controls the relative density of group g, with smaller variances resulting in positions closer together.

---

[1] The model is easily extended to networks with valued edges.

While we won't go into detail on the estimation of the model, the authors do propose two methods of obtaining parameter estimates. In the first method, they use a two-stage MLE technique that first estimates the latent positions and then second uses these estimates as an input to an expectation maximization routine to find cluster membership. The second method they propose is a fully Bayesian approach, which typically performs better (though it is slow).

Running Example: Scottish Schoolgirl Friendship Network

Returning to the friendship network among Scottish schoolgirls, in this section we begin by demonstrating how to estimate the LPCM using latentnet. At the end of the section, we will briefly introduce a different package, VBLPCM, which provides a much faster optimization algorithm but doesn't yet support binomial models.

Estimating the LPCM with ergmm is as simple as specifying the number of groups in the specification of the latent space. For example, a two-dimensional, two-cluster model can be specified with euclidean(d=2, G=2) in the model specification. In the code block below, we estimate two models for the friendship network, one with two clusters and one with three clusters.

```
## Note that we make some changes to the priors to help in the
       fitting process.
girls.2d.c2 <- ergmm(Girls ~ absdiff("smoke") + absdiff("drugs") +
                     euclidean(d=2, G=2, mean.var=1, var=1),
                     response="mentions", family="binomial",
                     fam.par=list(trials=3),
                     control=CONTROL,
                     seed=12)
girls.2d.c3 <- ergmm(Girls ~ absdiff("smoke") + absdiff("drugs") +
                     euclidean(d=2, G=3, mean.var=1, var=1),
                     response="mentions", family="binomial",
                     fam.par=list(trials=3),
                     control=CONTROL,
                     seed=12)
```

The summary output for these models has been omitted. Upon review, they didn't show anything new about the network. Coefficient estimates were in line with those of previous models: drug use homophily remained important to mentions of friendship and smoking remained marginally important as well. We will, however, show the graphical results of these models. The latent locations of the vertices for the two-cluster model are shown in the left panel of Figure 10.12, with the right panel showing the results for the three-cluster model (locations have once again been rotated to facilitate comparison).

In the plots, the large circles indicate the variance of the clusters, while the vertices themselves are shown as individual pie charts indicating the probability of cluster membership. From these results, it's clear that the individual groups are not particularly distinct from each other. In both of the models, the clusters overlap, but in the three-cluster model the third cluster is mostly contained within the other two clusters. This is a fairly good sign that the additional cluster structure introduced with the LPMC is not necessary for fitting a model to this network. However, there were some issue with estimating these models. It was somewhat difficult to get the parameters to mix well in a reasonable number of iterations.

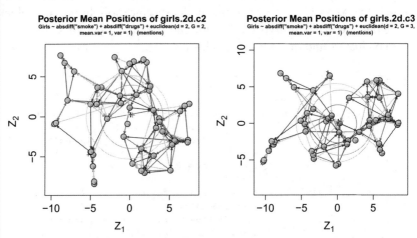

FIGURE 10.12 Estimated two-dimensional latent locations for the girls' friendship network models according to two-cluster and three-cluster LPMC. Vertices are represented by pie charts, which indicate the probability of cluster membership. Circles indicate the variance of the estimated cluster.

The lack of clarity in the results above provide the opportunity to test another tool for estimating the LPMC. Salter-Townshend (2015) provides an R package, VBLPCM, to estimate several models using a fast variational Bayes approximation. The package doesn't support binomial outcomes, and isn't as feature-rich as latentnet, but in situations where ergmm has a difficult time fitting a model well, VBLPCM is a good alternative. This is particularly true with large networks, where the algorithms employed by the package can make estimating a model possible. See Salter-Townshend and Murphy (2013) and Raftery et al. (2012) for details.

The model fitting process for VBLPCM is somewhat different than many other R packages. You begin by running a routine, vblpcmstart, that sets up the model and finds good starting values for the main fitting procedure. This function takes a network object as the first argument then optional argument to set the number of latent dimensions, clusters, and other possible parameters. After the vblpcmstart procedure has run, you then feed the result to the model fitting procedure, vblpcmfit. The code below takes these steps in fitting a three- and three-cluster model to the friendship networks (treating it as an unweighted network and excluding covariates).

```
1   vb.2d.c2.start <- vblpcmstart(Girls, G=2, d=2)
2   vb.2d.c2.fit <- vblpcmfit(vb.2d.c2.start)
3
4   vb.2d.c3.start <- vblpcmstart(Girls, G=3, d=2)
5   vb.2d.c3.fit <- vblpcmfit(vb.2d.c3.start)
```

The fitting of this network with VBLPCM takes much less time than ergmm. We can see the results below in Figure 10.13. Keeping in mind that these are not directly analogous to the results seen above for the binomial model including covariates, the differences in results are quite apparent. In both plots, it is clear that the variational Bayes approach has identified fairly distinct clusters of vertices in the network. In the plot on the left, two large clusters are apparent. In the right, three have been identified. From these you can't tell which model provides a better fit, but the model output (not shown) reports a BIC of approximately 1701 for the two-cluster model and 1637 for the three-cluster model, which suggests the three-cluster model is most appropriate (Handcock et al. 2007).

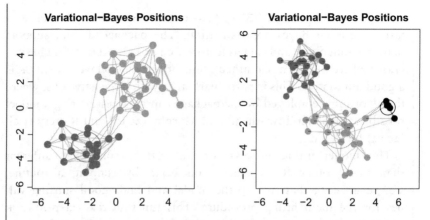

FIGURE 10.13 Estimated two-dimensional latent locations for the girls'
friendship network models according to 2-cluster and 3-cluster LPMC
estimated with a variational Bayes procedure. Circles indicate the variance of
the estimated cluster. The model excluded covariates and was estimated on
unweighted edges.

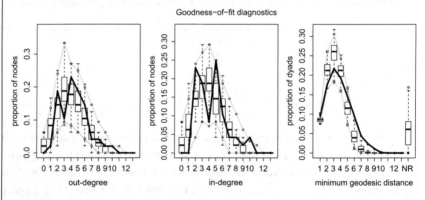

FIGURE 10.14 Goodness of fit diagnostics for the two-dimensional,
three-cluster LPCM estimated with the variational Bayes procedure. The
model excluded covariates and was estimated on unweighted edges.

The goodness-of-fit plots in Figure 10.14 show that the three-cluster
variational Bayes model fits the network well. In fact, keeping in mind
the lack of edge weights, the fit looks marginally better than those
originally estimated with ergmm. However, these results come with
one additional and potentially significant caveat: the two isolates were
removed from the network before the model was estimated.

10.4 RANDOM EFFECTS MODELS

It is a common feature of network research, and social research more broadly, that not all factors leading to edge formation are known and accounted for in the data. There are often vertex-level features that are associated with the propensity to form edges that are unknown or unknowable. Such unobserved heterogeneity can cause issues for model fitting and inference. Krivitsky et al. (2009) introduced a method for explicitly modeling the unobserved heterogeneity, which they refer to as random sender, receiver, and sociality effects, within the LSM and LPCM framework. This model will be reviewed in this section.

10.4.1 The Model

The LSM including the random sociality effects for undirected binary networks is presented in Equation (10.9). Once again, the model takes the usual form, with one small addition. In this version of the model, δ_i and δ_j represent random sociality effects for vertices i and j, which are assumed to follow the same distribution (typically Gaussian, centered at zero). A positive sociality effect indicates that the associated vertex is more likely to form edges than would be expected from the other factors included in the model, while a negative sociality effect indicates a lower probability than would be expected:

$$\Pr(N_{ij} = 1 \mid \beta_0, \mathbf{z}_i, \mathbf{z}_j, \delta_i, \delta_j,) = \mathrm{logit}^{-1}\{\beta_0 - d(\mathbf{z}_i, \mathbf{z}_j) + \delta_i + \delta_j\}$$
(10.9)

This model can easily be extended to directed networks. The necessary changes can be found in Equation (10.10):

$$\Pr(Y_{ij} = 1 \mid \beta_0, \mathbf{z}_i, \mathbf{z}_j, \delta_i, \delta_j,) = \mathrm{logit}^{-1}\{\beta_0 - d(\mathbf{z}_i, \mathbf{z}_j) + \delta_i + \gamma_j\}.$$
(10.10)

In this model, δ_i represents a random sender effect and γ_j is a random receiver effect. When δ_i is positive, that indicates i is more likely to send edges than would be expected, and when γ_j is positive, j is more likely to receive edges. These sender and receiver effects are usually modeled as independent Gaussians centered at zero. While the version specified here is for binary edges, the model can be easily altered to model valued edges as well.

Running Example: Scottish Schoolgirl Friendship Network

In this example, we once again use the `ergmm` function from `latentnet` to estimate receiver and sender random effects in the latent space model. This can be done by simply including the `rsender` and `rreceiver` terms in the model specification. Given some issues with model fit and convergence that we experienced with the models including clusters, we omitted clusters for this example. We do retain the smoking and drug use homophily terms and for our purposes restrict our model fitting to two-dimensional models.

The model results shown below are in line with those produced by previous models, with the homophily term for drug use remaining statistically significant and negative, as expected. In this model, the homophily term for smoking is once again statistically significant and also carries a negative sign, indicating that similar smoking behavior is important to friendship formation in this network. Interestingly, while not shown here, the inclusion of the random sender and receiver effects made this model somewhat easier to fit. This is probably due to the fact that these terms were able capture some of the random heterogeneity in the data that was not easy attributable to the other covariates. The goodness-of-fit statistics also improved marginally.

```
 1   > girls.2d.c2 <- ergmm(Girls ~ absdiff("smoke") +
         absdiff("drugs") +
 2                           rsender + rreceiver +
 3                           euclidean(d=2),
 4                   response="mentions", family="binomial",
 5                   fam.par=list(trials=3),
 6                   control=CONTROL,
 7                   seed=12)
 8
 9   ===========================
10   Summary of model fit
11   ===========================
12
13   Formula:   Girls ~ absdiff("smoke") + absdiff("drugs") + rsender
         + rreceiver +
14       euclidean(d = 2)
15   Attribute: mentions
16   Model:     binomial
17   MCMC sample of size 4000, draws are 100 iterations apart, after
         burnin
18       of 150000 iterations.
19   Covariate coefficients posterior means:
```

```
20                    Estimate    2.5%   97.5% 2*min(Pr(>0),Pr(<0))
21    (Intercept)      2.84374 2.30563  3.4440           <2e-16 ***
22    absdiff.smoke   -0.33679 -0.66050 -0.0053          0.0465 *
23    absdiff.drugs   -0.97504 -1.25961 -0.6924          <2e-16 ***
24    ---
25    Signif. codes:  0 '***' 0.001 '**' 0.01 '*' 0.05 '.' 0.1 ' ' 1
26
27    Sender effect variance: 0.3356859.
28    Receiver effect variance: 0.3667049.
29    Overall BIC:        1529.452
30    Likelihood BIC:      793.2718
31    Latent space/clustering BIC:      594.0645
32    Sender effect BIC:     66.77374
33    Receiver effect BIC:    75.3424
34
35    Covariate coefficients MKL:
36                    Estimate
37    (Intercept)     1.9868518
38    absdiff.smoke  -0.2720971
39    absdiff.drugs  -0.7562515
```

Figure 10.15 presents the estimated latent locations for this model. In the left panel, the vertices are scaled according to the posterior mean of the associated sender effects. In the right panel, the receiver effects are used to scale the vertices. Vertices are colored by the smoking covariate.

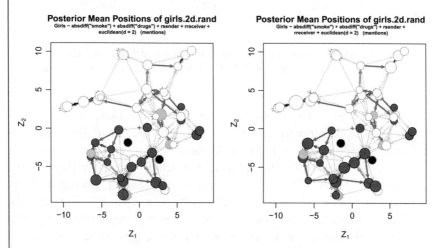

FIGURE 10.15 Estimated two-dimensional latent locations for the girls' friendship network models according to random effects LSM. Vertices are sized according to the magnitude of their sender effect (left panel) and receiver effect (right panel) membership. Vertices are shaded according to their stated tobacco use.

It's difficult to tell from Figure 10.15 the range of the random sender and receiver effects estimated in the model. For this reason, it's often useful to plot the sender and receiver posterior means for the vertices in the network. The code below does this by extracting the posterior means from the summary.ergmm object and produces a box plot for comparison.

```
sr <- rbind(data.frame(effect="sender",
                       re=summary(girls.2d.rand)$pmean$sender),
            data.frame(effect="receiver",
                       re=summary(girls.2d.rand)$pmean$receiver))
boxplot(re ~ effect, data=sr, horizontal=TRUE, xlab="Effect size")
```

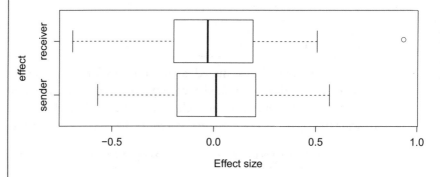

FIGURE 10.16 Distribution of posterior mean sender and receiver effects for the two-dimensional random effects LSM estimated on the girls' friendship network.

From Figure 10.16, we see that the distributions of the sender and receiver random effects are roughly the same (by construction, their means should have been close to zero). The only thing of note from this plot is the single outlier vertex in the receiver effects. This vertex, number 46, had a posterior mean receiver effect of nearly 1.0, which is a strong effect on the binomial scale. This indicates that the girl represented by this vertex is much more likely to receive edges than one would expect given her other exogenous covariates and connections in the network.

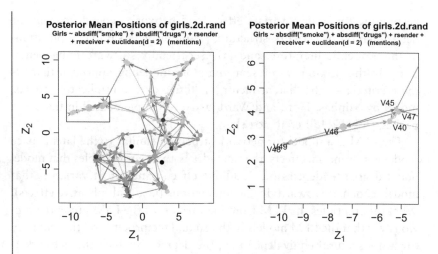

FIGURE 10.17 Latent positions for a subset of vertices in the two-dimensional random effects LSM estimated on the girls' friendship network.

Figure 10.17 shows two additional plots that makes it possible to see where this vertex lies in relation to the rest of the network. The plot on the left repeats the right panel from Figure 10.15, though now includes a box to indicate the portion of the plot presented in the right panel. In the zoomed panel, you can see why this girl is something of an outlier in the network. Of the five other girls in this group, girl 46 is mentioned by four of them as being a close friend in at least one period: girl 47 mentions her three times, girls 45 and 49 mention her two times each, and girl 40 mentions her in one of the surveys. In an extended analysis of this network and the social relationships it represents, girl 46 may be an interesting actor to investigate more closely. Identifying what makes her more popular than expected could shed light on additional factors driving friendships in adolescent girls.

10.5 THE ADDITIVE AND MULTIPLICATIVE EFFECTS LATENT FACTOR MODEL (LFM)

Throughout this book, we have presented modeling approaches that share three characteristics: (1) the capability of modeling and/or accounting for both covariate effects and network dependencies in the determination of network structure, (2) published example applications in the academic literature, and (3) user-friendly software implementations. In this section we present one more modeling approach that fits these criteria — the "latent factor," additive and multiplicative effects, model by Minhas, Hoff, and Ward (2019) — implemented in the amen package for R (Hoff et al. 2014).

The LFM is a model for network structure, similar to the latent space model with random effects, that includes both latent variables that model nodal degree tendencies (i.e., additive effects) and latent variables that model tendencies toward dyadic interactions (i.e., multiplicative effects). What differentiates the LFM from the variants of the LSM presented previously is that the LFM models both residual reciprocity and the tendency toward structural equivalence (i.e., the degree to which the network is characterized by pairs of vertices that are connected to the same sets of vertices).

Here we present the mathematical structure of the LFM for binary networks. In the LFM,

$$\Pr(y_{ij} = 1 \mid a, b, \beta, u, v, \Lambda) = \Pr(y_{ij}^* > 0 \mid a, b, \beta, u, v, \Lambda), \quad (10.11)$$

where a, and b are vectors of random sender and receiver effects, respectively, β is the vector of regression coefficients, u, and v are nodal sender and receiver coordinates, respectively, in the latent multiplicative space, and Λ is a diagonal matrix that is used to model the degree of structural equivalence reflected in the multiplicative effects term. The functional form of the LFM is given by

$$y_{ij}^* = a_i + b_j + \beta' x_{ij} + u_i' \Lambda v_j. + \epsilon_{ij}, \quad (10.12)$$

where ϵ_{ij} comes from a bivariate normal distribution with ϵ_{ji} that includes a correlation that models residual reciprocity. The distributions of the sender and receiver effects also includes variance components that capture (1) the heterogeneity across vertices in the scales of sender and receiver effects, modeling heterogeneity in the degree distributions, and (2) the tendency for a vertex's sender and receiver effects to be correlated, modeling the tendency toward general gregariousness of vertices.

Running Example: Scottish Schoolgirl Friendship Network

In this final example, we use the amen package to model the binary ties in the Scottish schoolgirl network via the LFM. The model includes all of the terms in the LFM presented above, and the covariates included are the homophily terms for drug use and smoking, as in the above examples. Unlike most of the other models we presented, the function for running the LFM, ame, does not take network objects as arguments or use the conventional formula framework to specify the model. Rather, the arguments include various matrix and array objects. To ease the manipulation of the data, we use the abind package in the construction of arrays (Plate & Heiberger 2016). The first step in setting up our data is to create two matrices in which the i, j elements are the absolute difference in, respectively, the smoking and drug use scores of vertices i and j. These matrices are used to model the homophily effects with respect to these two variables.

```
library(amen)
library(abind)

diff.smoke <- as.matrix(dist(get.vertex.attribute(Girls, "smoke"),
                        upper=TRUE))
diff.drugs <- as.matrix(dist(get.vertex.attribute(Girls, "drugs"),
                        upper=TRUE))

## dyadic covariate effects, bound into a 50x50x2 array
X <- abind(smoke=diff.smoke, drugs=diff.drugs, along=3)
```

The following code illustrates how we specify and estimate the model using ame. The first argument to the function is the adjacency matrix as extracted from the network object. Here we are using a directed, binary model, as indicted by symmetric=FALSE and model="bin". The dyadic covariates are included using the $50 \times 50 \times 2$ array, X, created above. rvar=TRUE and cvar=TRUE specify the inclusion of the row and column random effects components, while R=2 specifies a two-dimensional latent space.

```
girls.ame_2d <- ame(Girls[,], Xdyad=X, R=2, symmetric=FALSE,
    model="bin",
        rvar=TRUE, cvar=TRUE, nscan=500000, burn=10000, plot=FALSE,
        print=TRUE, seed=12)
```

The code following the estimation of the LFM draws upon the MCMC diagnostics from the `coda` package (Plummer et al. 2006) to assure that the Markov chains for the regression coefficients have converged. The function `geweke.diag` implements a test developed by Geweke (1992b), which amounts to a test that evaluates whether the mean of the Markov chain in the early part of the chain is different from that toward the end of the chain. The test statistics can be analyzed as *t*-statistics, and the smaller they are in magnitude the greater the evidence for convergence.

```
1   library(coda)
2     beta.mcmc <- as.mcmc(girls.ame_2d$BETA)
3     geweke.diag(beta.mcmc)
4
5   Fraction in 1st window = 0.1
6   Fraction in 2nd window = 0.5
7
8     intercept smoke.dyad drugs.dyad
9        1.1018     0.1732     0.4083
```

The `plot` function for `ame` model objects also provides useful diagnostics for model convergence as displayed in Figure 10.18:

Now that we have run the model and assured that tabl the MCMC has converged, we interpret the results in terms of the covariates. The results align with those of the analysis of these data using the LSM. Tie formation in this network exhibits homophily with respect to both smoking and drug use. The coefficient estimates are slightly different in terms of magnitude, but note that magnitudes cannot be directly compared between the LSM and the LFM, as (1) the different variance components in the two models distort the scales of the linear predictors and (2) because of the Gaussian structure of the errors in the LFM, the LFM is on the probit scale (as opposed to the logit scale with the LSM). Among the variance parameters, the "rho" term can be interpreted as a reciprocity effect on the correlation coefficient scale. The high posterior mean, and small posterior standard deviation indicate a strong tendency toward reciprocity.

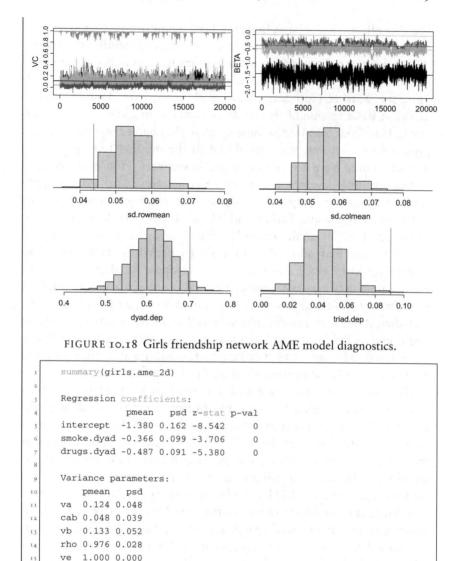

FIGURE 10.18 Girls friendship network AME model diagnostics.

```
 1    summary(girls.ame_2d)
 2
 3    Regression coefficients:
 4                  pmean    psd  z-stat  p-val
 5    intercept   -1.380  0.162  -8.542      0
 6    smoke.dyad  -0.366  0.099  -3.706      0
 7    drugs.dyad  -0.487  0.091  -5.380      0
 8
 9    Variance parameters:
10          pmean    psd
11    va    0.124  0.048
12    cab   0.048  0.039
13    vb    0.133  0.052
14    rho   0.976  0.028
15    ve    1.000  0.000
```

10.6 OTHER EXTENSIONS

The previous sections provided a review of three of the most important and useful extensions to the LSM, namely, the application of the model to valued-edge networks and the inclusion of vertex clustering and random sociality effects. There have, however, been a number of other extensions proposed and applied in the literature. Most prominently, this chapter did not include a discussion of the important bilinear mixed effect model of Hoff (2005), which itself has seen numerous applications and developments (Ward & Hoff 2007, Ward et al. 2007, 2013, Fosdick & Hoff 2015). A basic version of this model is available in latentnet (Krivitsky & Handcock 2008). Also missing from the chapter was the so-called projection model that was introduced in the original LSM paper, but doesn't seem to have been implemented in software (Hoff et al. 2002).

One exciting development in the LSM literature has been its application to dynamic (temporal) networks. For instance, not long after its initial implementation, Sarkar and Moore (2005) developed a version of the LSM for dynamic networks, which used several computational enhancements that allowed it to scale to networks with more than 10,000 vertices. Sewell and Chen (2015) propose an alternative model for dynamic networks with binary ties and use the case-control method of Raftery et al. (2012) to make computation on large networks feasible, including those with missing edges. Sewell and Chen (2016) provide an additional model for dynamic valued-edge networks. See Xu and Zheng (2009) and (Morgan 2015, Chapter 2) for additional applications and Kim et al. (2018) for a review of other dynamic LSMs.

Numerous other models for a variety of network types have also been proposed. As examples, Gormley and Murphy (2007) provide a model for rank data and apply it to voting data from an Irish election; Rastelli et al. (2016) develop what they call a Gaussian latent position model that incorporates a random effects component, making it capable of reflecting heavy-tailed degree distributions; Sweet, Thomas, and Junker (2013) propose a hierarchical LSM for education research; Austin, Linkletter, and Wu (2013) introduce an interesting model for the placement of new actors into the latent social space; and Smith, Asta, and Calder (2017) provide a detailed review of the properties of different latent spaces themselves, which should help guide future methodological development and novel applications.

10.7 WRAPPING UP

The latent space model provides a flexible framework for modeling network data. Off-the-shelf software exists to model a variety of valued-edge types. This includes count, binomial, and continuous edge types. The model has also been extended to capture unobserved heterogeneity in the form of random sociality, sender, and receiver effects and to accommodate clustering of vertices in the latent space. More recent work has further extended the model to temporal networks and to larger scale networks via variational Bayes estimation.

10.8 SELF-STUDY PROBLEMS

Select a weighted network dataset to study using extended variants of the LSM, but avoid using the data from `ina` that was used in this chapter. Be sure that the dataset includes at least one vertex attribute. If you do not have a dataset that you would like to use for this exercise, we recommend that you use the weighted `ACCBasketball` dataset from `ina`, which is introduced in the beginning of Chapter 7. Using this dataset, complete a report that includes the following information:

1. **Description of the dataset:** What does the dataset cover? Where did it come from? Has it been used in any prior studies?
2. **Hypotheses:** Describe and test at least one hypothesis regarding a vertex attribute.
3. **Model specification:** Identify a model specification that you believe is capable of testing your hypotheses, and is specified with the normal family via `ergmm`. Add a two-dimensional Euclidean latent space to the model. Specify a second model that reflects your hypotheses, but uses `amen` with a two-dimensional latent factor and the `model` option set to "nrm." Estimate the models and assure that they have converged.
4. **Estimates:** Present the coefficient estimates of the LSM and the LFM in either graphical or tabular form.
5. **Exploration:** Plot the latent positions from each model. Comment on whether you learn anything about the structure of the network from visualizing the latent space and latent factors.
6. **Interpretation:** Substantively interpret your results. Do you find support for your hypotheses? Do you think the effects that you find are large? Are the results consistent between the LSM and LFM.

References

Abramski, K. E. (2018), "A network based analysis of the international refugee crisis using GERGMs," PhD thesis, University of Rhode Island.

Adamic, L. A. & Adar, E. (2003), "Friends and neighbors on the web," *Social Networks* 25(3), 211–230.

Almquist, Z. W. & Butts, C. T. (2013), "Dynamic network logistic regression: A logistic choice analysis of inter- and intra-group blog citation dynamics in the 2004 US presidential election," *Political Analysis* 21(4), 430–448.

Amati, V. (2011), "New statistics for the parameter estimation of the stochastic actor-oriented model for network change," PhD thesis, Universitá degli Studi di Milano.

Amati, V., Schönenberger, F. & Snijders, T. (2015), "Estimation of stochastic actor-oriented models for the evolution of networks by generalized method of moments," *Journal de la Socit Franaise de Statistique* 156(3), 140–165.

Andrew, S. A., Short, J. E., Jung, K. & Arlikatti, S. (2015), "Intergovernmental cooperation in the provision of public safety: Monitoring mechanisms embedded in interlocal agreements," *Public Administration Review* 75(3), 401–410.

Arnold, L. W., Deen, R. E. & Patterson, S. C. (2000), "Friendship and votes: The impact of interpersonal ties on legislative decision making," *State and Local Government Review* 32(2), 142–147.

Atouba, Y. C. & Shumate, M. (2015), "International nonprofit collaboration: Examining the role of homophily," *Nonprofit and Voluntary Sector Quarterly* 44(3), 587–608.

Austin, A., Linkletter, C. & Wu, Z. (2013), "Covariate-defined latent space random effects model," *Social Networks* 35(3), 338–346.

Axelrod, R. (1984), *The Evolution of Cooperation*, Basic Books.

Axelrod, R. M. (2006), *The Evolution of Cooperation*, 2nd ed., Basic Books.

Bafumi, J., Gelman, A., Park, D. K. & Kaplan, N. (2005), "Practical issues in implementing and understanding Bayesian ideal point estimation," *Political Analysis* 13(2), 171–187.

Barabási, A.-L. & Albert, R. (1999), "Emergence of scaling in random networks," *Science* 286(5439), 509–512.

Barr, A., Dekker, M. & Fafchamps, M. (2012), "Who shares risk with whom under different enforcement mechanisms?" *Economic Development and Cultural Change* 60(4), 677–706.

Bartal, A., Pliskin, N. & Ravid, G. (2019), "Modeling influence on posting engagement in online social networks: Beyond neighborhood effects," *Social Networks* 59, 61–76.

Berardo, R. & Scholz, J. T. (2010), "Self-organizing policy networks: Risk, partner selection, and cooperation in estuaries," *American Journal of Political Science* 54(3), 632–649.

Berscheid, E. & Hatfield, E. (1969), *Interpersonal Attraction*, Addison-Wesley.

Besag, J. (1974), "Spatial interaction and the statistical analysis of lattice systems," *Journal of the Royal Statistical Society, Series B* 36, 192–236.

Betancourt, B., Rodrfguez, A. & Boyd, N. (2017), "Bayesian fused lasso regression for dynamic binary networks," *Journal of Computational and Graphical Statistics* 26(4), 840–850.

Biancani, S. & McFarland, D. A. (2013), "Social networks research in higher education," *in Higher Education: Handbook of Theory and Research*, Springer, pp. 151–215.

Block, P., Koskinen, J., Hollway, J., Steglich, C. & Stadtfeld, C. (2018), "Change we can believe in: Comparing longitudinal network models on consistency, interpretability and predictive power," *Social Networks* 52, 180–191.

Block, P., Stadtfeld, C. & Snijders, T. A. (2019), "Forms of dependence: Comparing SAOMs and ERGMs from basic principles," *Sociological Methods & Research* 48(1), 202–239.

Bochsler, D. (2009), "Neighbours or friends? When Swiss cantonal governments co-operate with each other," *Regional and Federal Studies* 19(3), 349–370.

Bonsón, E., Royo, S. & Ratkai, M. (2015), "Citizens' engagement on local governments' Facebook sites – an empirical analysis: The impact of different media and content types in Western Europe," *Government Information Quarterly* 32(1), 52–62.

Borg, I. & Groenen, P. J. F. (1997), *Modern Multidimensional Scaling: Theory and Applications*, Springer.

Box-Steffensmeier, J. M. & Christenson, D. P. (2014), "The evolution and formation of amicus curiae networks," *Social Networks* 36, 82–96.

Box-Steffensmeier, J. M., Arnold, L. W. & Zorn, C. J. (1997), "The strategic timing of position taking in Congress: A study of the North American Free Trade Agreement," *American Political Science Review* 91(2), 324–338.

Box-Steffensmeier, J. M., Freeman, J. R., Hitt, M. P. & Pevehouse, J. C. W. (2014), *Time Series Analysis for the Social Sciences*, Analytical Methods for Social Research, Cambridge University Press.

Bratton, K. A. & Rouse, S. M. (2011), "Networks in the legislative arena: How group dynamics affect cosponsorship," *Legislative Studies Quarterly* 36(3), 423–460.

Bull, S. B., Greenwood, C. M. & Donner, A. (1994), "Efficiency of reduced logistic regression models," *Canadian Journal of Statistics* 22(3), 319–334.

Butts, C. T. (2008), "Social network analysis: A methodological introduction," *Asian Journal of Social Psychology* 11(1), 13–41.

Butts, C. T. (2008), "network: a package for managing relational data in R," *Journal of Statistical Software* 24(2), 1–36.

Byrne, D. E. (1971), *The Attraction Paradigm*, Academic Press.

Caimo, A. & Friel, N. (2011), "Bayesian inference for exponential random graph models," *Social Networks* 33(1), 41–55.

Caimo, A. & Friel, N. (2014), "Bergm: Bayesian exponential random graphs in R," *Journal of Statistical Software* 61(2), 1–25.

Campbell, B., Cranmer, S. & Desmarais, B. (2018), "Triangulating war: Network structure and the democratic peace," *ArXiv e-prints* .

Cane, G. J. (1974), "Linear estimation of parameters of the cauchy distribution based on sample quantiles," *Journal of the American Statistical Association* 69(345), 243–245.

Canty, A. & Ripley, B. D. (2017), *boot: Bootstrap R (S-Plus) Functions*. R package version 1.3–20.

Casella, G. & Berger, R. L. (2001), *Statistical Inference*, Duxbury.

Castillo, E. & Colosimo, B. M. (2011), "Statistical shape analysis of experiments for manufacturing processes," *Technometrics* 53(1), 1–15.

Chandra, A., Copen, C. & Mosher, D. (2013), "Sexual behavior, sexual attraction, and sexual identity in the United States: Data from the 2006–2010 National Survey of Family Growth," in *International handbook on the demography of sexuality*, pp. 45–66. Springer.

Chen, B., Suo, L. & Ma, J. (2015), "A network approach to interprovincial agreements: A study of Pan Pearl river delta in China," *State and Local Government Review* 47(3), 181–191.

Chen, M. X. (2011), "Interdependence in multinational production networks," *Canadian Journal of Economics/Revue canadienne d'économique* 44(3), 930–956.

Christakis, N. A. & Fowler, J. H. (2011), *Connected: The Surprising Power of Our Social Networks and How They Shape Our Lives*, Back Bay Books.

Chu-Shore, J. (2010), "Homogenization and specialization effects of international trade: Are cultural goods exceptional?," *World Development* 38(1), 37–47.

Clark, J. H. & Caro, V. (2013), "Multimember districts and the substantive representation of women: An analysis of legislative cosponsorship networks," *Politics & Gender* 9(1), 1–30.

Corcuera, J. M. & Giummolè, F. (1999), "A generalized Bayes rule for prediction," *Scandinavian Journal of Statistics* 26(2), 265–279.

Cranmer, S. J. & Desmarais, B. A. (2011), "Inferential network analysis with exponential random graph models," *Political Analysis* 19(1), 66–86.

Cranmer, S. J. & Desmarais, B. A. (2016), "A critique of dyadic design," *International Studies Quarterly* 60(2), 355–362.

Cranmer, S. J. & Desmarais, B. A. (2017), "What can we learn from predictive modeling?," *Political Analysis* 25(2), 145–166.

Cranmer, S. J., Desmarais, B. A. & Kirkland, J. H. (2012), "Toward a network theory of alliance formation," *International Interactions* 38(3), 295–324.

Cranmer, S. J., Desmarais, B. A. & Menninga, E. J. (2012), "Complex dependencies in the alliance network," *Conflict Management and Peace Science* 29(3), 279–313.

Cranmer, S., Heinrich, T. & Desmarais, B. (2014), "Reciprocity and the structural determinants of the international sanctions network," *Social Networks* 36, 5–22.

Cranmer, S. J., Leifeld, P., Mcclurg, S. & Rolfe, M. (2017), "Navigating the range of statistical tools for inferential network analysis," *American Journal of Political Science* 61(1), 237–251.

Croft, D. P., Madden, J. R., Franks, D. W. & James, R. (2011), "Hypothesis testing in animal social networks," *Trends in Ecology & Evolution* 26(10), 502–507.

Dass, M. & Fox, G. L. (2011), "A holistic network model for supply chain analysis," *International Journal of Production Economics* 131(2), 587–594.

Dawid, A. P. (1980), "Conditional independence for statistical operations," *The Annals of Statistics* 8(3), 598–617.

Dekker, D., Krackhardt, D. & Snijders, T. A. (2007), "Sensitivity of MRQAP tests to collinearity and autocorrelation conditions," *Psychometrika* 72(4), 563–581.

De la Haye, K., Robins, G., Mohr, P. & Wilson, C. (2010), "Obesity-related behaviors in adolescent friendship networks," *Social Networks* 32(3), 161–167.

Dey, C. & Quinn, J. (2014), "Individual attributes and self-organizational processes affect dominance network structure in Pukeko," *Behavioral Ecology* 25, 1402–1408.

Denny, M. J., Wilson, J. D., Cranmer, S. J., Desmarais, B. A. & Bhamidi, S. (2017), *GERGM: Estimation and Fit Diagnostics for Generalized Exponential Random Graph Models*. R package version 0.11.2.

Desmarais, B. A. & Cranmer, S. J. (2010), "Consistent confidence intervals for maximum pseudolikelihood estimators," *Neural Information Processing Systems 2010 Workshop on Computational Social Science and the Wisdom of Crowds*.

Desmarais, B. A. & Cranmer, S. J. (2011), "Forecasting the locational dynamics of transnational terrorism: A network analytic approach," *in Proceedings of the European Intelligence and Security Informatics Conference (EISIC) 2011*, IEEE Computer Society.

Desmarais, B. A. & Cranmer, S. J. (2012a), "Micro-level interpretation of exponential radom graph models with application to estuary networks," *Policy Studies Journal* 40(3), 402 – 434.

Desmarais, B. A. & Cranmer, S. J. (2012b), "Statistical inference for valued-edge networks: The generalized exponential random graph model," *PLoS ONE* 7(1), e30136.

Desmarais, B. A. & Cranmer, S. J. (2012c), "Statistical mechanics of networks: Estimation and uncertainty," *Physica A: Statistical Mechanics and Its Applications* 391(4), 1865–1876.

Desmarais, B. A. & Cranmer, S. J. (2013), "Forecasting the locational dynamics of transnational terrorism: A network analytic approach," *Security Informatics* 2(1), 8.

Desmarais, B. A. & Cranmer, S. J. (2017), "Statistical inference in political networks research," in *The Oxford Handbook of Political Networks*, Oxford University Press, pp. 203–220.

Desmarais, B. A., Moscardelli, V. G., Schaffner, B. F. & Kowal, M. S. (2015), "Measuring legislative collaboration: The Senate press events network," *Social Networks* 40, 43–54.

Dianati, N. (2016), "Unwinding the hairball graph: Pruning algorithms for weighted complex networks," *Physical Review E* 93(1), 012304.

Dokuka, S., Krekhovets, E. & Priymak, M. (2017), "Health, grades and friendship: How socially constructed characteristics influence the social network structure," in *International Conference on Analysis of Images, Social Networks and Texts*, Springer, pp. 381–391.

Dokuka, S., Valeeva, D. & Yudkevich, M. (2015), "Formation and evolution mechanisms in online network of students: The vkontakte case," in *International Conference on Analysis of Images, Social Networks and Texts*, Springer, pp. 263–274.

Donovan, T. & Mickey, R. M. (2019), *Bayesian Statistics for Beginners: A Step-by-Step Approach*, Oxford University Press.

Dorff, C. & Ward, M. D. (2013), "Networks, dyads, and the social relations model," *Political Science Research and Methods* 1(2), 159–178.

Duque, M. G. (2018), "Recognizing international status: A relational approach," *International Studies Quarterly* 62(3), 577–592.

Duxbury, S. W. (2018), "Diagnosing multicollinearity in exponential random graph models," *Sociological Methods & Research*, online first, https://doi .org/10.1177/0049124118782543

Elman, M. F. (2001), "Falsification, generalization, and the democratic peace," *The International History Review* 23(4), 814–823.

Ernst, A. F. & Albers, C. J. (2017), "Regression assumptions in clinical psychology research practicea systematic review of common misconceptions," *PeerJ* 5, e3323.

Faber, J. (1987), "Measuring cooperation, conflict, and the social network of nations," *Journal of Conflict Resolution* 31(3), 438–464.

Falzon, L., McCurrie, C. & Dunn, J. (2017), "Representation and analysis of twitter activity: A dynamic network perspective," in *Proceedings of the 2017 IEEE/ACM International Conference on Advances in Social Networks Analysis and Mining 2017*, ACM, pp. 1183–1190.

Faust, K. (1988), "Comparison of methods for positional analysis: Structural and general equivalences," *Social Networks* 10(4), 313–341.

Faust, K. & Skvoretz, J. (2002), "Comparing networks across space and time, size and species," *Sociological Methodology* 32(1), 267–299.

Felmlee, D. & Faris, R. (2013), "Interaction in social networks," in *Handbook of Social Psychology*, Springer, pp. 439–464.

Fletcher, R. J., Revell, A., Reichert, B. E., Kitchens, W. M., Dixon, J. D. & Austin, J. D. (2013), "Network modularity reveals critical scales for connectivity in ecology and evolution," *Nature Communications* 4(1), 1–7.

Fletcher, R. J., Acevedo, M. A., Reichert, B. E., Pias, K. E. & Kitchens, W. M. (2011), "Social network models predict movement and connectivity in ecological landscapes," *Proceedings of the National Academy of Sciences* 108(48), 19282–19287.

Fosdick, B. K. & Hoff, P. D. (2015), "Testing and modeling dependencies between a network and nodal attributes," *Journal of the American Statistical Association* 110(511), 1047–1056.

Fowler, J. H. (2006), "Connecting the congress: A study of cosponsorship networks," *Political Analysis* 14(4), 456–487.

Frank, O. & Strauss, D. (1986), "Markov graphs," *Journal of the American Statistical Association* 81(395), 832–842.

Freckleton, R. & Watkinson, A. (2001), "Predicting competition coefficients for plant mixtures: Reciprocity, transitivity and correlations with life-history traits," *Ecology Letters* 4(4), 348–357.

Gallemore, C., Di Gregorio, M., Moeliono, M., Brockhaus, M., et al. (2015), "Transaction costs, power, and multi-level forest governance in Indonesia," *Ecological Economics* 114, 168–179.

Garlaschelli, D. & Loffredo, M. (2004), "Patterns of link reciprocity in directed networks," *Physical Review Letters* 93(26), 268701.

Gates, G. J. (2011), "How many people are lesbian, gay, bisexual, and transgender?" UCLA: The Williams Institute. Retrieved from https://escholarship.org/uc/item/09h684X2

Gelman, A. & Rubin, D. B. (1992), "Inference from iterative simulation using multiple sequences," *Statistical Science* 7(4), 457–472.

Genest, C. & MacKay, J. (1986), "The joy of copulas: Bivariate distributions with uniform marginals," *The American Statistician* 40(4), 280–283.

Geweke, J. (1992a), "Evaluating the accuracy of sampling-based approaches to the calculation of posterior moments," *in* A. Dawid & J. Berger, eds., *Bayesian Statistics*, Oxford University Press, pp. 169–193.

Geweke, J. (1992b), "Evaluating the accuracy of sampling-based approaches to the calculations of posterior moments," *Bayesian Statistics* 4, 641–649.

Geyer, C. J. (1990), "Likelihood and exponential families." University of Washington.

Geyer, C. J. & Thompson, E. A. (1992), "Constrained Monte Carlo maximum likelihood for dependent data," *Journal of the Royal Statistical Society, Series B* 54(3), 657–699.

Gill, J. (2008), "Is partial-dimension convergence a problem for inferences from MCMC algorithms?," *Political Analysis* 16(2), 153–178.

Goodreau, S., Handcock, M., Hunter, D., Butts, C. & Morris, M. (2008), "A statnet tutorial," *Journal of Statistical Software* 24(9), 1–26.

Gormley, I. C. & Murphy, T. B. (2007), "A latent space model for rank data," *in* E. Airoldi, D. M. Blei, S. E. Fienberg, A. Goldenberg, E. P. Xing & A. X. Zheng, eds., *Statistical Network Analysis: Models, Issues, and New Directions*, Springer pp. 90–102.

Haberman, S. J. (1988), "A stabilized Newton–Raphson algorithm for log-linear models for frequency tables derived by indirect observation," *Sociological Methodology* 18, 193–211.

Hafner-Burton, E. M. & Montgomery, A. H. (2008), "Power or plenty: How do international trade institutions affect economic sanctions?," *Journal of Conflict Resolution* 52(2), 213–242.

Handcock, M. S. & Gile, K. J. (2010), "Modeling social networks from sampled data," *The Annals of Applied Statistics* 4(1), 5.

Handcock, M. S., Raftery, A. E. & Tantrum, J. M. (2007), "Model-based clustering for social networks," *Journal of the Royal Statistical Society A* 170, 301–354.

Hanneke, S., Fu, W. & Xing, E. P. (2010), "Discrete temporal models of social networks," *The Electronic Journal of Statistics* 4, 585–605.

Harris, J. K., Moreland-Russell, S., Tabak, R. G., Ruhr, L. R. & Maier, R. C. (2014), "Communication about childhood obesity on twitter," *American Journal of Public Health* 104(7), e62–e69.

Hawe, P., Webster, C. & Shiell, A. (2004), "A glossary of terms for navigating the field of social network analysis," *Journal of Epidemiology & Community Health* 58(12), 971–975.

He, R. & Zheng, T. (2013), "Estimation of exponential random graph models for large social networks via graph limits," *in Proceedings of the 2013 IEEE/ACM International Conference on Advances in Social Networks Analysis and Mining*, ACM, pp. 248–255.

Heaney, M. T., Masket, S. E., Miller, J. M. & Strolovitch, D. Z. (2012), "Polarized networks: The organizational affiliations of national party convention delegates," *American Behavioral Scientist* 56(12), 1654–1676.

Hedayati, F. & Bartlett, P. L. (2012), "The optimality of Jeffreys prior for online density estimation and the asymptotic normality of maximum likelihood estimators," *in COLT*, p. 7–1.

Heidler, R., Gamper, M., Herz, A. & Eßer, F. (2014), "Relationship patterns in the 19th century: The friendship network in a German boys' school class from 1880 to 1881 revisited," *Social Networks* 37, 1–13.

Henry, A. D. (2011), "Ideology, power, and the structure of policy networks," *Policy Studies Journal* 39(3), 361–383.

Hoff, P. D. (2005), "Bilinear mixed-effects models for dyadic data," *Journal of the American Statistical Association* 100(469), 286–295.

Hoff, P. D., Raftery, A. E. & Handcock, M. S. (2002), "Latent space approaches to social network analysis," *Journal of the American Statistical Association* 97(460), 1090–1098.

Hoff, P., Fosdick, B., Volfovsky, A. & Stovel, K. (2014), *AMEN: Additive and Multiplicative Effects Modeling of Networks and Relational Data*. Package version 0.999.

Hogg, R. V. (2018), *Introduction to Mathematical Statistics*, Pearson Education Canada.

Holland, P. W. & Leinhardt, S. (1981), "An exponential family of probability distributions for directed graphs," *Journal of the American Statistical Association* 76(373), 33–50.

Holme, P. (2005), "Network reachability of real-world contact sequences," *Physical Review E* 71(4), 046119.

Hunter, D. R. (2007), "Curved exponential family models for social networks," *Social Networks* 29(2), 216–230.

Hunter, D. & Handcock, M. (2006), "Inference in curved exponential family models for networks," *Journal of Computational and Graphical Statistics* 15(3), 565–583.

Hunter, D. R., Handcock, M., Butts, C. T., Goodreau, S. M. & Morris, M. (2008), "ergm: A package to fit, simulate and diagnose exponential-family models for networks," *Journal of Statistical Software* 24 3, nihpa54860.

Hyvärinen, A. (2006), "Consistency of pseudolikelihood estimation of fully visible boltzmann machines," *Neural Computation* 18(10), 2283–2292.

Ingold, K. & Leifeld, P. (2014), "Structural and institutional determinants of influence reputation: A comparison of collaborative and adversarial policy networks in decision making and implementation," *Journal of Public Administration Research and Theory* 26(1), 1–18.

Jasny, L. (2012), "Baseline models for two-mode social network data," *Policy Studies Journal* 40(3), 458–491.

Johnson, R., Kovács, B. & Vicsek, A. (2012), "A comparison of email networks and off-line social networks: A study of a medium-sized bank," *Social Networks* 34(4), 462–469.

Karlberg, M. (1997), "Testing transitivity in graphs," *Social Networks* 19(4), 325–343.

Keller, F. B. (2016), "Moving beyond factions: Using social network analysis to uncover patronage networks among Chinese elites," *Journal of East Asian Studies* 16(1), 17–41.

Kim, B., Lee, K. H., Xue, L. & Niu, X. (2018), "A review of dynamic network models with latent variables," *Statistics Surveys* 12, 105–135.

King, R., Gimenez, O., Morgan, B. & Brooks, S. (2009), *Bayesian Analysis for Population Ecology*, Interdisciplinary Statistics Series, Chapman & Hall/CRC. https://www.routledge.com/Bayesian-Analysis-for-Population-Ecology/King-Morgan-Gimenez-Brooks/p/book/9781439811870

Kinne, B. J. (2013), "Network dynamics and the evolution of international cooperation," *American Political Science Review* 107(4), 766–785.

Konstantinos Kepaptsoglou, M. G. K. & Tsamboulas, D. (2010), "The gravity model specification for modeling international trade flows and free trade agreement effects: A 10-year review of empirical studies," *The Open Economics Journal* 3, 1–13.

Krackhardt, D. (1987a), "Cognitive social structures," *Social Networks* 9(2), 109–134.

Krackhardt, D. (1987b), "QAP partialling as a test of spuriousness," *Social Networks* 9(2), 171–186.

Krivitsky, P. N. (2012), "Exponential-family random graph models for valued networks," *Electronic Journal of Statistics* 6, 1100–1128.

Krivitsky, P. N. (2016), *ergm.count: Fit, Simulate and Diagnose Exponential-Family Models for Networks with Count Edges*, The Statnet Project. R package version 3.2.2.

Krivitsky, P. N. (2017), "Using contrastive divergence to seed Monte Carlo MLE for exponential-family random graph models," *Computational Statistics & Data Analysis* 107, 149–161.

Krivitsky, P. N. & Handcock, M. S. (2008), "Fitting position latent cluster models for social networks with latentnet," *Journal of Statistical Software* 24. Available at www.ncbi.nlm.nih.gov/pmc/articles/PMC5552185/.

Krivitsky, P. N. & Handcock, M. S. (2014), "A separable model for dynamic networks," *Journal of the Royal Statistical Society: Series B* 76(1), 29–46.

Krivitsky, P. N. & Handcock, M. S. (2019), *tergm: Fit, Simulate and Diagnose Models for Network Evolution Based on Exponential-Family Random Graph Models*, The Statnet Project (https://statnet.org). R package version 3.6.1.

Krivitsky, P. N., Handcock, M. S., Raftery, A. E. & Hoff, P. D. (2009), "Representing degree distributions, clustering, and homophily in social networks with latent cluster random effects models," *Social Networks* 31, 204–213.

Kronegger, L., Mali, F., Ferligoj, A. & Doreian, P. (2012), "Collaboration structures in Slovenian scientific communities," *Scientometrics* 90(2), 631–647.

Kuhnt, M. & Brust, O. (2014), "Low reciprocity rates in acquaintance networks of young adults – fact or artifact?," *Social Network Analysis and Mining* 4(1), 167.

Kuorikoski, N. (2010), "Anatomy of a lesbian relationship and its demise: The first lesbian relationship of the medical drama *Grey's Anatomy*," *Queers in American Popular Culture* 2, 47.

Lee, Y. & Nelder, J. (1996), "Hierarchical generalized linear models," *Journal of the Royal Statistical Society: Series B* 58(4), 619–678.

Lee, I.-W., Feiock, R. C. & Lee, Y. (2012), "Competitors and cooperators: A micro-level analysis of regional economic development collaboration networks," *Public Administration Review* 72(2), 253–262.

Leifeld, P. & Cranmer, S. (2014), "A theoretical and empirical comparison of the temporal exponential random graph model and the stochastic actor-oriented model," *Network Science* 7(1): 20–51.

Leifeld, P. & Cranmer, S. J. (2014), "A theoretical and empirical comparison of the temporal exponential random graph model and the stochastic actor-oriented model," *Network Science*.

Leifeld, P., Cranmer, S. J. & Desmarais, B. A. (2018), *xergm: Extensions for Exponential Random Graph Models*. R package version 1.8.3.

Leifeld, P., Cranmer, S. & Desmarais, B. (2019), "Temporal exponential random graph models with btergm: Estimation and bootstrap confidence intervals," *Journal of Statistical Software* 83(6), 1–36.

Lerner, J., Indlekofer, N., Nick, B. & Brandes, U. (2013), "Conditional independence in dynamic networks," *Journal of Mathematical Psychology* 57(6), 275–283.

Levy, M. A. (2016), "gwdegree: Improving interpretation of geometrically-weighted degree estimates in exponential random graph models," *The Journal of Open Source Software* 1(3), 36.

Li, G., Song, H. & Witt, S. F. (2005), "Recent developments in econometric modeling and forecasting," *Journal of Travel Research* 44(1), 82–99.

Li, J., Ziebart, B. & Berger-Wolf, T. (2018), "A game-theoretic adversarial approach to dynamic network prediction," *in Pacific-Asia Conference on Knowledge Discovery and Data Mining*, Springer, pp. 677–688.

Lin, K.-H. & Lundquist, J. (2013), "Mate selection in cyberspace: The intersection of race, gender, and education," *American Journal of Sociology* 119(1), 183–215.

Lind, B. (2012), "Lessons on exponential random graph modeling from *Greys Anatomy* hook-ups." Available at https://badhessian.org/2012/09/lessons-on-exponential-random-graph-modeling-from-greys-anatomy-hook-ups/.

Liu, X., Derudder, B. & Liu, Y. (2015), "Regional geographies of intercity corporate networks: The use of exponential random graph models to assess regional network-formation," *Papers in Regional Science* 94(1), 109–126.

Lomi, A. & Fonti, F. (2012), "Networks in markets and the propensity of companies to collaborate: An empirical test of three mechanisms," *Economics Letters* 114(2), 216–220.

Lu, Z., Savas, B., Tang, W. & Dhillon, I. S. (2010), "Supervised link prediction using multiple sources," *in 2010 IEEE 10th International Conference on Data Mining*, IEEE, pp. 923–928.

Lubell, M. & Robbins, M. (2017), "Climate adaptation, sea-level rise, and complex governance in San Francisco," *in Proc. 10th Annual Meeting of the Political Networks Section of the American Political Science Association*, American Political Science Association.

Lubetzky, E. & Zhao, Y. (2015), "On replica symmetry of large deviations in random graphs," *Random Structures & Algorithms* 47(1), 109–146.

Łuksza, M., Lässig, M. & Berg, J. (2010), "Significance analysis and statistical mechanics: An application to clustering," *Physical Review Letters* 105(22), 220601.

Lusher, D., Koskinen, J. & Robins, G. (2013), *Exponential Random Graph Models for Social Network Analysis*, Cambridge University Press.

Lyons, R. (2011), "The spread of evidence-poor medicine via flawed social-network analysis," *Statistics, Politics, and Policy* 2(1).

Mantel, N. (1967), "The detection of disease clustering and a generalized regression approach," *Cancer Research* 27(2 Part 1), 209–220.

Maslov, S., Sneppen, K. & Zaliznyak, A. (2004), "Detection of topological patterns in complex networks: Correlation profile of the internet," *Physica A: Statistical Mechanics and Its Applications* 333, 529–540.

Mazur, E. & Richards, L. (2011), "Adolescents' and emerging adults' social networking online: Homophily or diversity?," *Journal of Applied Developmental Psychology* 32(4), 180–188.

McDonald, S. & Benton, R. A. (2017), "The structure of internal job mobility and organizational wage inequality," *Research in Social Stratification and Mobility* 47, 21–31.

Michael, J. H. (1997), "Labor dispute reconciliation in a forest products manufacturing facility," *Forest Products Journal* 47, 41–45.

Michell, L. & Amos, A. (1997), "Girls, pecking order and smoking," *Social Science & Medicine* 44(12), 1861–1869.

Miller, B. & Kagan, K. (1997), "The great powers and regional conflicts: Eastern Europe and the Balkans from the post-Napoleonic era to the post Cold War era," *International Studies Quarterly* 41(1), 51–85.

Minhas, S., Hoff, P. D. & Ward, M. D. (2019), "Inferential approaches for network analysis: AMEN for latent factor models," *Political Analysis* 27(2), 208–222.

Mizruchi, M. S. (1990), "Determinants of political opposition among large American corporations," *Social Forces* 68(4), 1065–1088.

Molm, L. D. (2010), "The structure of reciprocity," *Social Psychology Quarterly* 73(2), 119–131.

Morgan, J. W. (2015), "Essays on Party System Institutionalization in East-Central Europe," PhD thesis, The Ohio State University.

Morris, M. & Kretzschmar, M. (1995), "Concurrent partnerships and transmission dynamics in networks," *Social Networks* 17(3–4), 299–318.

Morris, M., Handcock, M. S. & Hunter, D. R. (2008), "Specification of exponential-family random graph models: Terms and computational aspects," *Journal of Statistical Software* 24(4), 1548.

Mouw, T. & Entwisle, B. (2006), "Residential segregation and interracial friendship in schools 1," *American Journal of Sociology* 112(2), 394–441.

Neal, Z. (2014), "The backbone of bipartite projections: Inferring relationships from co-authorship, co-sponsorship, co-attendance and other co-behaviors," *Social Networks* 39, 84–97.

Neal, Z. P. (2017), "Well connected compared to what? Rethinking frames of reference in world city network research," *Environment and Planning A* 49(12), 2859–2877.

Newman, M. (2010), *Networks: An Introduction*, Oxford University Press.

Nomano, F. Y., Browning, L. E., Savage, J. L., Rollins, L. A., Griffith, S. C. & Russell, A. F. (2015), "Unrelated helpers neither signal contributions nor suffer retribution in chestnut-crowed babblers," *Behavioral Ecology* 26(4), 986–995.

Park, J. & Newman, M. (2004a), "Statistical mechanics of networks," *Physical Review E* 70(6), 66117–66130.

Park, J. & Newman, M. E. J. (2004b), "Solution of the two-star model of a network," *Physical Review E* 70(6), 066146.

Pattison, P. & Robins, G. (2002), "Neighborhood-based models for social networks," *Sociological Methodology* 32, 301–337.

Pearce, S., Ferguson, A., King, J. & Wilson, Z. A. (2015), "Flowernet: A gene expression correlation network for anther and pollen development," *Plant Physiology* 167(4), 1717–1730.

Pearson, M. & Michell, L. (2000), "Smoke rings: Social network analysis of friendship groups, smoking and drug-taking," *Drugs: Education, Prevention and Policy* 7(1), 21–37.

Pearson, M. & West, P. (2003), "Drifting smoke rings," *Connections* 25(2), 59–76.

Pearson, M., Steglich, C. & Snijders, T. (2006), "Homophily and assimilation among sport-active adolescent substance users," *Connections* 27(1), 47–63.

Peng, T.-Q., Liu, M., Wu, Y. & Liu, S. (2016), "Follower-followee network, communication networks, and vote agreement of the US members of Congress," *Communication Research* 43(7), 996–1024.

Plate, T. & Heiberger, R. (2016), *ABIND: Combine Multidimensional Arrays*. R package version 1.4-5.

Plummer, M., Best, N., Cowles, K. & Vines, K. (2006), "Coda: Convergence diagnosis and output analysis for mcmc," *R News* 6(1), 7–11.

Poast, P. (2010), "(Mis) using dyadic data to analyze multilateral events," *Political Analysis* 18(4), 403–425.

Poole, K. T. & Rosenthal, H. (1985), "A spatial model for legislative roll call analysis," *American Journal of Political Science* 29(2), 357–384.

Poole, K. T. & Rosenthal, H. (2000), *Congress: A Political-Economic History of Roll Call Voting*, Oxford University Press.

Raftery, A. E., Niu, X., Hoff, P. D. & Yeung, K. Y. (2012), "Fast inference for the latent space network model using a case-control approximate likelihood," *Journal of Computational and Graphical Statistics* 21(4), 901–919.

Rastelli, R., Friel, N. & Raftery, A. E. (2016), "Properties of latent variable network models," *Network Science* 4(4), 407–432.

Robins, G. & Pattison, P. (2001), "Random graph models for temporal processes in social networks," *Journal of Mathematical Sociology* 25(1), 5–41.

Rocca, M. S. & Gordon, S. B. (2010), "The position-taking value of bill sponsorship in Congress," *Political Research Quarterly* 63(2), 387–397.

Ryan, A. (2015), *On Hobbes: Escaping the War of All Against All*, Liveright Classics, W. W. Norton.

Rybarsch, M. & Bornholdt, S. (2012), "Binary threshold networks as a natural null model for biological networks," *Physical Review E* 86(2), 026114.

Salter-Townshend, M. (2015), "Vblpcm: Variational Bayes for the latent position cluster model for networks," Comprehensive R Archive Network. Version 2.4.4.

Salter-Townshend, M. & Murphy, T. B. (2013), "Variational Bayesian inference for the latent position cluster model for network data," *Computational Statistics & Data Analysis* 57(1), 661–671.

Sarkar, P. & Moore, A. W. (2005), "Dynamic social network analysis using latent space models," *ACM SIGKDD Explorations* 7(2), 31–40.

Sarkees, M. R. & Schafer, P. (2000), "The correlates of war data on war: An update to 1997," *Conflict Management and Peace Science* 18(1), 123–144.

Saul, Z. M. & Filkov, V. (2007), "Exploring biological network structure using exponential random graph models," *Bioinformatics* 23(19), 2604–2611.

Schmid, C. S. & Desmarais, B. A. (2017), "Exponential random graph models with big networks: Maximum pseudolikelihood estimation and the parametric bootstrap," in *2017 IEEE International Conference on Big Data*, IEEE, pp. 116–121.

Schmid, C., Thurner, P., Cranmer, S. J. & Kauermann, G. (2019), "Network interdependencies and the evolution of the international arms trade," *Journal of Conflict Resolution.* 63(7), 1736–1764.

Schneider, M., Scholz, J., Lubell, M., Mindruta, D. & Edwardsen, M. (2003), "Building consensual institutions: Networks and the national estuary program," *American Journal of Political Science* 47(1), 143–158.

Schweinberger, M. (2011), "Instability, sensitivity, and degeneracy of discrete exponential families," *Journal of the American Statistical Association* 106(496), 1361–1370.

Settle, J. E., Dawes, C. T., Christakis, N. A. & Fowler, J. H. (2010), "Friendships moderate an association between a dopamine gene variant and political ideology," *The Journal of Politics* 72(4), 1189–1198.

Sewell, D. K. & Chen, Y. (2015), "Latent space models for dynamic networks," *Journal for the American Statistical Association* 110(512), 1646–1657.

Sewell, D. K. & Chen, Y. (2016), "Latent space models for dynamic networks with weighted edges," *Social Networks* 44, 105–116.

Shalizi, C. R. & Thomas, A. C. (2011), "Homophily and contagion are generically confounded in observational social network studies," *Sociological Methods & Research* 40(2), 211–239.

Shmueli, G. (2010), "To explain or to predict?," *Statistical Science* 25(3), 289–310.

Shortreed, S., Handcock, M. S. & Hoff, P. D. (2006), "Positional estimation within a latent space model for networks," *Methodology* 2(1), 24–33.

Shrestha, M. K. & Feiock, R. C. (2009), "Governing US metropolitan areas self-organizing and multiplex service networks," *American Politics Research* 37(5), 801–823.

Shrum, W., Cheek, N. H. J. & MacD. Hunter, S. (1988), "Friendship in school: Gender and racial homophily," *Sociology of Education* 61(4), 227–239.

Simonsen, I., Eriksen, K. A., Maslov, S. & Sneppen, K. (2004), "Diffusion on complex networks: A way to probe their large-scale topological structures," *Physica A: Statistical Mechanics and Its Applications* 336(1), 163–173.

Simpson, S. L., Hayasaka, S. & Laurienti, P. J. (2011), "Exponential random graph modeling for complex brain networks," *PLoS ONE* 6(5), e20039.

Simpson, S. L., Moussa, M. N. & Laurienti, P. J. (2012), "An exponential random graph modeling approach to creating group-based representative whole-brain connectivity networks," *Neuroimage* 60(2), 1117–1126.

Sinke, M. R., Dijkhuizen, R. M., Caimo, A., Stam, C. J. & Otte, W. M. (2016), "Bayesian exponential random graph modeling of whole-brain structural networks across lifespan," *NeuroImage* 135, 79–91.

Smith, A. L., Asta, D. M. & Calder, C. A. (2017), "The geometry of continuous latent space models for network data," *arXiv preprint arXiv:1712.08641* .

Snijders, T. (2001), "The statistical evaluation of social network dynamics," *Sociological Methodology* 31(1), 361–395.

Snijders, T. A. (1996), "Stochastic actor-oriented models for network change," *Journal of Mathematical Sociology* 21(1–2), 149–172.

Snijders, T. A. (2002), "Markov chain Monte Carlo estimation of exponential random graph models," *Journal of Social Structure* 3(2), 1–40.

Snijders, T. A. (2017), "Stochastic actor-oriented models for network dynamics," *Annual Review of Statistics and Its Application* 4(1), 343–363.

Snijders, T. & van Duijn, M. (1997), "Simulation for statistical inference in dynamic network models," *in* R. Conte, R. Hegselmann & P. Terna, eds., *Simulating Social Phenomena*, Springer, pp. 493–512.

Snijders, T. A., Van de Bunt, G. G. & Steglich, C. E. (2010), "Introduction to stochastic actor-based models for network dynamics," *Social Networks* 32(1), 44–60.

Snijders, T., Pattison, P., Robins, G. & Handcock, M. (2006), "New specifications for exponential random graph models," *Sociological Methodology* 36(1), 99–153.

Snyman, J. (2005), *Practical Mathematical Optimization: An Introduction to Basic Optimization Theory and Classical and New Gradient-Based Algorithms*, Vol. 97, Springer Science & Business Media.

Song, H., Nyhuis, D. & Boomgaarden, H. (2019), "A network model of negative campaigning: The structure and determinants of negative campaigning in multiparty systems," *Communication Research* 46(2), 273–294.

Song, X., Yan, X. & Li, Y. (2015), "Modelling liking networks in an online healthcare community: An exponential random graph model analysis approach," *Journal of Information Science* 41(1), 89–96.

Steglich, C., Snijders, T. A. & West, P. (2006), "Applying siena," *Methodology* 2(1), 48–56.

Stevens, V. & Verhoest, K. (2016), "A next step in collaborative policy innovation research: Analysing interactions using exponential random graph modelling," *The Innovation Journal: The Public Sector Innovation Journal* 21(2), 1–20.

Stillman, P. E., Wilson, J. D., Denny, M. J., Desmarais, B. A., Bhamidi, S., Cranmer, S. J. & Lu, Z.-L. (2017), "Statistical modeling of the default mode brain network reveals a segregated highway structure," *Scientific Reports* 7(1), 11694.

Stillman, P. E., Wilson, J. D., Denny, M. J., Desmarais, B. A., Cranmer, S. J. & Lu, Z.-L. (2019), "A consistent organizational structure across multiple functional subnetworks of the human brain," *NeuroImage* 197, 24–36.

Strauss, D. & Ikeda, M. (1990), "Pseudolikelihood estimation for social networks," *Journal of the American Statistical Association* 85(409), 204–212.

Sweet, T. M., Thomas, A. C. & Junker, B. W. (2013), "Hierarchical network models for education research: Hierarchical latent space models," *Journal of Educational and Behavioral Statistics* 38(3), 295–318.

Tam Cho, W. K. & Fowler, J. H. (2010), "Legislative success in a small world: Social network analysis and the dynamics of congressional legislation," *The Journal of Politics* 72(1), 124–135.

Taylor, D., Myers, S. A., Clauset, A., Porter, M. A. & Mucha, P. J. (2017), "Eigenvector-based centrality measures for temporal networks," *Multiscale Modeling & Simulation* 15(1), 537–574.

Utz, S. & Jankowski, J. (2016), "Making 'friends' in a virtual world: The role of preferential attachment, homophily, and status," *Social Science Computer Review* 34(5), 546–566.

van Duijn, M. A., Gile, K. J. & Handcock, M. S. (2009), "A framework for the comparison of maximum pseudo-likelihood and maximum likelihood estimation of exponential family random graph models," *Social Networks* 31(1), 52–62.

Vera, E. R. & Schupp, T. (2006), "Network analysis in comparative social sciences," *Comparative Education* 42(3), 405–429.

Vögtle, E. M. & Windzio, M. (2016), "Networks of international student mobility: Enlargement and consolidation of the European transnational education space?," *Higher Education* 72(6), 723–741.

Wang, H., Iglesias, E. M. & Wooldridge, J. M. (2013), "Partial maximum likelihood estimation of spatial probit models," *Journal of Econometrics* 172(1), 77–89.

Wang, L. (2009), "Wilcoxon-type generalized bayesian information criterion," *Biometrika* 96(1), 163–173.

Ward, M. D. & Hoff, P. D. (2007), "Persistent patterns of international commerce," *Journal of Peace Research* 44(2), 157–175.

Ward, M. D., Ahlquist, J. S. & Rozenas, A. (2013), "Gravity's rainbow: A dynamic latent space model for the world trade network," *Network Science* 1(1), 95–118.

Ward, M. D., Siverson, R. M. & Cao, X. (2007), "Disputes, democracies, and dependencies: A re-examination of the Kantian peace," *American Journal of Political Science* 51(3), 583–601.

Warner, R. (2013), *Applied Statistics: From Bivariate through Multivariate Techniques*, Sage Publications.

Wasserman, S. & Faust, K. (1994), *Social Network Analysis: Methods and Applications*, Cambridge University Press.

Wasserman, S. & Pattison, P. (1996), "Logit models and logistic regressions for social networks: I. An introduction to Markov graphs and p^*," *Psychometrika* 61(3), 401–425.

Weible, C. M. & Sabatier, P. A. (2005), "Comparing policy networks: Marine protected areas in California," *Policy Studies Journal* 33(2), 181–201.

West, P. & Sweeting, H. (1996), "Background, rationale and design of the West of Scotland 11 to 16 Study," Technical Report 52, University of Aberdeen.

Wilson, J. D., Denny, M. J., Bhamidi, S., Cranmer, S. J. & Desmarais, B. A. (2017), "Stochastic weighted graphs: Flexible model specification and simulation," *Social Networks* 49, 37–47.

Wimmer, A. & Lewis, K. (2010), "Beyond and below racial homophily: ERG models of a friendship network documented on Facebook 1," *American Journal of Sociology* 116(2), 583–642.

Wyatt, D., Choudhury, T. & Bilmes, J. (2010), "Discovering long range properties of social networks with multi-valued time-inhomogeneous models," in *Proceedings of the Twenty-Fourth AAAI Conference on Artificial Intelligence*, AAAI, 630–636.

Xu, A. & Zheng, X. (2009), "Dynamic social network analysis using latent space model and an integrated clustering algorithm," in *Eighth IEEE International Conference on Dependable, Autonomic and Secure Computing, 2009. DASC'09*, IEEE, pp. 620–625.

Yeo, J. (2018), "Antecedents of border management network in El Paso, Texas: An exponential random graph model," *Journal of Homeland Security and Emergency Management* 15(3).

York, E. & Cornwell, B. (2006), "Status on trial: Social characteristics and influence in the jury room," *Social Forces* 85(1), 455–477.

Index